高等学校学术素养教育系列教材

SCI 论文阅读与写作技巧详解

刘进平 编著

中国林业出版社
China Forestry Publishing House

图书在版编目(CIP)数据

SCI 论文阅读与写作技巧详解 / 刘进平编著. —北京：中国林业出版社，2023.10(2024.5 重印)
ISBN 978-7-5219-2352-0

Ⅰ.①S… Ⅱ.①刘… Ⅲ.①科学技术-英语-论文-阅读教学-高等学校-教材
②科学技术-英语-论文-写作-高等学校-教材 Ⅳ.①G301

中国国家版本馆CIP数据核字(2023)第 177852 号

责任编辑：范立鹏
责任校对：苏　梅
封面设计：周周设计局

出版发行：中国林业出版社
　　　　　(100009，北京市西城区刘海胡同7号，电话 83143626)
电子邮箱：cfphzbs@163.com
网址：www.forestry.gov.cn/lycb.html
印刷：北京中科印刷有限公司
版次：2023 年 10 月第 1 版
印次：2024 年 5 月第 2 次
开本：787mm×1092mm　1/16
印张：13.5
字数：320 千字
定价：46.00 元

前　言

　　SCI论文阅读与写作是高年级本科生与研究生进行学术研究的基本技能，为使学生更好地掌握SCI论文阅读与写作技能，本教材通过大量例证详细介绍了SCI论文的阅读与写作技巧。SCI论文阅读与写作技能是紧密联系的两个方面：一方面，SCI论文写作是以大量的SCI论文阅读为基础的，可以说，不会阅读SCI论文就不会写作SCI论文；另一方面，如果没有SCI论文写作的经历，那么对SCI论文阅读的意义理解和实际效果也不会好。笔者在"SCI论文写作"课程教学过程中发现，课程的大部分时间实际上是在进行SCI论文阅读的教学，因为写作总是从阅读开始的，对于从未进行写作的学生而言，写作的技巧需要从阅读中加以体会和掌握。

　　本教材共分上、下两篇。上篇为SCI论文写作技巧，包括第一至第十三章，分别介绍了SCI论文的类型与结构、论文标题的写作、论文的署名与书写规则、摘要的写作、论文亮点和电子目录内容简介的写作、关键词的设置、引言的写作、材料与方法的写作、结果的写作、讨论的写作、结论的写作、致谢与参考文献的写作，以及初学者写作常见问题。下篇为SCI论文阅读技巧，包括第十四至第十九章，分别介绍了SCI论文阅读习惯的养成、SCI论文的查阅、下载与管理，阅读SCI论文的意义，SCI论文阅读的主要文字障碍，SCI论文阅读法之精读法、泛读法和串读法。

　　本教材的出版得到了海南大学教学名师工作项目（hdms202012）和海南大学作物学世界一流学科建设经费资助，另外，为了让初学者便于理解和掌握，本书引用了较多的期刊文献作为例证，在此一并表示感谢。

　　本教材可作为本科生与研究生文献阅读和论文写作的教材使用，也可供本科生、研究生和从事科研的初学者阅读参考。由于编写者水平有限，编写时间紧迫，不足和错误在所难免，广大读者如有意见和建议，请通过电子邮件（liu3305602@163.com）进行交流。

刘进平

2023年7月

目 录

前 言

绪 论 ……………………………………………………………… (1)

上篇 SCI 论文写作技巧 ……………………………………… (5)

第一章 SCI 论文的类型与结构 …………………………………… (6)
第二章 论文标题的写作 …………………………………………… (9)
第三章 论文的署名与书写规则 ………………………………… (14)
第四章 摘要的写作 ……………………………………………… (17)
第五章 论文亮点和期刊电子目录内容简介的写作 …………… (30)
第六章 关键词的设置 …………………………………………… (33)
第七章 引言的写作 ……………………………………………… (35)
第八章 材料与方法的写作 ……………………………………… (43)
第九章 结果的写作 ……………………………………………… (46)
第十章 讨论的写作 ……………………………………………… (53)
第十一章 结论的写作 …………………………………………… (61)
第十二章 致谢与参考文献的写作 ……………………………… (63)
第十三章 初学者写作常见问题 ………………………………… (69)

下篇 SCI 论文阅读技巧 ……………………………………… (81)

第十四章 SCI 论文阅读概述 …………………………………… (82)
第十五章 为什么阅读 SCI 论文如此重要 ……………………… (89)
第十六章 SCI 论文阅读的主要文字障碍 ……………………… (97)
第十七章 SCI 论文阅读法之精读法 …………………………… (104)
第十八章 SCI 论文阅读法之泛读法 …………………………… (173)
第十九章 SCI 论文阅读法之串读法 …………………………… (181)

参考文献 ………………………………………………………… (208)

绪 论

SCI 为科学引文索引（Science Citation Index）的英语缩写，是美国情报学家、"SCI 之父"——尤金·加菲尔德（Eugene Garfield）创立的美国科学信息研究所（Institute for Scientific Information, ISI）创办的一部世界著名的期刊文献检索工具。ISI 原隶属于汤森路透（Thomson Reuters）公司，现属于加拿大科睿唯安（Clarivate Analytics）公司。SCI 和科学引文索引扩展版（Science Citation Index Expanded, SCIE）收录了全球上万种学术期刊，涵盖数学、物理、化学、农学、林学、医学、生命科学、天文学、地理、环境、材料、工程技术等学科，涵盖了全世界最重要和最有影响力的研究成果。SCI 除作为文献检索工具外，还凭借其设立的影响因子（impact factor, IF）——某一期刊在过去两年中所发表的论文被引用的总次数与该刊在同一时期内发表论文的总数之比，对科技期刊学术质量、科学家和科研机构学术影响力（尤其是基础研究的水平）进行定量评价。ISI 每年发布《期刊引用报告》（*Journal Citation Reports*, JCR），即基于 SCI 数据库中期刊论文被引用情况对期刊 IF 值进行排名。需要指出的是，用 IF 值来定量评价学术水平虽然很流行，但不必过分盲信。

本书所指的 SCI 论文写作，实质是指用英语写作科技论文。但是要注意，英语虽已经成为国际科技交流的通用语言，但英语科技论文并不都是 SCI 论文，不仅因为有些英语科技期刊还未被 SCI 所收录，而且有相当一部分是美国科罗拉多大学丹佛分校图书馆馆员 Jeffrey Beall 所称的掠夺性期刊（predatory journals），就是收取高额的论文处理费，但基本没有质量检查和同行评审的开放存取或开源（open access, OA）期刊，俗称给钱就发的"水刊"。据研究，这类期刊上发表的论文读者非常有限，对促进科学研究发展的影响很小，因此很少引起科学家的注意。所以，强调用英语发表论文，就是指尽可能发表 SCI 论文。只有这样，才能更好地进行国际科技交流，增强论文成果的影响力，使研究成果获得同行承认。学术界向来有"不发表，就完蛋/灭亡"或"不发表，就出局/淘汰"（publish or perish）的说法，SCI 论文作为科研成果的一种形式，发表 SCI 论文对科学工作者个人的事业和前途至关重要。鉴于此，年轻学生在进入学术界之前，十分有必要学习 SCI 论文阅读与写作技巧。

本教材取名为"SCI 论文阅读与写作技巧详解"，是因为笔者在"SCI 论文写作"课程教学中体会到，教授 SCI 论文写作实质上很大的精力和时间是用来教学生怎样阅读 SCI 论文。对于 SCI 论文，有人称"不会读就不会写"，诚哉斯言。因为写作是以大量的阅读为基础的，没有足够的阅读量，就谈不上写出像样的 SCI 论文来。另外，如果没有动手写作 SCI 的经历，就体会不到阅读 SCI 论文有多重要，就不清楚如何有效地阅读 SCI 论文。因此，本教材将 SCI 论文阅读技巧和 SCI 论文写作技巧结合在一起来写作，并且将"SCI 论文阅读技巧"置于"SCI 论文写作技巧"之后，其意在于 SCI 论文阅读不只是着眼于获得论文中的信息，更重要的是从着眼于如何写作 SCI 论文的角度来谈 SCI 论文的阅读技巧。

谈到写作，很多人会说"文无定法"，说写作没有一定的法则，没有一定的模板，不过是随物赋形，随形赋意而已。这是一种误解，写作并非没有一定的规则和一定的技巧，而是不可生搬硬套，需要灵活运用而已。至于 SCI 论文（或者说英语科技论文），其本质上是一种应用文体，是需要遵循一定格式的。即便是高手写作，也只是在格式之内灵活腾挪罢了。对于初学者而言，就是要学习基本格式写作，等熟练之后，再寻求自由发挥。就像初学打拳，总是从基本的动作和套路开始练习，练到一定程度，这些动作才能内化，才能在具体实战中下意识发挥。

SCI 论文和普通英语写作本质上并没有多少区别。所以 SCI 论文写作与普通英语写作一样强调两样东西：一是大量阅读，二是从模仿开始。

如果将英语写作看作"输出"的话，那么英语阅读就是"输入"。只有大量地、不断地、高质量地"输入"，才能有效地"输出"。在教学方面，有人说"要给学生一杯水，教师要有一桶水"。这在英语写作方面也类似，要写出一篇好的论文，就要阅读大量的相关论文。复旦大学陆谷孙教授曾说："'输入'与'输出'，保持两者大致相当的比例，譬如说，'输入'一百万字的阅读量，最好保持一万字的写作'输出量'。写完最好找高手修改，且不断温习修改意见。"他还说："说英语要说得字正腔圆，只有亿万次的模仿，要减少母语干扰，对比最重要，譬如说，对比出英语的动词时态意识、与汉语迥异的数字意识等。"

在具体写作方面，模仿是最重要的步骤。选择写得好的论文细心阅读，写作时对其结构、句型和措辞加以模仿，日久天长，写作水平自然就会提高。北京大学王逢鑫教授说："学习写作要经历'天下文章一大抄'和'车轱辘话来回说'的过程。'一大抄'不是逐字逐句地抄袭，更不是原封不动地剽窃。'一大抄'强调模仿的重要性。英语不是我们的母语，我们遣词造句要有根有据，不可凭空杜撰。模仿是写作正确和得体英语的基础，而它的前提是记忆。现在许多学生不爱背书，认为这是机械地重复，浪费时间，没有意思。古人云：'熟读唐诗三百首，不会作诗也会吟。'熟读才能牢记单词和句型，用时方可信手拈来，脱口而出。……模仿总要经历由抄写到复用的过程。

'一大抄'是学习写作的必由之路：借用前人使用过的词汇、句型和搭配，重新排列组合，表达自己的思想感情，创造性写作总要建立在模仿的基础上。练习写作需要循序渐进。我从阅读到写作，从口头练习到笔头练习，从单句翻译到段落翻译，从单句造句到段落写作，从控制性写作到自由写作，从模仿性写作到创造性写作，一步一个脚印地踏踏实实去写。阅读是投入，写作是产出。不广泛涉猎名篇名著，是学习不到优秀语言的，写作的源泉就会枯竭。……'车轱辘话来回说'是一般写作的模式。'车轱辘话'，就是围绕一个中心思想来回反复阐述，即先用一个个中心句（top sentence）立意，再用若干支持性论点（supporting statement）详细说明，随后举上几个实例（example）证明观点，最后得出结论（conclusion），与开头的中心句遥相呼应。'来回说'，就是 paraphrasing，即同义表达，用不同的语言形式表达相同或相近的意思。"

与文学作品相比，科技论文写作更容易模仿。以丹尼尔·笛福（Daniel Defoe）的传统小说《鲁滨逊漂流记》（*Robinson Crusoe*）和詹姆斯·乔伊斯（James Joyce）的现代小说或意识流小说《尤利西斯》（*Ulysses*）为例，二者虽然都是小说，但二者的创作理念和叙述方式极不相同。而科技论文本质上是一种应用文体，其写作格式相当僵化和保守。科技论文对研究结果的写作是高度标准化和程式化的，也就是所称的 IMRD 或 IMRaD 结构形式，即论文包括 Introduction（引言）、Materials and Methods（材料和方法）、Results（结果）和 Discussion（讨论）几个主要的部分。这种结构称起源于 20 世纪 40 年代，并逐渐被广泛使用，是 20 世纪 80 年代以来唯一盛行的格式。此外，文学的语言以美感为追求，更讲究形象、变化和修辞，而科技语言则追求准确和逻辑，表达上更讲究清晰和简洁。写好论文的原则很简单，使文章更容易阅读和理解是论文写作的重要目标。因此，无论是格式还是语言，科技写作比文学写作更容易模仿。为了让读者体会文学语言与科学语言在表达上的差异，以下选取弗吉尼亚·伍尔夫（Virginia Woolf）关于散文小说（prose novel）和诗体小说（novel-poem）的比较，以及伯纳德·伍德（Bernard Wood）关于线粒体 DNA（mtDNA）和核 DNA（nuclear DNA）的区别为例来进行说明。

【例文 1】And indeed if we compare the prose novel and the novel-poem the triumphs are by no means all to the credit of prose. As we rush through page after page of narrative in which a dozen scenes that the novelist would smooth out separately are pressed into one, in which pages of deliberate description are fused into a single line, we cannot help feeling that the poet has outpaced the prose writer. Here page is packed twice as full as his. Characters, too, if they are not shown in conflict but snipped off and summed up with something of the exaggeration of a caricaturist, have a heightened and symbolical significance which prose with its gradual approach cannot rival. The general aspect of things-market, sunset, church-have a brilliance and a continuity, owing to the compressions and elisions of poetry, which mock the prose writer and his slow accumulations of careful detail. （实际上，如果我们把散文小说和诗体小说加以比较，散文也并不能尽领风骚。有时候，小说家会分别写

的十几个场景,在诗中被压成一个,许多页细致的描绘被融为一行,当你一页页读这样精练的叙述时,不禁会觉得诗人胜过散文作家。诗人的书页比散文容量大一倍。虽然诗中人物有可能是漫画式的剪影或夸张的概括,未能在冲突中徐徐展现,但却包含某种被提高了的、象征性的意义,这是采取渐进手法的散文无法与其竞争的。诗歌具有紧凑性和省略性,它可以借此睥睨散文家及其对细节的缓慢积累;也正因此,事物的总体方面——市场、落日、教堂——在诗中现出辉煌并具有某种连续性。)(黄梅,译)

说明:上文在比较诗体小说和散文小说时,句式丰富,措辞和表达方式多变,分别用了 triumphs, outpaced, rival, mock 来说明诗体小说胜过散文小说。

【例文2】For several reasons it focused on mtDNA and not on nuclear DNA. Mutations occur in mtDNA at a faster rate than they do in nuclear DNA, and unlike nuclear DNA mtDNA does not get reshuffled between chromosomes when germ cells divide. Nor does it have all of the innate mechanisms for DNA repair that are found in the nucleus. This may contribute to its higher mutation rate, and account for the observation that once mutations occur in mtDNA they tend to persist. (出于几方面的原因,该研究集中在线粒体DNA而不是核DNA上。线粒体DNA发生突变的速率远远高于核DNA发生突变的频率,而且在生殖细胞分裂时,线粒体DNA的染色体之间不会像核DNA的那样发生重组,也没有在核内发现的DNA的先天修复机制。这可能导致了它较高的突变频率,也说明了为什么只要线粒体DNA发生突变这些突变就会持续下去)(冯兴无,译)

说明:伯纳德·伍德在论述分子生物学手段应用于人类的进化与变异研究中线粒体DNA优于核DNA的原因,就十分简单、清晰和明确,这些措辞和句式也可在别的科技领域写作中模仿使用。

在模仿之前,需要在阅读文献时归纳和学习丰富多样的表达方法,记下可以模仿使用的句式和词语。目前,还可利用互联网资源和应用程序辅助写作,比如,可利用浏览器(如Google、Google Scholar、Bing和Yahoo)来搜索合适的词语搭配和包含特定词语的句子。此外,当代美国英语语料库(Corpus of Contemporary American English)、Ludwig、Linggle、Academic Phrasebank、Collocaid、NetSpeak、Hemingway Editor、Power thesaurus、Thesaurus 等网站和应用程序也可用来寻找包含特定词语的搭配、例句及同义词和近义词表达。在人工智能(artificial intelligence, AI)时代,ChatGPT可以作为SCI论文写作和润色修改的辅助工具,但不能完全依赖ChatGPT生成文本并列为共同作者,目前各大期刊与出版商抵制这种做法。除ChatGPT外,还有综合了改写(rewording)和重新措辞(rephrasing)的改写工具,如QuillBot、SciNote、Chat助手、科研者之家(Home for Researchers)等人工智能润色工具。

上篇

SCI论文写作技巧

英国伟大的物理学家、化学家——迈克尔·法拉第(Michael Faraday,1791—1867)一生独立发表论文450篇。他曾说过,科学只不过是"研究、发现和发表"。论文写作与发表是科学事业的重要环节,科学论文作为科学研究的一种产品(如同发明专利一样),是用来与其他科学家分享你自己的原始研究成果(研究性论文),或是用来评论其他人进行的研究(综述性论文)。写作SCI论文,有助于作者理解科学发现的过程,可以将研究成果记录和固定在出版物中,作为科研工作的一种产出,同时也是科学家之间最主要的交流方式和信息传播手段,是其他科学家进一步研究的基础。尽管"唯SCI论文评价"引发了一系列不良后果,但"SCI论文崇拜"和"SCI论文污名化"都不可取。SCI论文写作仍然是研究生的基本技能,SCI论文仍然是科技界的"硬通货"和"进身之阶"。

第一章　SCI 论文的类型与结构

一、SCI 论文的类型

SCI 论文可分为研究性论文和综述性论文两大类。前者是进行了新的实验研究/实地考察调研，获得数据和结果并加以讨论，获得新知识和原创性的科学贡献。后者是在阅读大量文献的基础上，对某一个领域的研究现状进行总结、评述和展望，有助于读者快速了解某一个领域的动态，把握学科的发展方向。

研究性论文从内容上讲，一般可分为研究性论文、技术或方法论文、数据论文等。技术或方法论文通常提出新的或改良的技术或工艺，或介绍新的分析软件、计算方法、工作流程或数据标准，一般会给出应用范例（如果是改良方法，则要提供优于原方法的数据）。数据论文提供科学记录、数据或数据集，并介绍数据采集、整理、编目、标准化或评估的过程。从内容篇幅和形式上来说，研究性论文又可分为长论文和短论文两类。长论文（articles, full articles）或一般研究性论文（original articles, research articles）篇幅较长，结构完整（正文具有引言、方法、结果、讨论各个部分）。这种论文详尽、完整地描述科学发现的背景、目的、方法、结果和意义，是 SCI 论文最主要的形式。短论文、简报（reports）、通讯（communications）、短讯（short communications）、短信（letters, correspondences, notes）篇幅较短，正文不会明确划分为引言、方法、结果、讨论等几个部分，在方法和结果方面相对没有长论文那么繁杂，多为对某一技术、方法突破性进展或新的理论发现进行快速报道。

综述（reviews）论文是在大量梳理文献的基础上，对某一领域或技术的历史和进展进行回顾和描述，以及对未来发展进行展望或就某一论题提出自己的看法。观点、述评、聚焦或快评（perspectives, spotlights, dispatches）论文是作者就某一新发表的论文、新的发现、新兴的研究课题或研究前沿进行评论，这类论文虽然也需要文献或图表数据支持自己的观点，但通常不如综述那么全面，篇幅也相对较短。

此外，医学领域还有介于研究论文和综述之间的荟萃分析(meta analysis)论文，这种论文是利用已发表的实证研究论文来提取数据，用统计学方法整理与分析，获得与目标问题有关的诸变量之间的明确关系或模式，从而得出较为确定性的结论。

二、SCI 论文的结构

SCI 论文作为科学界信息交流的方式，必须具有高度可读性，即清晰、准确和简洁；作为科技界的公共产品，不能是隐秘的或以自我为中心的。SCI 论文以期刊编辑、审稿人和相关领域的科学家为受众，编辑和审稿人决定论文是否适合发表，而相关领域的科学家决定是否阅读、参考和引用，因此，SCI 论文不能简单地按时间顺序叙述研究工作，而必须让期刊编辑、审稿人和相关领域的科学家相信所做的研究是重要的、有效的，并且是与同一领域的其他科学家相关的。为此，作者必须强调研究工作的动机和结果，而且必须包括足以证明这一结果的有效性证据。

英语科技论文或 SCI 论文最常见的结构为 IMRaD 结构形式，也就是论文包括 Introduction(引言)、Materials and Methods(材料和方法)、Results(结果)和 Discussion(讨论)几个主要的部分。其中引言介绍研究的是什么问题及为什么研究这个问题(相当于回答 Why?)，材料和方法介绍如何研究这个问题(相当于回答 How?)，结果介绍得到了什么发现(相当于回答 What?)，讨论解释这些发现意味着什么及可推出什么样的结论(相当于回答 So what?)。

传统上，科技论文的 IMRaD 结构应该像沙漏结构(图 1-1)。引言相当于倒金字塔或倒梯形结构，应当从介绍一个较为宽泛的领域或广泛关注的问题开始(沙漏结构的顶端开口)，然后通过文献综述缩小到一个非常具体的问题或假设(沙漏结构的颈部，也是其最窄的部位)。接着是材料与方法和结果(沙漏结构狭窄的中间部分)。最后是讨论/结论，相当正金字塔或正梯形结构，根据对方法和结果的讨论，得出一个较为一般或普遍的结论(沙漏结构的底端)。沙漏结构的顶端开口不能太窄，否则就不能吸引众多大同行读者的阅读和注意。沙漏结构的底端应当与顶端开口大小一致，否则读者对论文结论适用范围的期望就会落空。

如果完整地划分，研究性的长论文可分为以下几个部分：

  Title(论文标题)
  Author(s)(作者)
  Affiliation(s) and Address(es)(作者单位与地址)
  Abstract(摘要)
  Keywords(关键词)
  Body/Text(正文)

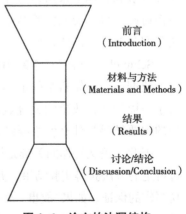

图 1-1 论文的沙漏结构

Introduction/Background(引言/背景)

　　Materials and Methods/Methods(材料和方法/方法)

　　Results(结果)

　　Discussion(讨论)

　　Conclusions(结论)

Authors' Contribution(作者贡献)

Acknowledgements(致谢)

Conflict of Interest(利益冲突声明)

Appendix/Supplementary Data/Supplementary Information/Additional Information(附录/附件)

Funding(项目资助)

References/Literature(参考文献/引文)

　　需要说明的是，不同的期刊在结构划分上可能会略有不同，例如，Results(结果)和Discussion(讨论)可根据论文写作具体情况合成一个部分 Results and Discussion(结果与讨论)。有的期刊论文没有单独的Conclusions(结论)部分，而是作为Discussion(讨论)的最后一小段。有的期刊没有单独的Funding(项目资助)，而是包含在Acknowledgements(致谢)中。有的期刊没有Authors' Contribution(作者贡献)和Conflict of Interest(利益冲突声明)。

　　需要说明的是，研究性论文虽然按照标题、摘要、引言、方法、结果、讨论、结论这样的顺序排列，但实际写作过程中，写作的先后顺序却不一定如此。往往是在拿到实验数据或结果后，通过查阅文献，进行构思立意，草拟一个题目。先写引言，介绍研究的问题，前人在这方面的研究情况，概述本研究的结果和意义。然后写方法(方法部分也可以在做试验之前或拿到实验结果之前完成)。论文结果并非对所有实验结果的记录，论文结果应该根据论文标题(也即中心观点或主要贡献)进行选择实验结果，只有那些能对中心观点或贡献有提供证据的实验结果才能作为论文的写作素材，通过分节和分标题来组织写作。结果中的图和表也可在实验过程中边做边整理。之后写作讨论部分，说明实验结果与引言(或背景)的关联，并推导出结论。最后要概括全文各部分要点，形成摘要。

　　Schimel 在《科学写作》(*Writing Science*)中强调，写论文要善于讲故事，否则只是一堆数据而已。做科学的根本目的不是获取数据，而是通过数据获得对自然的理解。对于一篇论文，故事的关键点就是：如何开头？提出怎样的具体问题或假设？论文工作的主要结果是什么？主要结论又是什么？

　　因此，论文写作的关键是构造一个完整的研究"故事"，挑出一个有意义的问题，通过特定的方法获得实验结果，并能支持作者在引言中提出的假设或主张，这些是论文成功写作的保证。如果"故事"的逻辑性不强，实验结果无法提供足够的证据，就需要补充试验或重新分析数据；或者重写引言，将现有的结果放在另外的背景下进行阐述。

第二章　论文标题的写作

一、论文标题的写作要求

论文标题相当于论文的标识或标签，是引发读者阅读兴趣的"钓饵"。一个好的论文标题十分重要。标题需要有吸引力，如果没有吸引力，就难以激起编辑、审稿人和普通读者的兴趣。编辑、审稿人和普通读者面对浩如烟海的论文，首先映入眼帘的就是论文标题，标题是否吸引人是促使他们继续阅读和获得他们关注的关键。因此，标题应当醒目且吸引人，以便给编辑、审稿人和普通读者留下良好的第一印象。此外，多数读者是通过网络搜索、浏览期刊目录或者文摘、索引而接触到论文标题的，论文标题的切合性直接决定是否进一步阅读摘要及全文的兴趣；对于论文搜索者而言，包含恰当的主题词和关键词才能让你的论文被检索到。因此，论文标题要尽可能简明扼要，高度概括论文的核心内容、中心贡献或学术创新点，同时包含必要的主题词和关键词。

拟定论文标题要符合 ABC 原则，也就是准确(accuracy)、简洁(brevity)和清楚(clarity)。准确包括两个方面要求：一方面要正确反映论文的主要内容，不至于文不对题；另一方面要保证语言的准确性。论文标题(包括摘要和摘要前面的亮点)是审稿人最先审阅的论文部分，要确保这些部分的写作是正确无误的，否则，糟糕的第一印象会让你的论文失去审稿人的阅读兴趣和审稿意愿。简洁就是要尽可能简短(不超过 20 个单词，以 10~12 个单词最好，在期刊页面标题排版不超过 2 行为宜)，同时能概括文章的主要发现或核心内容。清楚就是用修饰关系清楚的名词短语或简单句(要包含核心的主题词)来清晰地反映文章的主要发现或核心内容。一般而言，论文标题紧盯着的读者不应只局限于论文狭窄的研究领域，而使跨研究领域的读者或一般外行读者易于理解更好(顶级期刊尤其如此)。

Lockwood(2016)研究表明，尽管短标题的论文比长标题的论文引用率更高，但短标题并不一定就能使文章更引人关注。也有学者认为，由于网络时代的到来，网络检索是最主要的文献获取方式，因此，论文标题越长，被检索到的机会就越大。但是，检索到是一回事，会阅读和引用是另一回事。不仅是标题，摘要和全文中包含相应的主题词和关键词也足以使关注该研究领域的读者从网络检索中得到。因此，标题应宜长则长，宜短则短。此外，论文标题如果能清楚表明论文所做的研究工作、表明或证明某种结论，比没有做到这些更能吸引更多读者的注意。论文标题如果包含通用的或非专业的术语，或者包含有趣的或抓眼球的短语，会吸引更多读者的注意。将标题设为一个问题（即用问句作为标题）也可以增加文章下载的频率，但不一定有更高的 Altmetric 分数（代表论文出版后包括新闻、博客、社交媒体等在内的各种来源对论文引用或提及数据，即综合社会传播得分）。

在拟定论文标题时，题目不能过大或过于空泛，没有聚焦。同样，题目也不宜过长，过于详细具体，题目如果不能让人一目了然，读者留下的印象就不鲜明深刻。要避免使用国内惯用的"关于……的研究"（Study on..., Research on..., An investigation of..., Experiments of..., Experimental study of...）或"对……的思考""关于……的思考"（Thoughts on..., Regarding...）之类的套语。"……初报（或初探）"（An preliminary report/study of...）之类涉嫌研究不够全面深入，结论无法确定，也要尽量避免使用。同时，题目中不宜使用 novel、new 之类的形容词（一篇论文如果没有创新，为什么要发表呢？所以这种意思是不言而喻的，因此也没必要在论文标题中出现），如果要有形容词，可使用较为具体的、专指的或者以数据为基础的形容词，例如，

<u>Adaptive</u> mutability of colorectal cancers in response to targeted therapies, <u>Rapid nonuniform</u> adaptation to conformation-specific KRAS（G12C）inhibition, <u>Accelerated</u> viral dynamics in bat cell lines, with implications for zoonotic emergence.

慎用缩略语，尽可能避免使用化学式、上下角标、公式、特殊符号（数字符号、希腊字母等）和不必要的专业表达。但如果某些术语全称较长且缩写词已得到领域公知公用，是可以在标题中使用的。此外，分子式在化学或医学等领域的文章中有时也不可避免地出现。避免使用系列标题，因为这意味着论文是系列中的某一篇文章，内容是不完整的。

拟定论文标题时，应该用尽可能少的文字来描述论文内容，但是要做到正确、完整、简明、易懂。标题中应包含有助于编制索引和计算机搜索的主题词或关键词，但应使标题清晰易懂、具体、信息丰富。标题应该正确、完整和简明，这一点容易明白，例如，"Global-scale human impact on delta morphology has led to net land area gain"这样的标题要比"Global-scale human impact on delta morphology"要完整，而"B cells and tertiary lymphoid structures promote immunotherapy response"要比"The effects of B cells and tertiary lymphoid structures on immunotherapy response"要具体和清晰，因为 effects（效果、影响）可能是促进（promote），也可能是抑制（inhibit），后者就具体而清楚地表明这是一种促进作用。

题目怎么做到易懂呢？有一个技巧，就是对于人们不容易理解的名词，尤其是缩写名词，可用同位语成分略加解释。例如，《科学》(Science) 期刊中有一篇短论文或报告(report)的题目为：

Inhibition of Retroviral RNA production by ZAP, a CCCH-type Zinc finger protein.

在这个题目中，如果没有后面的同位语 a CCCH-type Zinc finger protein，读者若不读摘要和正文是很难明白 ZAP 是什么的。

再如，《自然》(Nature) 的一篇长论文(article)的标题为：

Molecular evolution of *FOXP2*, a gene involved in speech and language.

同样，这个题目如果没有同位语 a gene involved in speech and language 对 *FOXP2* 加以解释说明，读者也是很难明白 *FOXP2* 是一个什么样基因的。

在拟定论文标题时，往往将表达论文核心内容的主题词置于标题开头，这样会使创新内容十分醒目，有先声夺人之效。当这个主题词是一个很新的东西（如一个新的成分、分子或概念），这时候，可以采用同位语结构来对标题最开始的主题词加以解释说明，如下面 3 个标题：

SIR1, an upstream component in auxin signaling identified by chemical genetics.

GARNet, the Genomic Arabidopsis Resource Network.

SynCAM, a synaptic adhesion molecule that drives synapse assembly.

二、论文标题的语法结构和书写规则

标题最常见的结构为名词词组、动名词结构和简单句。简单句有陈述句和疑问句两种，多采用一般现在时。

名词词组为标题时，概括性很强，但应在各单词或词组之间用连词 and 和介词 of, in, for, from 等使它们之间的修饰关系清晰化，并尽可能将表达核心内容的主题词置于标题开头。例如，

A general theoretical and experimental framework for nanoscale electromagnetism.

Structural basis of DNA targeting by a transposon-encoded CRISPR-Cas system.

Undulating changes in human plasma proteome profiles across the lifespan.

Conversion of *Escherichia coli* to generate all biomass carbon from CO_2.

Direct observation of bimolecular reactions of ultracold KRb molecules.

Analysis of short tandem repeat expansions and their methylation state with nanopore sequencing.

动名词结构的标题通常用来表述一种新的方法或手段及所获得的结果。例如，

Visualizing poiseuille flow of hydrodynamic electrons.

Characterizing large-scale quantum computers via cycle benchmarking.

Cooling of a levitated nanoparticle to the motional quantum ground stat.

简单陈述句标题往往就是文章结论的概括，可以让读者对文章论证的核心内容一目了然。例如，

RGF1 controls root meristem size through ROS signaling.

Transient protein-RNA interactions guide nascent ribosomal RNA folding.

Disruption of the mouse *Shmt2* gene confers embryonic anaemia via foetal liver-specific metabolomic disorders.

PGRMC2 is an intracellular haem chaperone critical for adipocyte function.

Single-cell transcriptomics reveals expansion of cytotoxic CD4 T cells in supercentenarians.

有时也可用"主标题：副标题"结构，主副标题之间用冒号隔开，冒号在这里相当于系动词，但它比系动词连接成句更醒目。主标题通常为概括性的术语（主题词），而副标题是对主标题的解释和具体化说明。这种标题结构在综述论文中用得较多。例如，

CRUP: A comprehensive framework to predict condition-specific regulatory units.

The p53 pathway: Positive and negative feedback loops.

The capsaicin receptor: A heat-activated ion channel in the pain pathway.

Speak, friend, and enter: Signalling systems that promote beneficial symbiotic associations in plants.

目前，只有少数期刊还需要提供眉题（running title, running head）或短标题（short title）用于出版时印在期刊论文的页眉。眉题是对标题的核心内容进一步概括，一般不超过40个字符。例如，

标题：Dendritic cell immunoreceptor is a new target for anti-AIDS drug development: Identification of DCIR/HIV-1 inhibitors.

眉题：Inhibitors of DCIR limit HIV-1 infection.

标题单词书写格式因期刊不同而异，大体有两种：第一种是标题的第一个单词首字母大写，其他单词如果不是专有名词的话一律小写；第二种是标题中的所有实词首字母大写，介词、冠词和连词位于标题最前面首字母大写，其余位置小写。

第一种如：

DNA demethylase ROS1 negatively regulates the imprinting of *DOGL4* and seed dormancy in *Arabidopsis thaliana*.

Over-expression of 3-hydroxy-3-methylglutaryl-coenzyme A reductase 1 (*hmgr1*) gene under super-promoter for enhanced latex biosynthesis in rubber tree (*Hevea brasiliensis* Muell. Arg.).

第二种如：

RhNAC2 and *RhEXPA4* Are Involved in the Regulation of Dehydration Tolerance during the Expansion of Rose Petals.

A Single JAZ Repressor Controls the Jasmonate Pathway in *Marchantia polymorpha*.

也有标题中全部字母大写的情况，但相对较少，因此不再介绍。

注意：基因、蛋白质和物种学名在标题中有自己的书写规则：特定的基因和蛋白质除特殊情况外，一般野生型基因大写，而突变型基因小写，物种学名的属名首字母大写，而种加词首字母小写；基因和物种学名用斜体表示，蛋白质（包括酶）则用正体表示。如果题目为直接问句，则要加问号。另外，题目中逗号、冒号和连字符用得也较多。

第三章 论文的署名与书写规则

一、论文署名规则

论文作者(author 或 authors)是指列在论文标题之下,对论文工作作出直接贡献的人员。科技论文作者与文学作品的作者不同,科技论文通常需要在调查或实验的基础上来撰写,因此,作者不仅是执笔之人。但是也不能将与调查或实验工作关系不大的人员统统列为作者。关于什么人可作为作者,什么人不能作为作者,是大有讲究的。

国际医学期刊编辑委员会(International Committee of Medical Journal Editors Recommendation, ICMJE Recommendation)中将对论文工作有贡献的人分为作者(author)和非作者贡献者(non-author contributors)两类。只有同时满足如下4条标准的贡献者才能列为作者:

①对论文工作的思路或设计或为研究数据获取、数据分析或解释做出实质性贡献(Substantial contributions to the conception or design of the work; or the acquisition, analysis, or interpretation of data for the work)。

②论文撰写或对重要的论文知识内容起关键作用的论文修改(Drafting the work or revising it critically for important intellectual content)。

③对论文发表版本的最终批准或认可者(Final approval of the version to be published)。

④同意对论文所有事宜负责,确保与论文任何部分关于精确性与诚实性的问题能得到适当的调查和解决(Agreement to be accountable for all aspects of the work in ensuring that questions related to the accuracy or integrity of any part of the work are appropriately investigated and resolved)。

此外,作者除了要对自己所做的那部分论文工作负责外,还应确定共同作者(合著者)负责的论文工作的特定部分。同时,应该对共同作者(合著者)贡献的真实性有信心(In addition to being accountable for the parts of the work he or she has done, an author should be able to identify which co-authors are responsible for specific other parts of the work. In addition, authors should have confidence in the integrity of the contributions of their co-authors)。

而不能同时符合上述4项要求的贡献者不能列为作者，但可在论文致谢中加以感谢。例如，对项目资金和实验小组的一般性监督或一般性行政支持、写作协助、技术编辑、语言编辑和校对等人员属于非作者贡献者，不能列为作者。

一般而言，作者署名先后顺序应按照对论文的贡献大小进行排名，但以第一作者和通讯作者最为重要。第一作者往往是实验或调查工作的实施者、数据的获得者和处理者，同时也是初稿的执笔人。第一作者通常是做实验的研究生或博士后。通讯作者(correspondence author)是在稿件提交、同行评议和出版过程中负责与期刊沟通的作者，一般是导师、实验室或课题小组负责人、资深科学家或高级研究人员，这些人往往也是课题和论文工作的负责人，在实验设计、研究指导、论文修改等方面有贡献者。论文发表后，其他人寻求合作、索要实验材料、研究咨询等也通过通讯作者来进行。通讯作者一般都放在最后。简单地说，第一作者贡献最大，通讯作者起领导作用。

目前，随着科研合作的日益普遍，共同第一作者与共同通讯作者也应运而生。当一位或几位作者对论文工作作出主要贡献且贡献不分伯仲时，就列为共同第一作者。共同通讯作者一般是合作双方或多方的导师、实验室或课题小组负责人、资深科学家或高级研究人员。

作者在署名中的排列顺序往往由通讯作者确定，或者由论文工作的参与者集体决定，而且必须在投稿前加以确定。涉及科研合作的作者确定，需要在合作协议中加以规定。一般不能在投稿过程中随意增加或删除作者或改变作者顺序。如果作者在稿件提交后要求删除或增加作者，则须向期刊编辑提出申请，给出解释并签署所有作者的同意书。

二、姓名书写规则

西方人的姓名书写规则为"先名后姓"，跟我国的"先姓后名"结构有所不同。外国人姓名结构为：名字+中间名+姓氏。排在最前面的名字为出生时教士或父母给取的名字(教名)，英语中称为 first name、given name 或 forename，排在中间的为中间名(第二个名字)，英语中称为 middle name，排在最后的为姓氏，英语中称为 last name、family name 或 surname。例如，William Jafferson Clinton(威廉·杰弗森·克林顿)，William 是名，Jafferson 是中间名，Clinton 是姓。称呼时，姓要在前面加尊称，例如 Mr. Clinton，熟人则直呼其名 William。William Jafferson Clinton 也可写作"W. J. Clinton" "Clinton, W. J." "Clinton W. J."或"Clinton WJ"。

中国人的姓名按《中国人名汉语拼音字母拼写规则》(GB/T 28039—2011)书写，姓在前，名在后，姓和名的首字母大写，护照上以此为准，例如，Liu Jinping(刘进平)，简写为 Liu J.。事实上，也有不少人将双字名的两个字的拼音首字母大写，然后连字符连起来，如 Liu Jin-Ping，这样做可与单字名相区别；Liu Jin-Ping 简写为 Liu J.-P. 或 Liu J-P。不论哪一种书写法，最好在所有论文中保持一致，不至于在文献检索或论文引用时被误认为两个人。此外，向英语期刊投稿时，最好按西方人姓名"先名后姓"的规则书写，否则姓和名很容易被西方人混淆，在征引文献时发生错误。

三、单位和地址

论文需要提供作者的单位和地址[Affiliation(s) and Address(es)]，这不仅是论文成果的归属标记，也便于读者与作者联系。一般在作者后面对应地写出工作单位、联系地址、邮政编码、电子邮件地址或联系电话等信息。单位地址要尽可能详细，并要求写出全名。如果作者不止一个单位，则用数字或字母（通常用上标表示）按顺序前后标出。另外需要注意的是，英语单位地址的书写习惯为"先小单位（小地址）、后大单位（大地址）"。

第四章 摘要的写作

摘要(Abstract 或 Summary)也称为内容提要或概要,是对论文内容进行的简要概括,内容包括主要研究目的、研究方法、研究结果(或重要发现)、研究结论和意义。其作用主要是便于读者快速了解论文主要内容,以及信息检索。摘要一般不加注释和不进行评论,也不带有参考文献和图表。摘要最好避免使用化学结构式、数学表达式、角标、希腊文或罗马文等特殊符号。摘要字数一般控制在 150~250 个单词,不同期刊对其字数的要求不同。

摘要在许多方面是学术论文中最重要的部分,需要作者花大力气推敲。阅读摘要的人数是阅读全文人数的 10~500 倍。读者一般根据摘要来决定是否继续阅读全文。如果摘要写得不好,读者就没有兴趣继续阅读正文,编辑就可能直接拒稿。期刊编辑在寻找审稿人时,通常将论文的题目和摘要发给潜在的审稿人,由于审稿人为 SCI 期刊审稿一般为免费劳动,因此当摘要看起来很平庸时,很可能审稿人就会因缺乏兴趣而拒绝审稿。因此,作者要根据期刊要求,选择合适的摘要类型,简洁、清楚地概括全文信息,多花一点时间和精力,以吸引读者阅读兴趣为方针来进行摘要的写作。

一、摘要的分类

(一)报道性摘要

报道性摘要,也称资料性摘要或信息性摘要(informative abstract),为研究性论文的摘要类型。报道性摘要在简要概括的前提下,尽可能完整而准确地反映论文的各部分内容,也就是论文 IMRaD 结构中的 Introduction(引言)、Materials and Methods(材料和方法)、Results(结果)和 Discussion(讨论)等几个主要部分的内容。一般开头用一两句话介绍研究背景或研究目的,给出研究的领域或范围、问题提出的缘由和重要性。主要研究方法根据论文情况可单独说明,或者与的主要结果结合在一起来写,例如,用什么方法获得什么结果。摘要最重要的部分是结果,结果部分要给出主要发现和重要实验数据。最后用一两句话给出结论,并说明论文工作的理论价值或应用价值。如果结果有局限性或者有关问题有待进一步研究,也可一并说明。

【例文】引自"The F-box protein TIR1 is an auxin receptor"。

The plant hormone auxin regulates diverse aspects of plant growth and development. Recent studies indicate that auxin acts by promoting the degradation of the Aux/IAA transcriptional repressors through the action of the ubiquitin protein ligase SCF^{TIR1}. The nature of the signalling cascade that leads to this effect is not known. However, recent studies indicate that the auxin receptor and other signalling components involved in this response are soluble factors. Using an *in vitro* pull-down assay, we demonstrate that the interaction between transport inhibitor response 1 (TIR1) and Aux/IAA proteins does not require stable modification of either protein. Instead auxin promotes the Aux/IAA-SCF^{TIR1} interaction by binding directly to SCF^{TIR1}. We further show that the loss of TIR1 and three related F-box proteins eliminates saturable auxin binding in plant extracts. Finally, TIR1 synthesized in insect cells binds Aux/IAA proteins in an auxin-dependent manner. Together, these results indicate that TIR1 is an auxin receptor that mediates Aux/IAA degradation and auxin-regulated transcription.

(二) 结构化摘要

结构化摘要(structured abstract)与不分节的报道性摘要(也称为非结构化摘要,unstructured abstract)不同,结构化摘要的各个主要要素前面分别用小标题或黑体字加以标记,如 Background(背景)或/和 Objective(目的)、Methods(方法)、Results(结果)和 Conclusion(结论)。这种摘要更便于读者快速识别和理解。结构化摘要的格式因期刊而异,不同的期刊使用的结构形式不同。结构化摘要的格式是在 20 世纪 80 年代末 90 年代初由国际医学期刊编辑委员会制定的,目的是帮助医学卫生专业人员选择临床相关的并且方法有效的期刊文章。这种格式对作者和读者来说有若干优点:便于作者准确地总结论文内容;有助于推进编辑对论文鉴定及同行评审过程;利于计算机文献检索。因此,这种结构化摘要被生物医学专业期刊广泛采用。

《当代生物学》(*Current Biology*)期刊的摘要格式为:背景(Background)、结果(Results)和结论(Conclusions)。

【例文】引自"Patterns of auxin transport and gene expression during primordium development revealed by live imaging of the arabidopsis inflorescence meristem"。

Background: Plants produce leaf and flower primordia from a specialized tissue called the shoot apical meristem (SAM). Genetic studies have identified a large number of genes that affect various aspects of primordium development including positioning, growth, and differentiation. So far, however, a detailed understanding of the spatio-temporal sequence of events leading to primordium development has not been established.

Results: We use confocal imaging of green fluorescent protein(GFP)reporter genes in living plants to monitor the expression patterns of multiple proteins and genes involved in flower primordial developmental processes. By monitoring the expression and polarity of PINFORMED1 (PIN1), the auxin efflux facilitator, and the expression of the auxin-responsive reporter DR5, we reveal stereotypical PIN1 polarity changes which, together with auxin induction experiments, suggest that cycles of auxin build-up and depletion accompany, and may direct, different stages of primordium development. Imaging of multiple GFP-protein fusions shows that these dynamics also correlate with the specification of primordial boundary domains, organ polarity axes, and the sites of floral meristem initiation.

Conclusions: These results provide new insight into auxin transport dynamics during primordial positioning and suggest a role for auxin transport in influencing primordial cell type. PIN and AUX/LAX proteins: Their role in auxin accumulation.

《柳叶刀》(*The Lancet*)期刊的摘要格式为：背景(Background)、方法(Methods)、发现(Findings)和解释(Interpretation)。

【例文】引自"Efficacy and safety of nerinetide for the treatment of acute ischaemic stroke(ESCAPE-NA1): A multicentre, double-blind, randomised controlled trial"。

Background:

Nerinetide, an eicosapeptide that interferes with post-synaptic density protein 95, is a neuroprotectant that is effective in preclinical stroke models of ischaemia-reperfusion. In this trial, we assessed the efficacy and safety of nerinetide in human ischaemia-reperfusion that occurs with rapid endovascular thrombectomy in patients who had an acute ischaemic stroke.

Methods:

For this multicentre, double-blind, randomised, placebo-controlled study done in 48 acute care hospitals in eight countries, we enrolled patients with acute ischaemic stroke due to large vessel occlusion within a 12 h treatment window. Eligible patients were aged 18 years or older with a disabling ischaemic stroke at the time of randomisation, had been functioning independently in the community before the stroke, had an Alberta Stroke Program Early CT Score(ASPECTS)greater than 4, and vascular imaging showing moderate-to-good collateral filling, as determined by multiphase CT angiography. Patients were randomly assigned(1∶1) to receive intravenous nerinetide in a single dose of 2.6 mg/kg, up to a maximum dose of 270 mg, on the basis of estimated or actual weight(if known)or saline placebo by use of a real-time, dynamic, internet-based, stratified randomised minimisation procedure. Patients were stratified by intravenous alteplase treatment and declared endovascular device choice. All trial personnel and patients were masked to sequence and treatment allocation. All patients underwent endovascular thrombectomy and received alteplase in usual care when indicated. The primary outcome was a favourable functional outcome 90 days after randomisation, defined as a modified Rankin Scale(mRS)score of 0-2. Secondary outcomes were measures of neurological disability, functional independence in activities of daily living, excellent functional outcome (mRS 0-1), and mortality. The analysis was done in the intention-to-treat population and adjusted for age, sex, baseline National Institutes of Health Stroke Scale score, ASPECTS, occlusion location, site, alteplase use, and declared first device. The safety population included all patients who received any amount of study drug. This trial is registered with ClinicalTrials.gov, NCT02930018.

Findings:

Between March 1, 2017, and Aug 12, 2019, 1105 patients were randomly assigned to receive nerinetide($n=549$)or placebo($n=556$). 337(61.4%)of 549 patients with nerinetide and 329(59.2%)of 556 with placebo achieved an mRS score of 0-2 at 90 days(adjusted risk ratio 1.04, 95% CI 0.96-1.14; $p=0.35$). Secondary outcomes were similar between groups. We observed evidence of treatment effect modification resulting in inhibition of treatment effect in patients receiving alteplase. Serious adverse events occurred equally between groups.

Interpretation:

Nerinetide did not improve the proportion of patients achieving good clinical outcomes after endovascular thrombectomy compared with patients receiving placebo.

《新英格兰医学期刊》(*The New England Journal of Medicine*, NEJM)的格式则为背景(Background)、方法(Methods)、结果(Results)和结论(Conclusions)。

【例文】引自"Vitamin E acetate in bronchoalveolar-lavage fluid associated with EVALI"。

Background:

The causative agents for the current national outbreak of electronic-cigarette, or vaping, product use-associated lung injury(EVALI)have not been established. Detection of toxicants in bronchoalveolar-lavage (BAL) fluid from patients with EVALI can provide direct information on exposure within the lung.

Methods:

BAL fluids were collected from 51 patients with EVALI in 16 states and from 99 healthy participants who were part of an ongoing study of smoking involving nonsmokers, exclusive users of E-cigarettes or vaping products, and exclusive cigarette smokers that was initiated in 2015. Using the BAL fluid, we performed isotope dilution mass spectrometry to measure several priority toxicants: Vitamin E acetate, plant oils, medium-chain triglyceride oil, coconut oil, petroleum distillates, and diluent terpenes.

Results:

State and local health departments assigned EVALI case status as confirmed for 25 patients and as probable for 26 patients. Vitamin E acetate was identified in BAL fluid obtained from 48 of 51 case patients(94%)in 16 states but not in such fluid obtained from the healthy comparator group. No other priority toxicants were found in BAL fluid from the case patients or the comparator group, except for coconut oil and limonene, which were found in 1 patient each. Among the case patients for whom laboratory or epidemiologic data were available, 47 of 50(94%)had detectable tetrahydrocannabinol(THC)or its metabolites in BAL fluid or had reported vaping THC products in the 90 days before the onset of illness. Nicotine or its metabolites were detected in 30 of 47 of the case patients(64%).

Conclusions:

Vitamin E acetate was associated with EVALI in a convenience sample of 51 patients in 16 states across the United States.

(三)指示性摘要

指示性摘要(descriptive abstract),也称为说明性摘要或描述性摘要,只是简要概述论文涵盖的主题(主要议题),不具体涉及研究方法、论据、结果和结论,因此这类摘要更像一个段落形式的目录。它一般应用于介绍研究进展或专题内容的综述性文章。这类摘要只提供主题线索,以便读者决定是否阅读整个文档。与阅读报道性摘要不同,阅读指示性摘要不能代替阅读整个文档,因为它不能获得文章的内容,指示性摘要也不能实现报道性摘要的其他主要目标,因此,指示性摘要较不常用。

【例文】引自"The plant immune system"。

Many plant-associated microbes are pathogens that impair plant growth and reproduction. Plants respond to infection using a two-branched innate immune system. The first branch recognizes and responds to molecules common to many classes of microbes, including non-pathogens. The second responds to pathogen virulence factors, either directly or through their effects on host targets. These plant immune systems, and the pathogen molecules to which they respond, provide extraordinary insights into molecular recognition, cell biology and evolution across biological kingdoms. A detailed understanding of plant immune function will underpin crop improvement for food, fibre and biofuels production.

摘要的篇幅应与论文篇幅相匹配,较短的综述、评介性文章或短讯的摘要可更短一些。

【例文1】引自"Function of the ubiquitin-proteasome pathway in auxin response"。

The plant hormone auxin regulates many aspects of growth and development. Despite the importance of this hormone, the molecular basis for auxin action has remained elusive. Recent advances using molecular genetics in *Arabidopsis* have begun to elucidate the mechanisms involved in auxin signaling. These results suggest that protein degradation by the ubiquitin pathway has a central role in auxin response.

【例文 2】引自"Auxin transport: Why plants like to think BIG"。

The regulation of auxin transport via auxin efflux carriers likely plays a central role in a variety of physiological responses in higher plants. With the isolation of BIG, an *Arabidopsis* protein of enormous size, another potential regulator of auxin transport has been characterized.

(四) 融合型摘要

面对文献爆炸和期刊版面的紧张，期刊对论文格式也做出相应调整。以下是一篇《自然》长论文的摘要，相当于摘要与引言的融合。摘要后面没有引言，这意味着摘要功能上既作为摘要，也作为引言。

【例文】引自"Extensive signal integration by the phytohormone protein network"。

Plant hormones coordinate responses to environmental cues with developmental programs[1], and are fundamental for stress resilience and agronomic yield[2]. The core signalling pathways underlying the effects of phytohormones have been elucidated by genetic screens and hypothesis-driven approaches, and extended by interactome studies of select pathways[3]. However, fundamental questions remain about how information from different pathways is integrated. Genetically, most phenotypes seem to be regulated by several hormones, but transcriptional profiling suggests that hormones trigger largely exclusive transcriptional programs[4]. We hypothesized that protein-protein interactions have an important role in phytohormone signal integration. Here, we experimentally generated a systems-level map of the *Arabidopsis* phytohormone signalling network, consisting of more than 2,000 binary protein-protein interactions. In the highly interconnected network, we identify pathway communities and hundreds of previously unknown pathway contacts that represent potential points of crosstalk. Functional validation of candidates in seven hormone pathways reveals new functions for 74% of tested proteins in 84% of candidate interactions, and indicates that a large majority of signalling proteins function pleiotropically in several pathways. Moreover, we identify several hundred largely small-molecule-dependent interactions of hormone receptors. Comparison with previous reports suggests that noncanonical and nontranscription-mediated receptor signalling is more common than hitherto appreciated.

(五) 图形摘要

图形摘要(graphical abstract，GA)是书面摘要的直观呈现，旨在以单一、简洁的图像形式快速、清晰地传达论文的关键信息，以便读者第一眼就能了解论文的主要信息,确定哪些论文与他们的研究兴趣相关,从而吸引读者阅读、关注和引用。图文摘要依据期刊投稿指南要求制作,包括文件格式、字体类型、字体大小、线宽、颜色、图形尺寸等。图片可以是流程图、数据图、线条图、动态图、组织细胞图、化学结构图、仪器符号图等;图片要使用约定俗成的图例或公知公用的符号,需要时添加简洁而必要的文字注释;图片一般设有包含关键词的简短标题,类似于一张 PowerPoint 讲稿。图片摘要力求直观形象地反映论文的核心结果/结论,因此设计时应采取以突出重点、简洁明快、逻辑清晰和具有视觉冲击力的结构布局为要。

图形摘要在学术出版中越来越普遍,例如,爱思唯尔(Elsevier)、细胞出版社(Cell Press)的一些期刊就要求作者提交附有图形摘要的稿件。图形摘要可单独绘制,也可以是正文中使用过的概念图(conceptual figure)或合成图(synthesizing figure)。不同的期刊对图形摘要大小、像素、字体、文件类型都有不同的规定,但一般图像描述要按照视觉流动习惯从左到右和(或)从上到下设计,以彩图方式提供所获得结果或呈现过程的背景,例如,细胞研究要直观地显示所指的组织/物种类型、细胞/亚细胞器类型或分子类型如(DNA、RNA、蛋白质等)。只使用非专业人士也能明白的简单标签。图中文字使用大于 12 磅的 Arial、Helvetica 或 Myriad 等字体。图形摘要主要供在线浏览使用,可作为电子目录内容简介(eTOC blurb)的配图。

【例文】引自《发育细胞》(*Developmental Cell*):"A LncRNA-MAF: MAFB transcription factor network regulates epidermal differentiation"(图 4-1)。

与之相配合的电子目录内容简介为:

Lopez-Pajares et al. define dynamically altered genes during epidermal differentiation

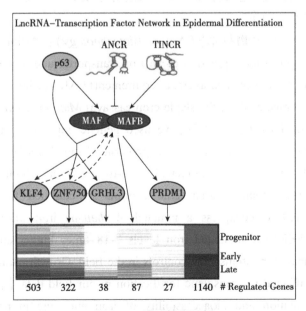

图 4-1 图形摘要示例

and use module mapping to identify transcription factors involved in this process. RISPR/Cas9-mediated ablation of MAF and MAFB in primary human tissue shows they are essential differentiation regulators. MAF: MAFB is regulated by lncRNAs and controls downstream key effector TFs.

二、摘要的写作要求

(一) 内容与要求

摘要尽可能包括引言(背景)、方法、结果和结论几个要素，尽可能详细而准确地对研究进行总结。收费期刊虽然不能免费下载全文，但摘要则能在检索时免费获得。因此，有不少研究人员可能只能读到文章的摘要而看不到全文。摘要如能提供准确而详尽的研究总结，这对于看不到全文或没时间看全文的研究者了解论文的工作很有好处。摘要可提供最重要的数据，但却不必列举方法和结果的细节。阅读摘要后对文章细节感兴趣的读者自然会下载和阅读全文。对于研究性论文，清晰而简洁地总结论文内容通常是一个挑战。初学者可以借鉴结构化摘要的结构来写作报道性摘要。因为结构化摘要每一节都有一个单独而清晰的标题，可以把每一个小节或类别归结成一个问题。例如，"背景"可以提炼为"关于这个问题的最新知识是什么"；"方法"可以提炼为"怎么获得结果的，采用何种方法"；"结果"可以归结为"发现了什么，得到了哪些数据或结果"，结果部分不能含糊其词，要明确地写出所发现的东西；"结论"可以归结为"结果说明什么，结果有什么意义"。与结构化摘要不同，非结构化摘要(报道性摘要)一般不分段落，也就是只有一个段落。但要注意的是，某些期刊的结构化摘要不要求作者写出完整的句子。

【例文1】引自《自然生物技术》(*Nature Biotechnology*)："Biofortification of field-grown cassava by engineering expression of an iron transporter and ferritin"。

Less than 10% of the estimated average requirement (EAR) for iron and zinc is provided by consumption of storage roots of the staple crop cassava (*Manihot esculenta* Crantz) in West African human populations.【描述背景】We used genetic engineering to improve mineral micronutrient concentrations in cassava. Overexpression of the *Arabidopsis thaliana* vacuolar iron transporter VIT1 in cassava accumulated three-to seven-times-higher levels of iron in transgenic storage roots than nontransgenic controls in confined field trials in Puerto Rico. Plants engineered to coexpress a mutated *A. thaliana* iron transporter (IRT1) and *A. thaliana* ferritin (FER1) accumulated iron levels 7-18 times higher and zinc levels 3-10 times higher than those in nontransgenic controls in the field. Growth parameters and storage-root yields were unaffected by transgenic fortification in our field data.【合并描述方法与结果】Measures of retention and bioaccessibility of iron and zinc in processed transgenic cassava indicated that *IRT1+FER1* plants could provide 40%-50% of the EAR for iron and

60%-70% of the EAR for zinc in 1-to 6-year-old children and nonlactating, nonpregnant West African women.【描述结论】

说明：由该非结构化论文，可见，报道性摘要包含的引言（背景）、方法、结果和结论等几个要素，但通常将方法与结果合并在一起来写。

【例文2】引自《自然》："Mechanism of auxin perception by the TIR1 ubiquitin ligase"。

Auxin is a pivotal plant hormone that controls many aspects of plant growth and development. Perceived by a small family of F-box proteins including transport inhibitor response 1 (TIR1), auxin regulates gene expression by promoting SCF ubiquitin-ligase-catalysed degradation of the Aux/IAA transcription repressors, but how the TIR1 F-box protein senses and becomes activated by auxin remains unclear.【描述背景】Here we present the crystal structures of the *Arabidopsis* TIR1-ASK1 complex, free and in complexes with three different auxin compounds and an Aux/IAA substrate peptide. These structures show that the leucine-rich repeat domain of TIR1 contains an unexpected inositol hexakisphosphate co-factor and recognizes auxin and the Aux/IAA polypeptide substrate through a single surface pocket. Anchored to the base of the TIR1 pocket, auxin binds to a partially promiscuous site, which can also accommodate various auxin analogues. Docked on top of auxin, the Aux/IAA substrate peptide occupies the rest of the TIR1 pocket and completely encloses the hormone-binding site. By filling in a hydrophobic cavity at the protein interface, auxin enhances the TIR1-substrate interactions by acting as a 'molecular glue'.【描述结果】Our results establish the first structural model of a plant hormone receptor.【描述结论】

说明：从该非结构化论文可以看到，当方法在领域内人所共知或方法较多难以概述时，可在摘要中忽略方法要素。因此，以上摘要包含引言（背景）、结果和结论，但没有描述方法。

（二）人称与语态

摘要过去多使用第三人称（或物称）和被动语态，以显示强调表述的客观性，同时将重要信息前置，主语部分承载较多的信息，有语义突出的效果。但目前使用第一人称（作者自己）和主动语态的摘要在大大增加，如 We used/applied..., We demonstrate/reveal/establish/characterize... 等。主动语态的表达更为直接、生动、简洁和清晰，动作的执行者和承受者可一目了然，能特别突出作者的科学贡献。

（三）时态

摘要的时态根据动作及表述的事实而定。介绍不受时间影响的普遍事实、实验结果和实验结论，使用一般现在时。描述某种研究趋势或发展动态，可用现在完成式。以第一人称叙述过去进行的实验或动作，用一般过去时，如 We investigated/explored..., We determined/assessed/measured/compared...，We calculated/computed/evaluated...，We developed/designed/derived/modeled/implemented... 等；但对于第一人称描述在论文中呈现、报告、描述或表明等的情况（而不是对过去所进行的实验描述）用一般现在时，如 We present...，We report...，We describe...，We show that...，We suggest that... 等，用一般现在时；对于以论文或报告为主语，对本论文或本报告呈现、描述、报告、提出等的情况描述，用一般现在时，如 This paper（或 This report）presents/describes/reports/proposes... 等。对于论文发现的意义描述，动词可用一般现在时（或利用 may、should、could 等情态动词）；描述论文发现对将来的影响可用将来时。

【例文1】引自"CRISPR-engineered T cells in patients with refractory cancer"。

CRISPR-Cas9 gene editing provides a powerful tool to enhance the natural ability of human T cells to fight cancer. We report a first-in-human phase I clinical trial to test the safety and feasibility of multiplex CRISPR-Cas9 editing to engineer T cells in three patients with refractory cancer. Two genes encoding the endogenous T cell receptor (TCR) chains, TCRα (*TRAC*) and TCRβ (*TRBC*) were deleted in T cells to reduce TCR mispairing and to enhance the expression of a synthetic, cancer-specific TCR transgene (NY-ESO-1). Removal of a third gene encoding PD-1 (*PDCD1*), was performed to improve anti-tumor immunity. Adoptive transfer of engineered T cells into patients resulted in durable engraftment with edits at all three genomic loci. Though chromosomal translocations were detected, the frequency decreased over time. Modified T cells persisted for up to 9 months suggesting that immunogenicity is minimal under these conditions and demonstrating the feasibility of CRISPR gene-editing for cancer immunotherapy.

说明：第一句"CRISPR-Cas9 gene editing provides a powerful tool to enhance the natural ability of human T cells to fight cancer"为描述背景，用一般现在时态。第二句对论文进行描述，句子 We report... 用第一人称（作者自己）和主动语态，采用一般现在时。后面的句子描述实验动作，第二句 Two genes...were deleted，第三句 Removal of...was performed 用物称（第三人称）和被动语态，采用一般过去时。最后一句的主句 Modified T cells persisted for up to 9 months 描述过去的动作，用一般过去时；用现在分词结构与一般现在时的从句，以及现在分词结构与名词词组一起来表述论文的结论和意义"suggesting that immunogenicity is minimal under these conditions and demonstrating the feasibility of CRISPR gene-editing for cancer immunotherapy"。

目前，SCI 论文摘要中利用第一人称（we）和主动语态来写作句子的情况逐渐增多，而且通篇采用一般现在时。

【例文2】引自"Strigolactone inhibition of shoot branching"。

A carotenoid-derived hormonal signal that inhibits shoot branching in plants has long escaped identification. Strigolactones are compounds thought to be derived from carotenoids and are known to trigger the germination of parasitic plant seeds and stimulate symbiotic fungi. Here we present evidence that *carotenoid cleavage dioxygenase 8* shoot branching mutants of pea are strigolactone deficient and that strigolactone application restores the wild-type branching phenotype to *ccd8* mutants. Moreover, we show that other branching mutants previously characterized as lacking a response to the branching inhibition signal also lack strigolactone response, and are not deficient in strigolactones. These responses are conserved in *Arabidopsis*. In agreement with the expected properties of the hormonal signal, exogenous strigolactone can be transported in shoots and act at low concentrations. We suggest that endogenous strigolactones or related compounds inhibit shoot branching in plants. Furthermore, *ccd8* mutants demonstrate the diverse effects of strigolactones in shoot branching, mycorrhizal symbiosis and parasitic weed interaction.

上面这个摘要中，全部采用一般现在时，且多用第一人称(we)和主动语态，如Here we present evidence that..., Moreover, we show that..., We suggest that...。但下面这两句用物称(第三人称)和被动语态，但时态仍是一般现在时：These responses are conserved..., In agreement with the expected properties of the hormonal signal, exogenous strigolactone can be transported...。

(四) 其他要求

摘要中第一次出现的物种名称，后面要用括号给出学名全称；第一次出现的缩略语、简称或代号也要用括号给出全称。摘要一般不引用文献，但在讨论、反驳、增补或评论类期刊文章中，也会征引文献。另外，某些期刊的通讯类文章中也可征引文献。

【例文1】引自《细胞》(*Cell*)的预评(preview)文章："The high road and the low road: Trafficking choices in plants"。

Polar transport of the signaling molecule auxin is critical for plant development and depends on both the polar distribution of auxin efflux carriers, which pump auxin out of the cell and the alignment of these polarized cells. Two papers in this issue of Cell(Michniewicz et al., 2007; Jaillais et al., 2007) address how polar transport of these carriers occurs and describe the endosomal pathways involved.【摘要需要征引文献】

【例文2】引自《自然》的通讯(Letter)文章："A novel sensor to map auxin response and distribution at high spatio-temporal resolution"。

Auxin is a key plant morphogenetic signal[1] but tools to analyse dynamically its distribution and signalling during development are still limited. Auxin perception directly triggers the degradation of Aux/IAA repressor proteins[2,3,4,5,6]. Here we describe a novel Aux/IAA-based auxin signalling sensor termed DII-VENUS that was engineered in the model plant *Arabidopsis thaliana*. The VENUS fast maturing form of yellow fluorescent protein[7] was fused in-frame to the Aux/IAA auxin-interaction domain (termed domain Ⅱ; DII)[5] and expressed under a constitutive promoter. We initially show that DII-VENUS abundance is dependent on auxin, its TIR1/AFBs co-receptors[4, 5, 6, 8] and proteasome activities. Next, we demonstrate that DII-VENUS provides a map of relative auxin distribution at cellular resolution in different tissues. DII-VENUS is also rapidly degraded in response to auxin and we used it to visualize dynamic changes in cellular auxin distribution successfully during two developmental responses, the root gravitropic response and lateral organ production at the shoot apex. Our results illustrate the value of developing response input sensors such as DII-VENUS to provide high-resolution spatio-temporal information about hormone distribution and response during plant growth and development.

(五) 常用句式

写作论文摘要有很多句式可以套用，初学者宜注意归纳和总结。

①描写论文背景可用：

The previous work on...had indicated that...

...have/has, however, been largely unexplored.

...have not been studied yet.

...has not yet been thoroughly investigated.

...but there is no generally accepted theory concerning...

Recent studies/although some research has established..., the role of...is not well known.

Although a number of papers have been published in the area of...

Little work has been carried out for...

Few studies have been done on...

②描写研究目标常用下面的短语开头：

This study examines/analyzes/identifies/determines/outlines/focuses on...

The study is aimed at...

A investigation was designed to...

The paper attempt to...

The paper is mainly devoted to...

To investigate/ascertain/identify/understand/elaborate...

For the purpose of...

The (main/primary) aim/goal/objective/purpose of the study/paper is to...

③描写方法常用下面的短语开头：

A quantitative study/a randomized controlled study/a qualitative survey/a literature review/a double blind trial is/was conducted/performed/carried out...

We describe a new approach to...

We present a test method to evaluate...

A novel technique has been developed to...

For measuring..., the...method was used/chosen in this study/experiment.

④描述结果常使用的句式有:

We describe...

We report...

Here we present evidence that...

We show that...

We demonstrate that...

The paper reports/presents/describes...

The results of observation/calculation show that...

It is found that...

The structure/function/mechanism/relationship (between...and...) is characterized by...

X was statistically significant.

Variable A has a negative correlation with Variable B.

⑤描述结论可用以下句式:

Our results illustrate...

We suggest that...

To sum up, we have revealed...

We concluded that...

It is concluded that...

The result of the present work implied that...

The conclusion of our research is...

The research has led to the discovery of...

摘要要尽可能少使用领域特别狭窄的行话或专业术语。有研究者对大约20 000篇论文的标题和摘要中的行话或专业术语进行统计,发现当行话或专业术语达到摘要的1%或更多时,论文的被引数量会急剧下降。尤其是像《自然》和《科学》这类顶级期刊,更是要求论文要有跨领域的意义。因此,摘要中使用过多特别专门的行话和术语显然会影响论文的阅读和引用。

第五章　论文亮点和期刊电子目录内容简介的写作

目前，有些期刊还要求作者在提交稿件时提供论文亮点（Highlights）和期刊电子目录的内容简介（eTOC blurb，其中 TOC 是 Table of Content 的缩写），以便让读者在网络出版环境和文献爆炸时代快速了解论文的主要内容，从而获得更多的读者和引用。这两种要素的写作都要求使用完整的句子，语言要简洁平易，概括文章的核心发现，传达研究的本质及其独特性，但最好不要直接拷贝摘要中的语句。为了将论文中大量复杂的信息压缩到一个非常小的文本空间中，需要去除多余单词，缩短短语和句子，使用主动语态；在字符数而不是单词数限制的情况下，尽可能使用简单的词汇或用较短的同义词替换较长的单词。文章的关键词和关键短语最好能在出现在论文亮点和期刊电子目录的内容简介，但要避免使用非标准缩写词，如有必要，则须在第一次使用时写出全称。为了面向广泛的或一般的读者，避免使用生僻的行话和高度技术性的语言。这两种要素一般在论文（包括摘要）完成后最后写作。

论文亮点要求将一篇研究文章的核心发现浓缩成 3~5 个要点，通常有字符数限制，例如，爱思唯尔期刊要求每条亮点包括空格在内不超过 85 个字符。这些亮点之间内容不要重叠，也不要做任何解释，同时不要包含废话和复杂的信息。亮点要准确而简洁地向读者呈现论文中最令人兴奋的结果或主要创新点，但不要包括论文摘要中有关背景、方法等信息。

需要写作论文亮点的期刊有爱思唯尔旗下的《工业作物与产品》（*Industrial Crops and Products*）、《植物生理学与生物化学》（*Plant Physiology and Biochemistry*）、《基因》（*Gene*）等。以下是发表在 2020 年《植物生理学与生物化学》的题目为 "Jasmonate and aluminum crosstalk in tomato: Identification and expression analysis of *WRKYs* and *ALMTs* during JA/Al-regulated root growth" 的论文亮点。

- Jasmonic acid enhanced aluminum-induced root growth inhibition in tomato.
- Aluminum induced the expression of genes related to JA biosynthesis and signaling.
- SlMYC2-VIGS seedlings and *jasmonic acid insensitive mutant jai* 1-1 were employed

to evaluate the expression patterns of WRKY transcription factors and ALMT genes.

• WRKY and ALMT regulatory module was involved in jasmonic acid-mediated root growth inhibition under aluminum stress.

期刊电子目录的内容简介一般不超过3行（不超过50个单词或60个单词，不同期刊要求不同），使用第三人称[以第一作者等（First Author et al.）或通讯作者及其同事（Corresponding Author and Colleagues）起头]和以简洁、平实和浅易（非专家能看得懂）的语言介绍论文的主要内容，可包括描述论文核心发现的背景和意义信息（这对范围广泛的不同领域读者理解论文发现是必要的），但不要描述实验细节。另外，有的期刊电子目录的内容简介需要配图。

需要写作期刊电子目录内容简介的期刊有 Cell Press 旗下的期刊 *Cell, Current Biology, Cell Stem Cell, Cell Reports Physical Science* 等。

Cell 在写作期刊电子目录内容简介时使用的作者为通讯作者，如2020年的一篇论文："A universal design of betacoronavirus vaccines against COVID-19, MERS and SARS"，其期刊电子目录内容简介如下：

Gao et al. present the structure-guided design of a coronavirus immunogen comprised of two protein subunits each containing the of virus spike receptor binding domain fused together via a disulfide link. The immunogen elicits strong immunogenicity in mice and protects them against viral challenge. The vaccine design strategy can be universally applied to SARS, MERS, COVID-19 and other CoV vaccines to counter emerging threats.

也可以不使用作者开头，直接而简洁地概括论文的主要结果、结论和意义，如2020年的一篇论文"Major impacts of widespread structural variation on gene expression and crop improvement in tomato"，其期刊电子目录内容简介如下：

Comprehensive structural variant identification in tomato genomes allows insight into the evolution and domestication of tomato and serves as a resource for phenotype-directed breeding.

《当代生物学》在写作期刊电子目录内容简介时使用的作者为第一作者，如2020年的一篇论文："Tyrosine phosphorylation of the myosin regulatory light chain controls non-muscle myosin II assembly and function in migrating cells"，其期刊电子目录内容简介如下：

Aguilar-Cuenca et al. determine the cellular function of myosin light chain (RLC) phosphorylation on tyrosine. Phospho-Tyr155 RLC mainly appears at lamellipodia, preventing the interaction of the regulatory light chain with myosin heavy chain II, impairing formation of functional myosin hexamers and limiting myosin assembly during protrusion.

当然也可以在前面用一句话来介绍论文发现的背景，如"Vast differences in strain-level diversity in the gut microbiota of two closely related honey bee species"的期刊电子目

录内容简介如下：

Bacteria have highly flexible gene content; functions of bacterial communities therefore depend on their strain-level composition. Using metagenomics, Ellegaard et al. find major differences in composition and diversity in the gut microbiota of two related honey bees, raising new questions on function and evolution of host-associated bacteria.

在写作这两种要素时，都需要了解期刊"作者须知"中的写作要求，同时参照最新几期论文的格式来写作。

第六章　关键词的设置

摘要之后通常是由作者选择的、能反映论文内容的关键词（Keywords）。设置关键词的目的是满足文献索引或检索工作的需要，一般从论文中提取出最能反映论文研究主题、研究领域或方向、主要方法、核心结果的词或词组作为关键词。关键词一般为3~8个，以5个关键词居多，但不同期刊所要求列出的关键词数量有不同规定，有时甚至要求提供可供参考的关键词清单。

挑选关键词有两个原则：一是选择的关键词要能反映或切合论文的内容，因为相关性越强，在检索结果列表中就越靠前，显示度就越高；二是选用一组意义宽窄不同的术语组合，最大限度地使文章被潜在的读者检索到。应该避免只使用一般性短语（general phrases）；一定要包括能反映文章特殊内容（细节）的描述性词汇（detailed descriptive words）。如果关键词过于笼统，则很可能会面临大量文章使用的相同关键词的竞争。关键词应该指出一般性主题，但是不应太宽泛。例如，一篇关于表观遗传调控因子（epigenetic regulator）的论文，就不宜使用诸如"细胞生物学（cell biology）"或"遗传学（genetics）"之类的过于宽泛的关键词，这些术语几乎既不能反映与论文的相关性最强的内容，也不是潜在读者搜索这篇论文使用的合适关键词。因此，要挑选摘要中出现的、能反映论文特殊性的关键术语。另外，如果关键词过于具体，那么搜索这些关键词的读者数量也不会很多，从而减少潜在的阅读者。

从实际搜索行为来看，读者一般用短语或完整的句子来搜索目标论文，这是因为单词搜索产生的结果列表比预期的要宽泛得多，其中大多数文章可能都不相关。这样看来，"关键词"其实表述不当，称"关键词组"也许更好。在实际选择关键词时，要尽可能选择包含二到四个单词的短语作为关键词。

挑选关键词时，要避免使用标题中已经出现的术语。因为论文标题本身是可搜索的并将被加权（通过编程代码标记为具有更大的权重），因此，关键词应是补充标题内容，但可以使用标题中出现的重要词语的替代词语作为关键词，不过要注意缩写词往往是多种单词的缩写，可能在不同领域中具有不同的含义，如 ARC 这个术语在许多领域都有意义，如计算机编程、工程、数学和生物学等。因此，如果是指 ARC 文件格式（ARC file format），那就应该使用短语"ARC file format"作为关键词。

如果研究涉及一个关键的方法或技术，应确保这种方法或技术的术语出现于论文的标题或关键词中，并要注意拼写形式，搜索引擎在默认情况下会忽略大小写规则，但连字符可能是一个问题。因此，应确保使用的是每个关键词的官方/正式认可的书写形式，否则，有可能会导致论文检索率降低。

关键词的设置要遵守期刊规定。例如，大多数临床论文使用的关键词来自美国国家医学图书馆的医学主题标题（US National Library of Medicine's Medical Subject Headings，MeSH），还有一些期刊规定使用单词而不是短语作为关键词。

保险起见，可在准备论文初稿或在提交论文之前测试设置的关键词。当把关键词输入各种期刊和学术数据库中（如 Google Scholar），结果是否包括与待发论文主题相似的论文，如果没有，就修改到能如此为止。

第七章　引言的写作

引言（Introduction）也称导言、前言或背景（Background），是正文的开头部分。引言回答为什么做某项研究的问题，重点介绍论文工作的背景信息和研究目的。引言介绍一篇论文工作，要选择最吸引人的切入点来写。不同的切入点决定一批实验数据的取舍和组织，因而引言的写作也决定了论文后面结果和讨论部分的写作角度或方向。

一、引言的内容与结构

引言主要内容包括：研究领域与方向的介绍，相关研究的历史、现状与进展，前人研究的不足与局限，本研究所要解决的问题（与理论假说），本研究工作的发现及意义。

引言的结构为倒三角形、倒金字塔或漏斗形结构（图 7-1）。首先对自己研究所属的一个较宽泛领域或方向及其重要性（相当于倒三角形底边、倒金字塔的基础或漏斗

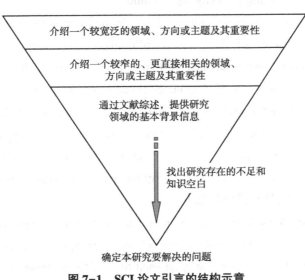

图 7-1　SCI 论文引言的结构示意

的喇叭口)加以介绍，然后收窄到对一个相关性更直接的领域或方向(及其重要性)加以介绍；之后对其研究进展进行综述和概括，说明哪些问题已经解决，还有什么问题没有解决，也就是要找出研究存在的不足和知识空白，然后确定本研究要解决的问题(相当于倒三角形顶点、倒金字塔的塔尖或漏斗的管口)。作者可在此处提出自己的假说或猜想。引言部分最后是对论文的主要发现进行概括或预览。

以下就《自然》期刊标题为"The JAZ family of repressors is the missing link in jasmonate signalling"论文的引言为例，来说明引言的这种结构。

Life on earth relies on a complex equilibrium of biotic and abiotic interactions.【介绍一个较宽泛的领域、方向或主题及其重要性】Plant small signalling molecules such as the jasmonates, structurally similar to prostaglandins in metazoans[1,2], are essential for plant survival in nature, and thus contribute to modulation of this equilibrium. Jasmonates (jasmonic acid and other oxylipin derivatives) are key regulators of plant responses to environmental stresses and biotic challenges, such as ozone exposure, wounding, water deficit, and pathogen and pest attack[1-4]. They are also involved in important plant developmental processes, such as root growth, tuberization, fruit ripening, tendril coiling, reproductive development and senescence[1-4]. Their importance beyond the plant kingdom has been recently highlighted by their suggested anti-cancer activity in humans[5].【介绍一个较窄的、更直接相关的领域、方向或主题及其重要性】

More than four decades after the discovery of methyl jasmonate as a major lipid constituent of the jasmine scent[6], understanding of the biosynthetic (octadecanoid) pathway of jasmonates from linolenic acid is now well established[7]. In contrast, our current knowledge about the jasmonate signalling pathway lags behind[3,8].

Efforts to dissect the signalling pathway have defined two steps. The first one comprises components and regulators of SCF (Skip/Cullin/Fbox) E3 ubiquitin ligase complexes (SCF^{COI1})[9-13]. The second step is defined by transcription factors, such as MYC2 and ERF1, which orchestrate the expression of jasmonate-related effector genes[14-16]. However, these two steps remain unlinked and major questions about the molecular details of the jasmonate signaling pathway remain unanswered. For example, the jasmonate receptor is unknown, the link between jasmonate perception and SCF^{COI1} is unidentified, and the connection between this SCF complex and the activation of transcription factors remains unresolved.【通过文献综述，提供研究领域的基本背景信息】

The existence of these two types of jasmonate-signalling components has led to the hypothesis that activation of jasmonate responses by transcription factors requires ubiquitin-mediated degradation of a repressor that is targeted to the 26S proteasome by the SCF^{COI1} after jasmonate perception. However, more than a decade after the molecular identification of COI1, the F-box component of the SCF^{COI1} complex, the identity of this hypothetical repressor remains unknown.【找出研究存在的不足和知识空白，确定本研究要解决的问题】

Here we report the identification of *JASMONATE-INSENSITIVE 3*(*JAI3*) and show that it belongs to a novel family of jasmonate-regulated nuclear targets of SCF^{COI1}, named JAZ (jasmonate ZIM-domain) proteins. JAI3 and other JAZs physically interact with COI1, and jasmonate treatment induces their SCF^{COI1}-dependent proteasome degradation. The *jai* 3-1 allele encodes a mutant protein resistant to degradation that also inhibits degradation of the wild-type JAI3 and other JAZs, explaining its dominant jasmonate-insensitive phenotype. Additionally, JAI3 and JAZ1 interact with MYC2, the key transcriptional activator of jasmonate-regulated gene expression, suggesting a model of JAI3/JAZ action as repressors of MYC2. Our results demonstrate that JAZs are direct targets of the SCF^{COI1}, linking ubiquitin-mediated protein degradation to transcriptional activation of jasmonate responses. Moreover, our results show that MYC2 and JAZs are involved in a negative regulatory feed-back loop that provides a mechanistic explanation for the pulsed response to jasmonate and the subsequent desensitization of the cell.【对论文的主要发现进行概括或预览】

二、引言的写作要求

引言目的是向读者提供足够的论文背景信息，使读者明白选题的依据或研究的论据，介绍相关工作的来龙去脉和研究进展，识别知识链上缺失一环，作为着手研究的问题。引言与讨论是 SCI 论文最难写的部分。引言既要有逻辑性，段落之间一环套一环，富有逻辑性和层次感，又要有一定的趣味性，能吸引读者一直读下去。

引言写作的重点是处理好结构。单主题文章的引言结构如前所述，而对于一个涉及两个或两个以上主题的文章，引言部分的写作首先需要处理好这些主题的主次关系。通常以一个主题作为主要主题或第一主题，首先加以介绍，然后介绍次要主题或第二主题。不同主题模块之间要有合理的过渡语句，不要给人突兀之感。

对于研究对象和主题本身比较普遍和重要的论文，引言按部就班写作基本没有什么问题，但是对于研究对象（如地方性的生物）和主题（区域性的问题）本身比较特殊的论文，在前言中怎样开篇和立意对于高影响因子期刊接收至关重要。因为这些期刊大多喜欢能引起国际性的或跨领域专业读者普遍兴趣（general interest）的稿件，因此，宜在引言中避免一开始就从地方性的生物或区域性的问题写起，而应该从可引起普遍关心的主题来组织写作前言，在引言中谨慎提及仅具有开创性意义的信息（至少不要在引言的第一段中论述，而是放到其后的文献综述或引言最后的陈述部分作为解决某个宏大或普遍意义问题的个案研究提及），甚至根本不必在引言中提及（例如，可在方法与材料中给出）。

引言难写的原因在于以下几点：

①对于新手而言，如何在引言开头用一两句话介绍一个较宽泛领域、方向或主题及其重要性是比较困难的，一般人都会有"一部二十四史，不知从何说起"这样的感觉。因此，这一两句话的开场白就十分见功力，高手既能做到开门见山，高屋建瓴，有见识，有气势，又不至于无限宽广，不着边际。

②从一个较宽泛领域、方向或主题过渡到一个相关性更直接的领域、方向或主题（及其重要性），要富有鲜明的层次感和很强的逻辑性，让人感觉过渡自然，而不能有突兀之感。第一次出现的术语，要加定义和解释，第一次出现的物种要用括号给出学名，第一次出现的缩略语或代号，要用括号给出全称。

③对相关研究的进展进行综述和概括，找出研究存在的不足和知识空白，作为论文选题依据，这需要建立在文献的批判性阅读基础之上，否则就不能识别真正的科学问题。文献综述部分是为了帮助作者提炼研究问题及阐明作者的主张，因此，这部分不能写成一个篇幅浩大、面面俱到的综述文章，而是应该对文献进行过滤，将论述方向聚焦到论文工作要解决的问题上来。批判性阅读是指基于对所研究问题的了解，对前人工作进行客观评价，分析前人的贡献和不足，识别研究的缺陷和空白。对前人工作的评价，要客观而公正，负面评价要出言慎重且要留有余地，而不可利用言辞加以贬损。这部分要对问题背景和意义进行简明而恰当的论述，通过引用真正相关的文献概述之前所做的工作，要让读者明确什么工作前人已经完成，什么工作还没有完成；哪些问题是前人已经解决的，哪些问题是本篇论文工作要解决的；如果本篇论文工作是以前研究工作的延续，那么既要交代与前面所做工作的连续性，又要明确区分本篇论文工作如何不同于以前出版的相关论文工作。但是要注意，为了激发论文读者（包括期刊编辑、审稿人和普通读者）的兴趣，为论文工作选题提供了一个令人信服的理由，仅仅是一个从未被研究过的现象本身并不是研究这个现象的充分理由。

这部分写作同样要有逻辑性和层次性，要根据一定的逻辑有层次地论述，要用观点来统率文献，而不能简单地罗列作者和文献（例如，张三做了什么，李四做了什么，王五又做了什么），因为这样会显得逻辑性不强。根据引用方式的不同，可分为作者突显式引用和非作者突显式引用。

作者突显式引用就是引述突出作者，通常将"作者（出版年）"或"作者[参考文献序号]"置于句子的开头。例如，

Specifically, Tupy (1976) showed that bark application of ethylene enhanced the invertase activity and sucrose utilization in latex by increase of latex pH. Liu *et al.* (2007) constructed and screened two ethephon-induced latex SSH cDNA libraries, and found that the cDNAs associated with sucrose metabolism, regulation of coagulation, stability of lutoids and signal transduction were up-regulated and might be related to the ethephon action.

非作者突显式引用就是在引述中不突出作者，通常将"作者，出版年"或"[参考文献序号]"置于引述内容的句子结尾。例如，

The circadian clock is an endogenous timekeeper mechanism which regulates a vast array of biological processes such as growth, metabolism, flowering, and biotic and abiotic stress(Greenham and McClung, 2015; Nagel and Kay, 2012; Seo and Mas, 2015; Bendix *et al.*, 2015). As a master regulator, approximately one-third of Arabidopsis genes are under the circadian control and it also regulates a large proportion of genes in hormone-responsive pathways(Covington *et al.*, 2018; Mizuno and Yamashino, 2008).

一般将参考文献的标注或著录分为著者-出版年制和顺序编码制两种。前者在正文中采用著者-出版年标注，后者在正文中用序号标注引文。需要说明的是，如果利用著者-出版年制标注，则只出现作者的姓，而不是全名。

由于引言部分在介绍研究主题及其重要性，以及通过文献综述介绍主题目的背景信息时都需要通过征引参考文献来进行。那么，对文献的概述与回顾，就不要遗漏领域内经典的、最新的文献，因为审稿人都是熟读文献的同行专家，如果没有引用经典文献，会让审稿人觉得你"不知古"，而没有跟踪到最新文献（包括刚刚上线还未正式印刷出版的文献），会让审稿人觉得你"不知今"。所引文献不能全是5年前或10年前的文献，让人感觉你的选题没有新意，是在"炒冷饭"；也不能只引用支持自己说法的文献，而忽视不支持自己论点的文献，要实事求是、一五一十地引用正方和反方的相关文献，归纳研究存在的不足和知识空白。引用文献忌多忌滥，要有切合性，不相关的文献不需要引用，相关的文献不能遗漏；同样，要对文献进行过滤、综合、概括和提炼观点，不能够对每一篇文献都大篇幅详细描述，显得只是材料或观点的堆积，使引言篇幅过大，废话太多。可以引用综述文章来避免大量引用相关性不是很强的文献，但引用的文献又不能全部来自综述文献，重要的、原创性的研究性论文还是要加以引用。同样，也不能只引用自己发表的文章（自引过高是不恰当的），而不引用同行的论文。引用文献中的论据要准确，没有亲自阅读过原文，只是根据别的论文的参考文献来转引的文章，态度不够审慎；如果第一个引用者出现误解，后面的作者人云亦云地转引，就会将错误累积在文献中。一般引用要用自己的话来加以概述（间接引用），如果原封不动地引用原文（直接引用），要加引号并注明，否则就是抄袭。

④通过综述文献识别论文所要解决的问题。通过综述文献，提出一个明确的和具体的科学问题或知识空白（knowledge gap），并说明采用何种方法解决这个问题。鉴于一般的科学研究通常起始于问题，然后根据已有的知识提出合理的假说（hypothesis），然后通过研究来验证假说，因此，如果属于"假说-检验"型论文，要说讲明作者有什么样的假说，利用什么样的思路来验证这个假说。常用的表达句式有：We hypothesize (d) that..., Our hypothesis is/was that..., The hypothesis that...was tested experimentally using..., 等等。

⑤引言的最后一部分是对论文的主要发现进行概括或预览，要突出自己论文工作的创新性，给读者或审稿人留下深刻的印象。虽然在摘要、讨论和结论中也有概括成

果和突出创新性的机会,但要注意这里不要逐字重复出现在论文其他地方的句子。

⑥引言要有逻辑性和层次感,实现这一点除内容本身的安排要具有逻辑性外,利用过渡词是最明显也是最常用的方法。例如,表示拓展的过渡词有:and, also, moreover, similarly, likewise 等;表示因果的过渡词有:because, that is why, for, then, thus, therefore, accordingly, as a result 等;表示例证的过渡词有:for example, for instance 等;表示时间的过渡词有:meanwhile, before, after, until, eventually 等;表示转折的过渡词有:however, but, although, in spite of, despite, nonetheless, while, whereas, even as, even so 等,尤其是 however 和 but,其在点出前人研究不足和空白时是最常用的。常用的句式有:

However, little information is available to…

However, little is known about/of…

However, few investigations have…

However, little work has been done to date to examine…

Few attempts, however, have been made to…

However, there has been little discussion about how…

However, to date, published data are very scarce…

However, the results were inconclusive in…

However, it is unknown (not clear) whether/how…

However, large uncertainties still exist in…

However, uncertainties still exist, in particular for…

However, large discrepancies still exist in the estimates of…

However, large discrepancies between…and…have revealed major uncertainties that still exist in…

However, the reasons why…have been largely unknown.

However, (despite…) …remains elusive/unclear/unknown/unresolved/to be elucidated/very poorly understood.

However, previous research has strongly suggested that…

⑦增加引言的趣味性可通过以下方式实现:引经据典,说明问题的经典性和重要性。例如,生物进化和系统发育的很多问题可追溯到达尔文的论述,追根溯源有利于读者、编辑和审稿人对论文工作的重视,如《自然遗传学》(*Nature Genetics*)的一篇论文:"The genome sequence of the orchid *Phalaenopsis equestris*",其引言就从达尔文的名著 *Fertilization of Orchids* 开始论述。利用全球性的重大问题,可突显问题的重要性。例如,关于植物对高温、干旱等的反应与耐性研究,可以联系到全球气候变暖上来,其意义会更宏大,如发表在《植物杂志》(*The Plant Journal*)的一篇文章:"Plant tissue succulence engineering improves water-use efficiency, water-deficit stress attenuation and salinity tolerance in Arabidopsis",其引言就从全球气候变暖对农业生产的影响大篇幅论述开始。使用一些时髦的或形象的词来描述研究对象,例如,暗物质(dark matter)原指天文物理学中可能存在于宇宙中尚不为人所知的一种不可见的物质,现在常用来形容非编码 RNA(noncoding RNA,ncRNA)或长链非编码 RNA(lncRNAs)作为生物学或基因组的暗物质。如《国际分子科学杂志》(*International Journal of Molecular Sciences*)的一篇文章:"Non-coding RNAs: The 'dark matter' of cardiovascular pathophysiology",其在引言中这样写道:For many years the role of these molecules remained unknown, so ncRNAs were called the "Dark Matter" of biology.

⑧与摘要类似,引言较多使用物称(第三人称)和被动语态,但在叙述作者的工作时,可适当使用第一人称(we 或 our)和主动语态,以明确地表示作者自己的科学贡献,加深对审稿人的印象。叙述目前的状态,不受时间影响的实验结论和普遍事实,用一般现在时;介绍研究趋势或发展动态,尤其是叙述目前已完成的实验或已证实的结论,可用现在完成式;叙述过去进行的实验或动作,用一般过去时。

以下就《自然》期刊标题为"The F-box protein TIR1 is an auxin receptor"论文的引言第一段为例,来说明时态在引言中的使用。

Since its discovery over 70 years ago, the plant hormone auxin or indole acetic acid (IAA) has been implicated in virtually every aspect of plant growth and development[1,2].【叙述研究取得的进展和目前的研究状态,有现在完成时】In some tissues auxin regulates cell elongation, while in others the hormone promotes cell division.【叙述不受时间影响的实验结论和普遍事实,用一般现在时】Recent studies also indicate that auxin acts as a morphogen during embryogenesis and in the root meristem[3,4].【叙述目前的状态,用一般现在时】Despite the importance of auxin to the plant, many aspects of auxin signalling are poorly understood.【叙述目前的状态,用一般现在时】In particular, the identity of the auxin receptor(s) is unknown.【叙述目前的状态,用一般现在时】The best-characterized candidate receptor, the auxin binding protein 1 (ABP1), was identified by virtue of its auxin binding activity[5].【叙述过去进行的实验或动作,用一般过去时】Although some characteristics of ABP1 are consistent with receptor function, the role of this protein in auxin signalling has not been determined.【叙述目前的结论和研究状态,有一般现在时和现在完成时】

论文引言中虽然使用一般过去时较多,但也会用到现在完成时。与现在完成时相比,一般过去时强调真实客观地叙述过去发生的事情本身,因此成为科技论文、新闻报道、历史传记等常用的时态。现在完成时表示过去发生(无须指明具体时间)而现在已经完成,或者持续到现在的动作或状态,或者对现在有影响的动作。与强调动作发生在过去某一时间的一般过去时相比,现在完成时更强调过去动作与现在的关系,强调说明现在的情况或状态,强调表达过去动作或发生的事对现在的影响。如果同一件事既可用一般过去时也可用现在完成时表达，通常用现在完成时表示最近若干年所完成的事，而用一般过去时描述过去较长一段时间完成的事。例如，

【例文 1】The last two decades have seen substantial advances in our knowledge of the molecular genetics directing floral meristem and organ identity development, leading to a clear picture of how floral organ identity is acquired(Robles and Pelaz, 2005).

【例文 2】Finally, the circadian clock has been implicated in the regulation of the photoperiodic induction of flowering(Kreps and Kay, 1997). Several circadian clock-associated Arabidopsis genes(e. g. , *CCA1*, *LHY* , *FKF1*, and *ZTL*) have been shown to control flowering time.

【例文 3】The genetic networks underlying differentiation of valves, valve margins, and repla have been extensively studied in the last few years, leading to the proposal of a well-supported and detailed model for patterning on the transversal plane of the ovary(Dinneny and Yanofsky, 2005; Alonso-Cantabrana et al. , 2007).

现在进行时态表示现在进行的动作或正在发生的事情，虽在科技论文中应用较少，但也存在。例如：

【例文 1】We are only now beginning to understand the genetic pathways directing floral organ patterning.

【例文 2】The signal transduction network that is responsive to these photoreceptors is beginning to be elucidated, and several factors involved in phytochrome signal transduction have been defined.

⑨引言写作要避免自觉不自觉地抄袭。一般而言，引用别人的文献，即便是标明出处，也要用自己的话来重述。如果完全拷贝别人的原话，要用引号标出。如果引用别人 40 个或更多的单词，则要作为左缩进半英寸的一整段来引用(这种情况在自然科学的 SCI 论文中极少见)。

第八章 材料与方法的写作

在以实验为基础的研究性论文中,专门有一节为材料和方法(Materials and Methods)或方法(Methods),这一部分通常在引言之后、结果之前,但也有期刊把它置于讨论与结论之后、参考文献之前。这一部分详细描述和说明论文工作的实验对象或实验材料、处理条件和处理方法、实验设计、实验步骤或计算推导过程等。

这部分写作的基本要求是,实验方法与过程的描述要具体完整,尽可能提供详尽的细节,一方面保证研究方法正确可行,足以获得可靠的实验结果,另一方面也便于他人能够重复或再现论文的实验结果。如果表述不清或故意隐瞒甚至误导,就会使论文的研究结果不能被重复,不仅造成整个社会科研资源的极大浪费,阻碍科研进程,还会让别的研究者质疑论文的科研成果。发表论文就意味着在科学界共享方法与成果,故意隐瞒方法是不道德的,也是一种学术不端的行为。

材料和方法的写作一般首先对材料进行描述,然后根据逻辑关系、实验顺序或时间先后,分节对论文涉及的方法和步骤按照先后分若干小节进行说明,每一小节前面可设置一个精练而恰当的标题,一般以实验名称(或实验目标与实验方法相结合)作为标题。一般情况下,方法部分的写作顺序可与结果部分相对应,这样写作有助于读者理解,提高论文的可读性。

以生物医学为例,实验对象或实验材料一般为植物、动物、微生物和人(病患或参试者)或者这些生物的一部分(分子、细胞、组织与器官)。实验对象或实验材料来源要明确,要清楚其种属世系、性别、年龄、遗传组成和生理状况,还需要介绍其生长、培养或栽培条件,采样或实验的时间和地点(经纬度),实验时的大小或培养时间长短等。如果研究对象是人,则需交代调查或实验对象的种族、身高、体重,以及是否具有某种习惯或疾病史等可能对实验结果或统计学处理的影响因素。如果是物理学或化学材料,那么需要说明材料的来源、成分、结构、特性等。对特定对象或材料的选择,要说明其选择标准和理由。

在实验之前,如果需要对实验对象或实验材料进行处理,则需要说明处理条件和处理方法。方法中需要说明所用的实验设计和数据统计分析方法，如对照是什么，采用什么样的区组设计，设置多少次(组)重复，采用何种统计学检验等。不恰当的实验设计和统计分析往往会使论文结果无效，导致论文无法发表。常见的这类错误包括：样本群体过小(这样很容易使结果偏离正态分布)、缺乏适当的对照组及数据未经统计分析(说明不同处理组之间或处理组与对照组之间的差异，应该用 ANOVA 或 T-test 进行显著性检验)，以及多重比较后未进行适当校正。生物医学论文中还需说明实验处理过程是否符合相应的伦理学要求等，具体来讲，就是要在课题设计完成后、试验前，获得动物伦理和临床试验的伦理批准，课题设计完成后进行临床试验注册。

实验过程说明清楚、详细。领域内人所共知的常规操作方法可简述；对实验影响重大的细节和数据(通常也是读者同行最关注的那部分信息)一定要翔实可靠；作者首创的方法需要详述细节并交代其原理；采用已有的方法可简述并列出相应的参考文献；如果对已有方法进行改进，要清楚地说明在哪些地方做了改进及其理由。对于较为复杂的实验步骤或操作流程，可借助流程示意图来加以说明。实验步骤要按前后顺序描述，上下步骤之间的关系要交代清楚，不能让读者产生误解或混乱印象。实验中用到的关键仪器要说明商品名称、规格型号，用括号补充交代其生产厂家、厂址与国别，重点化学试剂或药品也要说明品名和规格，用括号补充交代其制造商、产地与国别，必要时还要说明其主要化学和物理性质。最后要说明实验数据的处理方法或统计分析方法(statistical analysis)，说明采用何种分析软件，交代其版本与网址并列出相应的参考文献。数学符号公式要用 MathType 插入 Word 文档中。

为了叙述清楚实验步骤的前后顺序和相互关系，这部分经常要用到一些表示顺序和承接的过渡词语，如 first, second, third, at the beginning, at first, then, next, later, afterwards, subsequently, meanwhile, before, after, immediately, gradually, briefly, finally 等。为了让读者明白使用某种方法或某步操作的目的，通常要在句子前面使用带 to 的动词不定式或 for 的介词短语来表示实验目的。这部分由于动作者或实验者为读者已知的作者，要突出被实验对象和操作方法，因此，使用被动语态较多，但是，也可用第一人称(we)和主动语态。由于实验是过去发生的，因此，除非陈述不受时间影响的事实或没有时间变化的实验原理采用一般现在时态外，实验操作主要采用一般过去时。

以下以《自然》期刊标题为 "Root microbiota drive direct integration of phosphate stress and immunity" 论文的方法第二小节 "Census study experimental procedures" 标题下前 3 段为例，来说明语态和时态在材料与方法中的使用。

For experiments in wild soil, we collected the top-soil (approximately 20 cm) from a site free of pesticide and fertilizer at Mason Farm (North Carolina, USA; +35° 53′ 30.40″, −79° 1′ 5.37″)[19]. Soil was dried, crushed and sifted to remove debris. To improve drainage, soil was mixed 2∶1 volume with autoclaved sand. Square pots (2×2 inch square) were filled with the soil mixture and used to grow plants. Soil micronutrient analysis is published in ref. 19.

All Arabidopsis thaliana mutants used in this study were in the Columbia (Col-0) background (Supplementary Table 16). All seeds were surface-sterilized with 70% bleach, 0.2% Tween-20 for 8 min, and rinsed 3× with sterile distilled water to eliminate any seed-borne microbes on the seed surface. Seeds were stratified at 4 °C in the dark for 2 days.

To determine the role of phosphate starvation response in controlling micro-biome composition, we analysed five mutants related to the Pi-transport system (pht1;1, pht1;1; pht1;4, phf1, nla and pho2) and two mutants directly involved in the transcriptional regulation of the Pi-starvation response (phr1 and spx1;spx2). All these genes are expressed in roots[13-18].

从上例可见，除第一段和第三段的第一句使用第一人称和主动语态外，其余的句子全用物称（第三人称）和被动语态。时态除说明方法出处（Soil micronutrient analysis is published in ref. 19.）和结果（All these genes are expressed in roots[13-18]）用现在时，所用描述实验操作的句子都用一般过去时。

第九章 结果的写作

结果是论文的核心。论文的结果部分是基于翔实的数据，利用文字与图表，呈现对所研究问题的全部证据或解决方案。引言是介绍问题的由来及提出解决思路（或假说），而在结果部分，就需要将实验所得的结果，按一定的逻辑，组织成一环扣一环的证据链条，来支持假说并排除其他可能的解释。并非全部实验结果都要写入论文，实验结果要根据论证的问题来选择和组织，与问题无关的实验结果可置之勿论。或者说，结果和数据要有选择性，使用的数据能集中解决引言中提出的问题，要围绕引言中所提出的问题来组织数据。除少数情况下将结果与讨论合并在一起写作外，一般将结果与讨论分开写作。

一、提炼结果，分条论证

从实验所得的原始结果到论文结果，需要一个提炼、概括和总结的过程。实验数据或观察到的现象不能不加选择地全部写入论文，而是要有所选择和提炼，只有与问题相关的、能够论证作者主张的代表性数据才能写入论文结果，无关的数据只会干扰论文的论证效果。通常原始数据需要经过统计学处理才能写入论文结果，例如，将多次重复观测数据计算平均值与标准偏差，或者转换为百分数，是否具有显著性差异，并要说明统计学差异程度的意义。另外要注意的是，数据与结论之间的相关关系（correlation）和因果关系（causation）要区分清楚，不可将只具有相关关系的结果诠释为因果关系。

由于论证需要分步骤来进行，那么结果部分也需要按论证步骤分成若干小节，每一小节由一组相关的证据组成，每一小节都有一个子标题，子标题通常也就是这一组数据论证的论点。通常在实验之前就需要清楚要做哪些相关实验，获得什么样的数据，来论证什么样的论点。据此在写作时确定写作提纲，可直接转换为结果中的子标题。小节前后顺序可按逻辑论证思路来安排，也可按实验过程或时间顺序由先到后、程度由浅到深或由表及里、重要性程度由小到大来安排。

二、文字与图表相结合论述

目前，科技论文往往涉及大量的数据，图表远比文字更能形象、直观、准确地表达数据传递的信息，因此，几乎所有的论文结果都是用文字与图表相结合论述。图表不仅在撰写论文时最先制作，往往也是读者浏览论文时留下第一印象的部分。读者往往在看完题目或摘要后马上浏览图表，因为图表是最直观的证据。为了绘制漂亮的图表，作者除了要掌握最简单常用的软件外，如 Excel、PowerPoint、PhotoShop、ImageJ，还应该学会常用绘图软件，如 Origin、Phthon(Matplotlib)、Paraview、Adobe Illustrator、draw.io、Tecplot、R-ggplot2、Visio、Matlab 等。一般对于照片或图像的裁剪、旋转、拼接、亮度和对比度调整等，可用 PhotoShop 和 ImageJ，数据分析所作的折线图、柱状图等可用 Excel、Matlab、Origin 等绘制，而流程图可用 PowerPoint 和 Visio 绘制。数据转化为图表可用在线图表制作工具，如花火 hanabi、Python 数据可视化开发库 Plotly。

图表的标题和注解应简洁、全面并具自明性。文字与图表相结合论述有以下几点要求：

①表格和图片要具有自明性，即图表及其标题和注释应准确而清楚地表达数据反映的意义，读者可不依赖文字叙述直接从图表了解它所传达的信息，或者说图表及其标题和注释可在不参考文字描述的情况下易于理解。标题和注解中出现的任何符号、缩写和测量单位都要加以说明。具体而言，完整的图例(figure legend)包括一个概括图版(包含多个小图)的简短标题，对于图版中的每个图片，要顺序编号，概括说明所示实验结果，通常还要简要描述所使用的材料种类和来源、培养条件、处理方法、所用技术等细节。图中用到的符号、缩写、图例、线条、颜色、比例尺、误差线(标准差 SD 或标准误差 SEM)、统计学分析的 P 值要注释说明。

②同一批数据要么表述为图，要么表述为表，图片和表格不要重复表述同一批数据，但可以在正文中以图片呈现，但同一批数据的表格作为附件(supplemental information, supplemental data)上传。

③正文不能简单地重复描述图表中的数据，而应概括性地阐述图表所反映的趋势和规律，必要时可提及关键性的数据。

④所有的图和表必须在正文中提及，并且图和表在正文中应当按照出现顺序加以编号并引用。

⑤不同期刊往往对论文中的图表数量加以限制，作为直接证据的图表可放在正文中，而表示原始数据或支持性数据的图表可作为附件或附录(appendix)上传。

图和表各具优势。表格适合展现大量数据，能呈现具体精确的数字，也便于不同样本、阶段、地区或处理之间的数据比较，但图片不仅形式多样，而且能更直接、清晰和形象地展示数据，使读者更易于理解和把握不同组数据间的差异、关联、因果和变化趋势，从而快速、准确地获得关键结果信息。与文字描述和表格数据相比，图片更能突显所要传达的关键信息，也更具视觉冲击力，因而在 SCI 论文中图片使用要比表格更为普遍。

表格分普通表格与三线表（只有顶线、底线和栏目线 3 条横线，没有竖线）两种，科技论文常用三线表，因为它更为简洁明了。对于容易用文字描述的一组一个变量的若干项数据，以及多组多个变量的一项数据，可以不用表格。涉及多组多个变量的多个项目数据就需要用表格来呈现，但要注意将重要的或读者感兴趣的数据置于最后一行或最后一列，这样可以给读者留下深刻印象。表格中的数据格式（如小数点保留位数、平均值还是平均值+标准差表示）要保持一致，表示显著性差异的字母（A、B、C、D、E 或 a、b、c、d、e）或星号（*）标在数据的右侧或右上角，代表显著性水平分析的 P 值要在表下注明。如果表中变量、项目或单位使用缩写，也要在表下注释清楚。

照片图让人感觉真实，显微照片要用字母或代号标出各个部分的名称，目标部分要用箭头指出，显微放大倍数要用标尺刻度说明。流程图是用箭头、线条和不同形状的图形符号来表示实验步骤、方法流程和算法程序。示意图是用简单的图形来说明相对复杂的过程、猜想、原理、结构和装置，容易解释抽象的原理或理念。折线图适合显示随时间或程序连续变化的数据趋势，柱状图或直条图可用于不同处理之间（或不连续变化）的差异对比以及表现数据变化趋势。折线图的横轴、纵轴要注明单位与数字刻度，数字刻度应等距或具有一定规律性（如对数尺度）。当图中用不同形状或颜色线条代表不同事物时，应该用清晰的图标在空白处注明。柱状图或直条图用横轴表示不同类别或不同处理组，纵轴表示测量值；柱或直条的宽度应一致，不同类之间的间隙应相等，同一类型柱状图中的不同亚组要用不同颜色表示，并用图标表示。每个柱或直条表示的数值应该用误差线标记误差范围和显著性差异。扇形图（扇形统计图）和饼图适于表示各部分与总体的比例关系，但各个部分要用不同颜色标明。如果想表示数据的离散分散情况或对多组数据分布特征进行比较，可使用箱形图、盒式图或盒形图。论文中如使用地图，一定要根据权威出版社的地图绘制，不能使用有损国家领土和主权完整的地图，图片应有以 "km" 为单位的比例尺，图注中要说明采用的投影方式（如墨卡托投影、等距或等面积投影）以及原因。图片可以是黑白、灰度和彩图；不论什么类型的图片，都要求简洁、清晰和对比度强；彩图只有在能比黑白或灰度图片更有效提高图片可读性时使用，且要避免使用背景色彩浓重、没有足够的对比度的图片。最后要说明的是，图片中使用的缩写和显著性水平分析的 P 值要在图注中加以注明。

一张图片胜过千言万语。数量适当、精心准备、易于理解、信息丰富的图片可为论文增色不少。面对大量的论文稿件，富于创造性和经过深思熟虑的插图会让编辑和审稿人青眼相加，增大了论文发表的可能性。图片不仅在结果部分大量使用，对于复杂的方法描述，使用流程图可以使方法描述更简短和清晰；而概念图或合成图既可在引言部分来帮助呈现论文的研究背景、目前尚不能回答的问题及研究将要测试的假设，也可以在讨论部分来形象地展示根据论文结果提出的假说、原理和机制，并可以大大简化讨论部分的文字描述。

图片要按照打印版图片的尺寸和比例来进行制作，使图片中的文字、线条和点的大小适当。论文通常以单列宽度(79 mm)、2/3页面宽度(110 mm)和整页宽度(168 mm)来配图，图片最大高度为 230 mm。不按这些尺寸设计的图片，在最后出版时将被缩小或扩大，并有可能导致图像的细节难以辨别。图片大小要适当、一致，避免图版中的图片大小不一以及图形周围出现大片空白。图片要尽可能简明而易识别，一张图所包含的曲线(折线)图或柱状图不要太多，且要用不同的形状或颜色加以区分。折线图和柱状图要有误差线。切记不要一图多用(原图或对图片进行旋转、截图或美化后在不同论文中使用)，使用已发表论文的图片要注明。期刊对图片的分辨率和格式设有规定。一般而言，矢量图更清晰和保真，为 .eps 或 .pdf 格式；摄影图像的分辨率为 300 dpi，格式可以是 .jpg 或 .tif；如果是艺术线条和摄影图像相结合的图片，无法以矢量图格式保存，就使用高分辨率的 .jpg 或 .tif 格式(即 600~800 dpi)。包含多幅单张图片的图版要合成一个文件，每个图片或图版文件小于 10 MB，并且以其编号命名。

目前，期刊文章中多数以一组相关的图片排列成一个图版，来支持一个特定的论点。图表要有一个简明扼要的标题，小节的标题通常与对应的图表标题内容一致，但最好不要完全重复同样的表述。也就是说，文本中不要重复图表的标题，各节的标题也不要与图表的标题完全一样。一般表的标题在表的上方，图的标题在图的下方。虽然正式发表文章中图表插在文章结果部分的适当位置，但投稿时图表是单独上传的，整合后的 PDF 投稿论文中图表位于文末的参考文献之后。

三、结果的叙述方式

如果结果与讨论不合在一起写的话，那么，结果部分不需要对数据结果进行详尽的讨论，但需要解释数据的统计学意义，例如利用 t 检验、方差分析和卡方检验等统计学比较的具体的 P 值和差异是否显著(注意 significant 用来形容统计学上的显著性差异)，说明这些数据显示的趋势、规律、支持或否定某个论点。论文的引言解释为什么研究这个课题，材料与方法说明如何获得这些结果，而讨论则阐述这些结果蕴含的意义和可推导的结论。结果主要是提供证据，不能喧引言和方法的"宾"，也不能夺讨论的"主"。但是，为了让读者明白每个实验的目的和用意(或者说背景)，在每一个小节或每一段之前介绍某个具体实验的目的是有益的。

例如，在《植物细胞》(*The Plant Cell*)标题为"A secreted effector protein of *Ustilago maydis* guides maize leaf cells to form tumors"的论文结果中，小标题"The see1-SGT1 interaction has functional relevance"之下的第一段(画线部分为实验目的)：

To further investigate the role of See1 in targeting SGT1, we checked if the identified phosphorylation at Thr-150 in Zm-SGT1 is required for SGT1 function. To address this point, we first performed a yeast complementation assay using *sgt1* cell cycle mutants to test for the complementation ability of phosphomimic and phosphonull mutants of Zm-SGT1 at this position. This assay did not show any differences in the complementation ability compared with the wild-type SGT1 (Supplemental Figure 21). This suggests that the phosphorylation site we identified in planta is not required for the cell cycle-related SGT1 function in yeast. Because the relevant phosphorylation site is specific to monocot SGT1 homologs and not present in yeast, one could not expect a function of this residue in yeast.

结果部分一般无须引用参考文献，但是为了说明某个实验的具体目的和用意，提供理解结果的背景，有些期刊允许在结果中征引参考文献。例如，在《植物细胞》*Plant Cell*标题为"Direct and indirect visualization of bacterial effector delivery into diverse plant cell types during infection"的论文结果中，小标题"Effectors are delivered into multiple cell types in arabidopsis leaves"之下的最后一段（画线部分为实验背景）：

Epidermal pavement cells in Arabidopsis display a wide size distribution with dimensions ranging 10 to 200 μm, correlated with endopolyploidy of the cell (Melaragno et al., 1993). In contrast, the average size of an epiphytically colonizing *P. syringae* is 1.2 μm (Monier and Lindow, 2003a). The size disparity between bacterial and host cells at the leaf surface could enable multiple bacterial cells to attach and deliver effectors into the same host cell from discrete locations. In order to investigate the ability of *Pst* DC3000 to deliver effectors at multiple sites within each cell, we quantified the number of distinct fluorescent foci within an individual cell from confocal micrographs. The number of fluorescent foci per cell differed depending on the effector and ranged from 1 to 25 (Supplemental Figure 5). Compared with other effectors, AvrPto-GFP$_{11}$ exhibited a significantly higher number fluorescent foci in pavement cells at 48 hpi, but a significantly lower number of foci in mesophyll cells at 24 hpi (Supplemental Figure 5). At 24 hpi, AvrB-GFP$_{11}$ was not only delivered into more mesophyll cells than AvrPto-GFP$_{11}$, but the number of distinct foci in a single mesophyll cell was also significantly higher (Supplemental Figures 5C and 5D). Taken together, these data demonstrate that the GFP strand system allows analysis of native promoter driven effector delivery during natural infection and the positive detection of cells targeted for effector delivery.

从上面这两个例子可知，结果中既可用被动语态，也可用第一人称（作者自己We）和主动语态。涉及不受时间影响的推论或结论，或没有时间变化的实验原理采用一般现在时，而描述过去所做的实验或调查时，采用一般过去时。论述图表总是使用现在时，例如，Table 1 shows different specialised cells and the average number of mitochondria each cell contains. 实验数据或结果表明某个具体结论也用现在时。例如，These results <u>indicate</u> that one of the main functions of MpJAZ is repressing the synthesis of secondary metabolites such as terpenoids, carotenoids, flavonoids, and phenylpropanoids. 又如，DNA sequence homologies for the purple gene from the four congeners(Table 1) <u>show</u> high similarity, differing by at most 4 base pairs.

此外，为了表述简洁，通常在说明结果的句子末尾引用图表(将引用的图表序号置于括号中)。例如，Dip inoculation of Arabidopsis Col-0 with virulent *P. syringae* pv *tomato*(*Pst*)DC3000 carrying an empty vector(EV)did not result in trypan blue staining of leaf cells 14 h postinoculation(hpi)(Figure 1A). In contrast, Col-0 infection with *Pst* carrying the AvrB effector resulted in activation of RPM1-mediated resistance and accumulation of the trypan blue stain in the epidermal pavement and guard cells as well as internal mesophyll cells(Figure 1A)，而不是突出图表来造句说明，例如，Figure 1A shows/indicates/illustrates that... 或 From the Figure 1A we can see that... 或 As seen in Figure 1A, ... 或 As Figure 1A indicates, ...

在结果或图表描述中，要了解常用的表达和高频词。例如，表达"一般性上升或增加"的高频词有 increase, rise, grow, expand, go up, ascend, climb, be on the increase, be on the rise；表达"急剧上升或增加"的高频词有 jump, surge, soar, rocket, skyrocket, shoot up；表达"到达最高点"的句式有 peak at..., reach a/the peak at..., reach the highest point at..., hit/reach a record high at...；表达"一般性下降或减少"的高频词有 decrease, fall, decline, drop, sink, slump, dip, descend, go down, be on the decline, be on the wane, take a downtrend, 表达"急剧下降"或"减少"的高频词有 plunge, plummet；表达"持平"或"稳定"的高频词有 level off/out at, hover at, stabilize, settle, hardly change, have little change, keep steady, remain stable at..., remain steady at..., remain constant at..., stay constant at..., plateau out, bottom out at...；表达"到达最低点"的句式有 fall to/hit/reach/sink to a record low at..., hit a trough at...；表达"上下波动"的高频词有 fluctuate(around)..., fluctuate between...and..., see a fluctuating pattern, peak and troughs, rebound to...；表达"变化幅度大"的高频词有副词 significantly, considerably, substantially 和形容词 significant, considerable, substantial, marked, noticeable；表达"变化幅度小"的高频词有副词 slightly, modestly, moderately, marginally 和形容词 slight, modest, moderate, marginal；表达"变化速度快"的高频词有副词 rapidly, sharply, dramatically, drastically, steeply 和形容词 rapid, sharp, dramatic, drastic, steep；表达"变化速度缓慢"的高频词有副词 slowly, gradually, gently 和形容词 slow, gradual, gentle；表达"变化速度持续"的高频词有副词 continuously, consistently, steadily 和形容词 continuous, consistent, steady；表达"不同变量之间的关系"的句式有 be dependent on..., be independent of..., be(positively/negatively)correlated with…, be determined by…; 表达"大约"的高频词有 about, approximately, roughly, around; 表达"占多少份额"的高频词有 account for, make up, represent, constitute; 表达"分别的""对应的"的高频词有副词 respectively, correspondingly 和形容词 respective, corresponding 及名词 conterpart。

英语和汉语在表达倍数比较、倍数增加和倍数减少时存在区别，汉语中大（长、重等）或增加 N 倍是不包括基数在内的，英语则否。如表达"A 的大小（长度、重量等）是 B 的 N 倍"或"A 比 B 大（长、重等）N-1 倍"的英语是"A is N times as large（long, heavy…）as B""A is N times larger（longer, heavier…）than B""A is N times the size（length, height, weight…）of B""A is larger（longer, heavier…）than B"; 表达"增加到 N 倍"或"增加了 N-1 倍"要用英语"increase by N times""increase N fold""increase by a factor of N"; 表达"A 减少到 B 的 1/N"或"A 比 B 减少了（N-1）/N"的英语是"decrease/reduce/drop N times""N fold reduction/decrease""N times less than…""reduce/decrease by a factor of N"。

第十章 讨论的写作

讨论(Discussion)位于结果之后,是论文十分重要的组成部分,也是最难写作的部分之一。讨论是在征引参考文献的基础上,对论文结果的有效性和重要性进行解释和评价,并指出研究过程中出现的问题和可能的解决办法。讨论之所以重要,是因为它是解释如何理解结果(How?)的,也就是论文的结果和证据是否回答了引言中设定的问题。如果说引言介绍相关工作的来龙去脉和研究进展,识别知识之链上缺失的一环,作为论文工作研究的问题,那么讨论就是对结果加以解释和推导,找到缺失的那一环来闭合知识之链,从而将论文的学术贡献在人类对某一领域或问题的认识进程中给予一个恰当的位置。讨论之所以难写,是因为它需要作者对所提问题和结果有深刻的理解,需要作者对相关文献有相当程度的熟悉和把握,否则,既不能对结果进行合理的解释,也不能做出恰当的评价。无论论文的结果如何漂亮,讨论写不好也很难让读者理解论文工作的创新性,也会让论文的重要性大打折扣。

一、讨论的内容

讨论的内容应该包括:①回应引言中的背景、问题与假设,讨论是否解答引言中设定的问题或支持引言中提出的可检验的假设。②概述论文的主要结果,征引参考文献,指出与前人结果的异同,并推测其原因。③对结果加以说明和解释,说明其背后的原因或机理,并根据现有结果(自己的和前人的)推导出一般的结论或模型。④分析影响研究结果有效性的因素,指出研究结果的局限性和不足,并提出克服的方法与下一步工作的方向。⑤论述结果或结论的意义和应用,突出论文成果的重要性与影响力。

二、讨论的结构

讨论部分的结构多样,不易概括。如果讨论的点比较多,为了鲜明起见,可分成若干小节来进行,每一节前面都加一个简洁清晰的小标题;如果讨论的点不多,则无须分节进行。总体来讲，与引言从一般到特殊或从宽泛到狭窄的"倒三角形"结构不同，讨论可以根据情况，从具体的结果推导出一个较一般的结论、假说或模型来。

在讨论部分的开始，可以对论文的中心贡献或核心结果进行概括，并指出其创新性和重要性。也可首先利用参考文献，简述最直接的问题或背景，然后概括论文的中心贡献或核心结果，并指出其创新性和重要性。无论哪一种方式，此处重点回应引言中设定的问题或引言中提出的可检验假设。

接下来是分段对论文若干主要发现、主要结果或主要步骤（或某一发现、结果或步骤的重要环节、因素、角度等）进行讨论。结构可以是从要回答的具体问题或背景出发，然后简述论文结果，再征引文献对结果进行解释，对其有效性或适用性进行评价，论述其影响因素及可能的不足和局限。也可以就某一问题，先简述前人的答案和解释如何，然后介绍本文的结果和对这一问题的回答和解释，是否支持或反对某一方观点，或者另提出新的观点。

讨论的最后可归纳总结一个结论，或者根据情况推导出一个更一般的假说或模型，评价论文成果如何推进了本领域的研究。另外，需要指出哪些环节和部分还有待进一步研究或证实，并指出下一步的研究对策和对应用前景的展望。

三、讨论写作注意事项

（一）讨论点不必面面俱到

初学者最大的问题要么是"老虎吃天，无从下口"，不知该讨论什么，往往重复叙述结果了事；要么就是"眉毛胡子一把抓"，什么都讨论一番。讨论无须面面俱到，不必对所有结果进行讨论，而应选择重要的结果或研究中发现的重要问题进行讨论，对不太重要的枝节问题可以忽略不提。与前人一致的结果可简单提及或一笔带过，对能体现论文研究创新性的结果一定要浓墨重彩，突出讨论。论文的重要性在于其创新性的结果，只有创新性的结果才是对人类知识版图的扩展或知识总量的增加，如果只是简单地重复别人的工作或得出与别人一致的结果，那就没有太大的意义。因此，论文要在讨论中重点对独特性的思路或实验设计以及创新性的结果进行讨论。此外，对论文结论有效性关系重大的环节和因素也要重点关注。对论文结果的解释或原理的探讨，不能置之勿论，而是越深入越好，越透彻越好，并且要考虑多种可能的解释。

（二）讨论应使论文自洽、完整

论文需要讲一个自洽的、完整的故事，讨论在这方面需要利用结果和参考文献，来回应引言，基本回答引言设定问题或支持引言提出的假设。如果实验结果不能回答引言设定的问题或不支持引言中提出的假设，那说明要么是论文的实验设计和方法有问题，要么结果无法提供足够的证据来回答引言设定的问题，或者是引言设定的问题有误。如果论文引言、材料与方法、结果都没有问题，那么讨论就应努力使论文自洽、完整。讨论针对的要点不要超出论文结果的范围；没做的实验结果，就不必加以讨论。讨论的思路需要理顺，参考文献需要吃透，使讨论与引言前后呼应，使读者读后没有混乱、矛盾和残缺之感。

(三) 不回避研究的局限和不足

就像新闻写作讲究观点平衡一样，论文写作也讲究观点平衡。也就是既要明确表示论文的科学贡献，也要指出研究的局限和不足。对于结果的解释，不能简单化和独断处理，要考虑多种备选的解释，对于暂时无法成立的理由或与前人解释冲突的证据，要实事求是地写明。讨论写作重要的一点是，结合参考文献，清晰地解释、阐述和论证实验结果，让读者清楚地明白哪些结果是确定无误的，哪些结果是无法判断的，哪些结论是确信无疑的，哪些结论是假设猜测的。有些作者往往不愿意在讨论中指出研究的局限和不足，生怕编辑或审稿人看低了自己的论文，这其实是个误解。任何研究都会有这样或那样的不足与局限，一篇论文不可能回答所有问题。指出研究的局限和不足，正是需要进步和改进之处，而必要的推测也是将来需要进一步证实或证伪的地方，这不仅对后来的研究者重要，对科学进步本身也很重要。作者应该客观、诚实地审视自己的研究结果，既不夸大研究成果，也不回避局限性，同时，在明确的结果或结论的基础之上，再提出新的假设和进一步研究的建议。

(四) 需要征引参考文献

初学者写讨论通常还存在一个大的问题——自说自话，不引用参考文献。讨论的重要功能是将论文得出的结果或结论，关联到整个人类知识库或知识之链上，如果不引用参考文献，就无法体现这个功能，读者也就不能在整个文献知识背景下，来系统深入地理解论文的研究结果。不引用参考文献，就无法做到将论文结果与研究背景和引言中设定的问题关联起来；不引用参考文献，就无法做到将论文的研究发现与前人已经确立的或广泛接受的知识体系联系起来；不引用参考文献，就无法令人信服地提供结果有效性和重要性的证据；不引用参考文献，就无法表明前人研究的局限性和突出论文工作的创新性。但是要注意，引用文献不能只引支持论文结果或结论的文献，而有意回避或忽略不支持论文结果或结论的文献；同样，也不能为了强调论文研究结果的创新性，而故意不引前人已有的相关研究成果。显然，恰当征引参考文献的前提是阅读文献、熟悉文献和理解文献。

(五) 讨论可结合图表进行

如有必要，讨论过程中可引用结果或附件中的图表并加以说明。如果作者在自己论文结果或结论的基础上，整合前人的成果，提出了新的解释、假想或理论模型，那么，在讨论部分绘制一个示意图，图文并茂地加以说明，这将会使讨论写作提升到一个新的高度，会令编辑和审稿人刮目相看。

四、讨论写作的语言

讨论部分往往需要概述结果，但不要简单拷贝结果中的语句，概括论文的主要发现及其重要性也不要用摘要、引言最后一段用同样的语言，措辞和语句表达要有所变化。讨论部分最忌讳语言叙述让读者分不清哪些工作是作者的，哪些工作是别人的。因此，在叙述论文发现或论述论文成果时，可用第一人称（we 或 our）和主动语态明确表示，这种方式本身就有对自己创新成果强调的作用。如《自然》期刊标题为"The *Arabidopsis* F-box protein TIR1 is an auxin receptor"的论文，其讨论部分前两段的开头两句分别如下：

We had previously reported that auxin acts to promote SCF^{TIR1} - Aux/IAA interaction, and hence Aux/IAA degradation, by modifying SCF^{TIR1} rather than the Aux/IAAs[22]. Here we have shown that this modification is the direct binding of auxin to TIR1 and thus that TIR1 is an auxin receptor that mediates transcriptional responses to auxin.

As well as providing key evidence of an auxin receptor function for TIR1, our work with heterologously expressed TIR1 also answers the previously open question of whether TIR1 binds Aux/IAA targets directly or indirectly through some kind of adaptor protein, indicating that binding is direct and that in all probability no additional components are required. If this is indeed so, we further conclude that SCF^{TIR1} and associated protein degradation machinery, the Aux/IAAs, and their binding partners the ARFs represent a complete signal transduction cascade from auxin to gene expression.

讨论写作中经常用到因果推理，表达因果关系的英语词语十分丰富，常用的连词有：because, since, as, for, thus, so, therefore, hence, hereby, thereby, why；介词有：because of, due to, owning to, thanks to, on（the）account of, on the ground of, as a result of, by virtue of；副词有：consequently, eventually, then, admittedly, inevitably, as a result, as a consequence, because of this, for this reason, on the account；动词有：result from/in, follow from, base on, account for；名词有：basis, result, consequence, reason；动名词有：seeing that, considering that。讨论部分免不了对结果与结论、证据与论点、现象与原因之间的关系进行表述，为了精确地表达，要对诸如 prove, demonstrate, establish, confirm, ascertain, determine, show, reveal, indicate, found, suggest, imply 这些近词语进行辨析，如果表达类似于数学定理证明那样坚实的逻辑和确凿的证据证明某种结论或表明某种观点的真实性，就用 prove, demonstrate 表示；如果表示确立或证实某种观点，可用 establish, confirm, ascertain, determine 表示；如果表示展示、显示、指出、发现或表明某种现象、结果或结论，就用 show, indicate, found 表示；如果表示某种不确定性的推测，就用 suggest, imply 表示。以 show, reveal, indicate 为例：show（显示、表明）最为常用；reveal（揭示）意味着结论并不明显，需要对

数据进行分析或解释才能得出结论；indicate（表明）与 show 类似，但意味着作者避免明确的陈述，解释有一定的不确定性，论文中不宜使用过多。类似地，情态动词 can, will, should, probably, may, might, could, possibly 依次表示论点或论断由强到弱的确定性程度，在选用时要加以分辨。以最常用来表示推测的 may, might, could 为例，即便英美作者也可能混淆使用。"It may rain."表示很有可能要下雨（It is likely that It will rain.）；"It might rain."表示有可能要下雨，但谁也没有十足的把握（There is only a possibility that it will rain but no one is very sure.），而"It could rain."则表示有下雨这种可能，但可能性很小（It is less likely that it will rain.）。因此，作者在写作讨论时根据情况选用合适的词语。

在时态使用方面，叙述论文过去所做的实验或得出的结果用一般过去时，论述本论文中呈现的结果，论述这些结果的意义、推论或结论用一般现在时，而讨论论文成果对该领域将来的影响，可用将来时。

讨论往往在开始一段概括论文的主要发现或重述结果。这部分常用的动词（下划线所示）和例文如下：

【例文1】We identified NGA3/TOP1, in an activation tagging mutagenized population, by the severe phenotype observed in gynoecium development caused by NGA3/TOP1 overexpression.

【例文2】Here, we developed a highly efficient virus-induced gene silencing (VIGS) vector for use in papaya by modifying an artificially attenuated infectious clone of papaya leaf distortion mosaic virus (PLDMV; genus: Potyvirus), PLDMV-E, into a stable Nimble Cloning (NC)-based PLDMV vector.

【例文3】The results of this study show that CKI1 is expressed in the ovule and endosperm, but not in the embryo, based on the expression patterns of a CKI1::GUS reporter construct in transgenic plants.

【例文4】Analyses of CKI1 mutants suggest that CKI1 is involved in female gametophyte development and homozygous cki1 mutant is lethal.

【例文5】Analyses of AHP-green-fluorescent protein (GFP) fusions reveal that AHP1 and AHP2, but not AHP5, are translocated from the cytoplasm to the nucleus in a cytokinin-dependent manner.

【例文6】These studies indicate that plant phytochromes have diverged from the ancestral His protein kinase as Ser/Thr kinases with a new activity.

【例文7】The functional importance of hybrid His protein kinases implicates the necessity of another player in the HIS-to-ASP phosphorelay to serve as an intermediate by acquiring and transferring phosphate to separate receiver proteins, ARRs.

【例文8】Functional complementation analysis using a yeast *ypd1* mutant demonstrated that AHP1, AHP2, and AHP3 could act as phosphorelay intermediates.

讨论还需要对论文引言提出的问题或假设做出回应，也就是对结果进行评论。这部分常用的动词搭配（下划线所示）和例文如下：

【例文1】These experiments <u>provide compelling/strong evidence</u> that CRE1/AHK4/WOL is a cytokinin receptor and perceives extracellular cytokinins.

【例文2】The results <u>support the idea</u> that AHPs form a physical link between the plasma membrane-localized sensor kinase and the nuclear response regulators in cytokinin signaling.

【例文3】These results <u>confirm known associations with</u> iron measures and <u>give unique evidence of</u> their role in different ethnicities, suggesting origins in a common founder.

【例文4】These findings <u>are consistent with/ in line with/ in agreement with</u> a modulating effect of placebo (under analgesic expectation in humans) on a potent nociceptive, pro-inflammatory cytokine(IL-18) and underlying relationships with endogenous opioid activity, a neurotransmitter system critically involved in pain, stress, and mood regulation.

【例文5】We <u>established a link</u> between the gut microbiota and body weight.

【例文6】This sequence divergence and the failure of cytokinin binding to CKI1 in yeast <u>argue against</u> the function of CKI1 as a cytokinin receptor.

之后，讨论还需对重要结果进行解释和评估，提出理由，进行推测。这部分常用的词汇（下划线所示）和例文如下：

【例文1】Dysbiosis of the gut microbiome can <u>result from</u> other factors too, like antibiotics. This type of medication is linked to weight gain <u>because</u> they disrupt the microbial communities in your gut, either by preventing and slowing bacterial growth, or killing them.

【例文2】This suggests that gut bacteria could affect weight. This may <u>be due to</u> the effect of bacteria on the digestion of different foods.

【例文3】Bed bug infestations have resurged since the 1980s for reasons that are not clear, but <u>contributing factors</u> may be complacency, increased resistance, bans on pesticides, and increased international travel.

【例文4】There are <u>several possible explanations</u> to the paucity of studies on RSVH. First, rates of this kind of homicide may in fact be very low. Second, and in line with this, there are reasons to believe that it would take a multi-centre design to obtain a sample size large enough for a satisfactory quantitative study.

【例文5】Together with these genetic factors, auxin <u>appears to</u> play a key role in the specification of the different domains along the apical-basal axis of the Arabidopsis gynoecium. This was first suggested by the phenotypes of mutants affecting auxin transport or signaling.

【例文 6】Another possibility is that CKI1 might be part of a cytokinin receptor complex or recognizes cytokinins in a manner distinct from that of CRE1/AHK4/WOL.

【例文 7】Therefore, we conclude that ARR3 and ARR4 play a role in the control of hypocotyl length under light/dark cycles, possibly acting on phyB stability.

【例文 8】Considering the larger number of sensors and response regulators, His protein kinases probably converge on and share AHP proteins to direct different signals on response regulators.

【例文 9】Nitrate application also activated ARR3 through ARR9 expression, presumably due to the elevation of cytokinin levels by nitrate.

【例文 10】Because these five proteins perform partially redundant functions, it is possible that they form complexes and carry out the phosphotransfer process.

【例文 11】Currently, we cannot exclude the possibility that overexpression of CKI1 provides higher kinase activities that nonspecifically activate unrelated signaling pathways.

【例文 12】We analyzed F2 seedlings from a cross between arr3, 4, 5, 6 and arr5, 6 for segregation of a long period and observed the long period in one-sixteenth of the seedlings (data not shown), consistent with segregation of two genes and ruling out the possibility of an unlinked third mutation.

最后，讨论要说明实验存在哪些局限或缺陷，或哪些问题还需进行进一步研究和探讨。这部分的常用的搭配（下划线所示）和例文如下：

【例文 1】It remains to be investigated whether the effects of stress hormones on fear retrieval also generalize across different contexts.

【例文 2】The counterpart that modulates *MYC2* activation in these processes including leaf senescence remains to be an interesting topic for future investigations.

【例文 3】Much work is needed to determine which factors or mechanisms are involved in the circadian control of blood pressure.

【例文 4】Further investigation is needed to determine which light signals regulate the expression of *PIF4/PIF5* mRNA through ELF3 during senescence.

【例文 5】Extensive genetic mapping or other experimental approaches will be needed to identify the determinants of ELF3-TR-dependent background effects.

【例文 6】Further research is necessary to determine whether ELF3 or the evening complex are thermosensors.

【例文 7】Further investigation into the physiological significance of these interactions should help determine the feasibility of targeting the clock clinically for the treatment of diabetes and other metabolic disorders.

【例文 8】PIF4 and ELF3 are emerging as key hubs for integrating developmental responses to the environment, and it will be interesting to see if their role in thermoresponsiveness is conserved in crop plants.

【例文 9】As the PrD and intrinsically disordered protein sequences are widespread within eukaryotes19, it will be interesting to see whether they have been recruited to provide thermosensory behaviour through phase transitions in other signalling contexts.

第十一章 结论的写作

结论(Conclusions)是指位于正文末尾,对论文主要发现或核心成果及其理论意义或应用前景的概括总结。

初学者在写作结论时,很容易拷贝结果当作结论。需要注意的是,结果是调查、观察或实验获得的数据,是得到某一结论的证据,而结论是在结果的基础上分析得出的观点、见解和理论。

论文的结论宜精练而具体,忌笼统和泛泛而论。同样,在指出研究的意义时,也应当说明具体的意义,而不是仅仅是"对……有意义"或"有助于认识……"。结论和意义都应当是具体而明确的。此外,虽然也有论文结论会提及研究的不足之处和对后续工作的展望与设想,但是,最好在论文的讨论部分加以论述,在结论部分指明研究的缺陷和不足会暴露研究的缺点,弱化论文的结论,贬低论文的贡献。

不同期刊论文结论的写作格式往往不同,有的期刊论文需要在讨论之后单独设一个带标题(也就是 Conclusions)的小节来写结论,有的期刊论文虽然没有单独一个小节来写结论,但在讨论的最后一段实质上就是结论内容,还有的期刊论文既没有单独结论部分,也不会在讨论的第一段或最后一段包含结论内容。如果属于前两种情况,要注意写作时不要简单地拷贝摘要、引言、结果或讨论中的句子。摘要、引言最后一段、讨论的第一段往往在内容上与结论差不多,但是最好不要简单重复,作者要利用好论文中这几个机会,对论文创造性成果加以强调,以便给编辑和审稿人留下深刻的印象。另外要注意的是,结论是前文结果的概括总结,不应包含前文中未出现的新事实。结论部分是否需要引用图表或参考文献,视情况而定。

结论的长短可根据文章长短来设定,一般为 50~200 个单词,短论文的结论可短一点,长论文的结论可稍长一点。

下面为《科学》期刊上标题为"A NAC gene regulating senescence improves grain orotein, Zinc, and iron content in wheat"的一篇短论文或简报(report)的结论。

The cloning of *Gpc-B1* provides a direct link between the regulation of senescence and nutrient remobilization and an entry point to characterize the genes regulating these two processes. This may contribute to their more efficient manipulation in crops and translate into food with enhanced nutritional value.

下面为《美国科学院院刊》上标题为"OsNAP connects abscisic acid and leaf senescence by fine-tuning abscisic acid biosynthesis and directly targeting senescence-associated genes in rice"的一篇研究性论文(长度在《自然》和《科学》的短文与长文之间)的结论。

Overall, we propose a functional model of OsNAP's role in rice leaf senescence (Fig. 6). The leaf-aging signal triggers the accumulation of *OsNAP* transcripts, and this accumulation initiates the onset of senescence. The validity of this mechanism is supported by our observations that OsNAP directly or indirectly regulates the expression of genes known to control senescence in an age-dependent manner, including CDGs, nutrient transportrelated genes, and other SAGs. In addition, ABA participates in leaf senescence by modulating *OsNAP* expression, although high *OsNAP* expression levels also could regulate ABA biosynthesis via a feedback mechanism. Thus, OsNAP appears to act as a key regulator linking the ABA-signaling and leaf senescence processes.

下面是《自然》期刊上标题为"Root microbiota drive direct integration of phosphate stress and immunity"长论文(article)的结论。

Plant responses to phosphate stress are inextricably linked to life in microbe-rich soil. We demonstrate that genes controlling PSR contribute to assembly of a normal root microbiome. Our SynCom enhanced the activity of PHR1, the master regulator of the PSR, in plants grown under limited phosphate. This led to our discovery that PHR1 is a direct regulator of a functionally relevant set of plant immune system genes. Despite being required for the activation of JA-responsive genes during PSR[24], we found that PHR1 is unlikely to be a general regulator of this response (Extended Data Fig. 9c-e, Supplementary Table 12). Rather, PHR1 may fine-tune JA responses in specific biological contexts.

We demonstrate that PSR and immune system outputs are directly integrated by PHR1 (and, probably, PHL1). We provide a mechanistic explanation for previous disparate observations that PSR and defence regulation are coordinated and implications that PHR1 is the key regulator[8,11,12,24]. We provide new insight into the intersection of plant nutritional stress response, immune system function, and microbiome assembly and maintenance; systems that must act simultaneously and coordinately in natural and agricultural settings. Our findings will drive investigations aimed at utilizing microbes to enhance efficiency of phosphate use.

第十二章 致谢与参考文献的写作

一、致谢

致谢(Acknowledgements)在论文的结论之后,可以表达对不包含在作者名单中的人员提供的帮助(如审读论文、一般性的技术和设备支持等)或机构、团体、企业提供的资助表示感谢。这部分写作要尽可能具体,个人帮助要说明什么方面的帮助,项目资助要写清编号与资助主体单位。

致谢个人常用的句式如:We thank ××× for critical reading of the manuscript/for critical comments on the manuscript/for helpful suggestions/for useful discussions, for construction of the ××× (具体质粒名称)vector, and ××× for technical assistance.

感谢资金资助的句式如:This work/project was supported by grant ××× (项目编号)from the ××× (资助主体)to ××× (作者),Support by ××× (资助主体)grant ××× (项目编号)to ××× (作者),××× (作者) was supported by ××× (资助主体)grant ××× (项目编号),××× (作者) was supported/funded by the ××× (资助主体)(项目编号 ×××)。

二、参考文献

参考文献(References 或 Literature)为撰写论文引用的文献来源,通常置于论文的最后。参考文献的作用是提供文献引用或参考的来源,是论文立题或评判的重要依据,也为读者对论文相关内容溯本求源带来便利。同时,参考文献可明确前人的学术贡献,是尊重前人科研成果的表示。引用参考文献可使论文论述精练、节省篇幅。

选择参考文献时,要考虑时效性、相关性、代表性、可靠性、客观性、权威性等因素。时效性是指尽可能引用近 5 年(尤其是上一年或当年)的文献。相关性要求参考文献要与论文内容密切相关,应当与论文切题,避免滥引。代表性是指文献要具有代表性,不要漏掉领域内的重要的或经典的文献。可靠性是要确保所引文献来源真实可靠,内容没有疑问。客观性是指不要因为论文观点倾向性而回避不利于自己论点的文献，或者倾向性地引用某些文献（包括自己的文献）而不引另外一些文献。权威性是指参考文献尽可能是领域内权威期刊或主流期刊论文。

作者在引用参考文献前要确保阅读过所引文献，格式遵循拟投稿期刊最新论文的体例要求，在论文提交时，要核对文献各著录项，如期刊论文的作者姓名、出版年、论文题目、期刊名或专著名、卷、期、页码、著作的作者、章节名、编辑、著作名、出版单位、出版地点、出版年份及页码，确保没有错误。一般情况下，参考文献只能使用已出版的文献（如果只是线上出版还未来得及出版纸质版的论文，此时尚没有卷期号及页码，需要注明 doi 编号或 URL 网址）。有些学科期刊也可将预印本文库中的论文或已被出版社接收而正处于出版过程中的"待刊"论文或专著列为参考文献。对于"待刊"论文或专著，可用"（in press）"标注表示。

每种期刊都会在投稿须知或作者须知中规定其参考文献的著录格式，不同的期刊参考文献著录格式千差万别，但总体上分著者-出版年制和顺序编码制两种。

著者-出版年制（name-year system 或 Harvard system）是指在正文中利用作者姓（author's surname）和出版年（publication year）来征引文献，单个作者格式为"（作者 年）"或"（作者，年）"，例如，（Hurd 1996）。两个作者格式为"（第一作者 and 第二作者 年）"，例如，（Johnson and Young 2003）。3 个或 3 个以上作者格式为"（第一作者 et al. 年）"或"（第一作者 et al.，年）"，例如，（Pace et al. 2004）。当有多个文献来源时，括号内各个文献来源之间用逗号或分号隔开，按出版年次序或著者字母顺序先后排列，例如，（Smith 1920; Walker 1963; Schuster and Coyne 1974; Vidaver 1981; Mount and Lacy 1982; Starr 1984; Billing 1987; Nester 2004）。篇末参考文献按作者姓的字母顺序升序排列（alphabetical list of references）。同一作者的不同出版年的文献来源，括号内不同出版年之间用逗号隔开，例如，（Hassanein 1997，2001）。同一作者相同出版年的不同文献来源时，参考文献中按出版年先后排列，用出版年后的小写英语字母顺序加以区别，引用格式为"（作者 年+小写字母）"，例如，（Sabo and Power 2002a）。

Despite the occurrence of apomixis in more than 400 species belonging to over 40 families of angiosperms, it is found scarce in agriculturally important crops (Bicknell and Koltunow 2004; Carman 1997). Harnessing its full potential would depend on the successful introduction of the apomixis trait to a crop variety via an introgression-based approach or genetic engineering method (Spillane et al. 2001). However, the introgression of apomixis through back-crossing program has been largely unsuccessful and the engineering of conditional apomixis through biotechnology has been limited by the lack of the understanding of molecular mechanisms that trigger apomixis (Barcaccia and Albertini 2013; Spillane et al. 2001; van Dijk et al. 2016).

References

Barcaccia G, Albertini E (2013) Apomixis in plant reproduction: a novel perspective on an old dilemma. Plant Reprod 26: 159-179.

Bicknell RA, Koltunow AM (2004) Understanding apomixis: recent advances and remaining conundrums. Plant Cell 16 Suppl: S228-245.

Carman JG (1997) Asynchronous expression of duplicate genes in angiosperms may cause apomixis, bispory, tetraspory, and polyembryony. Biol J Linn Soc 61: 51-94.

Spillane C, Steimer A, Grossniklaus U (2001) Apomixis in agriculture: the quest for clonal seeds. Sex Plant Reprod 14: 179-187.

van Dijk PJ, Rigola D, Schauer SE (2016) Plant Breeding: Surprisingly, Less Sex Is Better. Curr Biol 26: R122-124.

顺序编码制(citation-order system 或 citation-sequence system)是指在正文中按照参考文献的排序，利用数字编号来征引文献，格式为"数字编号"或"[数字编号]"(上标或正常格式)，两个或多个不连续文献来源之间有逗号隔开，3个或3个以连续文献来源用连字符(-)置于最前与最后来源之间表示。篇末参考文献按正文中出现或引用顺序先后来排列编号(numbered list of references)。

Stable gene transfer can be developed for gene function studies at whole plant level. Much progress has been made in cassava genetic transformation of both *Agrobacterium tumefaciens*-mediated and biolistic-mediated system [1-3]. However, the transformation efficiency is relatively low and genotypic dependent[4], and the process requires well-trained tissue culture specialists, is lengthy and difficult to repeat[5, 6].

References

1. Zhang P, Legris G, Coulin P, Puonti-Kaerlas J. Production of stably transformed cassava plants via particle bombardment. Plant Cell Rep. 2000; 19: 939-45.

2. Siritunga D, Sayre R. Generation of cyanogen-free transgenic cassava. Planta. 2003; 217: 367-73.

3. Siritunga D, Sayre R. Engineering cyanogens in cassava. Plant Mol Biol. 2004; 56: 661-9.

4. Zhang P, Puonti-Kaerlas J. PEG-mediated cassava transformation using positive and negative selection. Plant Cell Rep. 2000; 19: 1041-48.

5. Nyaboga EN, Njiru JM and Tripathi L. Factors influencing somatic embryogenesis, regeneration, and *Agrobacterium*-mediated transformation of cassava (*Manihot esculenta* Crantz) cultivar TME14. Front Plant Sci. 2015; 6: 411.

6. Zainuddin IM, Schlegel K, Gruissem W, Vanderschuren H. Robust transformation procedure for the production of transgenic farmer-preferred cassava landraces. Plant Methods. 2012; 8: 24.

还有一种参考文献的著录格式为著者字母-顺序编号制(alphabet-number system)，

参考文献按字母顺序排列编号，正文利用数字编号来征引文献。这种著录格式在科技论文中较少见。

不论哪一种引用和著录格式，都需要注意，征引的文献来源应尽可能靠近所引的信息内容或相关的主题。引用位置一般在句尾或句中，视情况而定，但总体原则是信息来源具体明白、清晰无误。

例如，下面的征引方式是正确的：

Several NGS-based approaches have been developed to identify SNPs, such as restriction site associated DNA sequencing(RAD-seq)(Baird et al., 2008), genotyping-by-sequencing(GBS)(Elshire et al., 2011), 2b-RAD(Wang et al., 2012), specific length amplified fragment sequencing(SLAF-seq)(Sun et al., 2013), double digest RAD(ddRAD)(Dacosta and Sorenson, 2014) and amplified-fragment single nucleotide polymorphism and methylation(AFSM)(Xia et al., 2014).

但下面这样引用就不恰当：

Several NGS-based approaches have been developed to identify SNPs, such as restriction site associated DNA sequencing(RAD-seq), genotyping-by-sequencing(GBS), 2b-RAD, specific length amplified fragment sequencing (SLAF-seq), double digest RAD (ddRAD)and amplified-fragment single nucleotide polymorphism and methylation(AFSM)(Baird et al., 2008)(Elshire et al., 2011; Wang et al., 2012; Sun et al., 2013; Dacosta and Sorenson, 2014; Xia et al., 2014).

此外，参考文献序号或著者-出版年在句子中的具体标注位置分两种情况。

第一种情况：如果句子中没有出现作者或信息来源（报告、文章等），参考文献序号或著者-出版年一般标注在句尾或句中的适当位置，也就是完整引述内容的结尾。例如，

Senescence is the age-dependent deterioration process at the cellular, tissue, organ, or organismal level, leading to death or the end of the life span [48].（顺序编码制）

It is well-recognized that anthocyanin biosynthesis is tightly regulated at the transcriptional level by the evolutionarily conserved MYB-bHLH-WD repeat (MBW) complex(Xu et al., 2015; Lloyd et al., 2017; Naing and Kim, 2018).（著者-出版年制）

第二种情况：如果句子中（尤其是句首）出现作者或信息来源，参考文献序号或著者-出版年一般标注在作者或信息来源后面。例如，

Recently, Castelblanque et al. [7] discovered genes involved in cell wall remodeling in laticifers of *Euphorbia lathyris*.（顺序编码制）

These reports [13, 14] suggest that many more molecular and chemical studies are still needed to give us a better understanding of latex functionalities and limitations in plant defense.（顺序编码制）

The most accepted classification of laticifers was proposed by De Bary [30], who described two types of laticifer: articulated and nonarticulated [1, 31, 32] (Box 1). (顺序编码制)

Zhou et al. (2008) reported the transformation of *A. andraeanum* callus with the C-repeat binding factor 1 (CBF1) gene mediated by *A. tumefaciens*. (著者-出版年制)

A recent study by Ishikawa et al. (2011) demonstrated that the wound signal promotes the expression of *CYCD;1* at the wound site and through its binding to CDKA, upregulates CDKA activity. (著者-出版年制)

According to Jones (1968), ethylene can increase or decrease the quantity of a-amylase in two ways: By affecting the synthesis of the enzyme and by influencing the a-amylase release. (著者-出版年制)

The activity of a-amylase was measured as described by Black and others (1996), with some modifications. (著者-出版年制)

以上只是一般的期刊论文参考文献著录和引用格式，专著、著作析出文献、会议论文、学位论文又有所不同。对于多作者参编的专著或论文集，如果主编或编辑者只有一位，一般在主编或编辑者姓名后用括号(Ed.)或(ed.)表示；如果不止一位主编或编辑，那么就用(Eds.)或(eds.)表示。不同的期刊参考文献著录和引用格式也会存在一些差异，需要在投稿前根据期刊网站对参考文献著录和引用格式进行准备，这可以利用手工对文献进行排列整理，也可利用 EndNote 软件自动按照期刊要求的格式来整理。无论哪一种方式，参考文献的著录格式要严格遵守期刊的规定，这是对期刊编辑的尊重，也显示一定的投稿诚意。

《植物细胞》的参考文献著录格式如下：

单个作者期刊文章的著录格式：

Eisenstein, M. (2015). Disease: Closing the door on HIV. Nature 528: S8-9.

两个作者期刊文章的著录格式：

Gutnisky, D. A. and Dragoi, V. (2008). Adaptive coding of visual information in neural populations. Nature 452: 220-224.

3 个作者期刊文章的著录格式：

Alby, K., Schaefer, D., and Bennett, R. J. (2009). Homothallic and heterothallic mating in the opportunistic pathogen Candida albicans. Nature 460: 890-893.

3 个以上作者期刊文章的著录格式：

Okita, K., Nakagawa, M., Hyenjong, H., Ichisaka, T., and Yamanaka, S. (2008). Generation of mouse induced pluripotent stem cells without viral vectors. Science 322: 949-953.

单个作者著作的著录格式：

Tsui, J. B. -Y. (2004). Fundamentals of Global Positioning System Receivers (John Wiley & Sons, Inc.: Hoboken, NJ).

主编著作的著录格式：

Kole, C. ed(2006). Cereals and Millets(Springer: Berlin, Heidelberg).

主编著作析出文献的著录格式：

Rozowsky, J., Bertone, P., Royce, T., Weissman, S., Snyder, M., and Gerstein, M. (2005). Analysis of Genomic Tiling Microarrays for Transcript Mapping and the Identification of Transcription Factor Binding Sites. In Advances in Bioinformatics and Computational Biology: Brazilian Symposium on Bioinformatics, BSB 2005, Sao Leopoldo, Brazil, July 27-29, 2005. Proceedings, J. C. Setubal and S. Verjovski-Almeida, eds, Lecture Notes in Computer Science. (Springer: Berlin, Heidelberg), pp. 28-29.

学位论文的著录格式：

Muenyong-Zinner, S. (2017). Care First Wound Healing Center a Business Plan.

《美国科学院院刊》的参考文献著录格式如下：

期刊文章的著录格式：

J. -M. Neuhaus, L. Sticher, F. Meins, Jr., T. Boller, A short C-terminal sequence is necessary and sufficient for the targeting of chitinases to the plant vacuole. *Proc. Natl. Acad. Sci. U. S. A.* 88, 10362- 10366(1991).

主编著作析出文献的著录格式：

A. V. S. Hill, "HLA associations with malaria in Africa: Some implications for MHC evolution" in Molecular Evolution of the Major Histocompatibility Complex, J. Klein, D. Klein, Eds. (Springer, 1991), pp. 403- 420.

预印本文献的著录格式：

H. Luetkens *et al.*, Electronic phase diagram of the LaO1-xFxFeAs superconductor. arXiv: 0806. 35331(21 June 2008).

从上面我们可以看到，《植物细胞》与《美国科学院院刊》的参考文献著录格式很明显的区别在于：两者的姓名格式书写不同，所列作者数量不同，出版年的位置不同。

第十三章 初学者写作常见问题

初学者写作最常见的问题是写作格式问题和简单语法问题。对复杂的表达犯错，一般审稿人不会抱怨，但是对于满目的书写格式错误和简单语法错误，是最不能忍受的。

一、书写格式

(一) 物种学名的书写格式

物种的学名格式问题是 SCI 论文写作常遇到的格式问题。瑞典著名的植物学家林奈(Caroius Linnaeus，1707—1778)提出"双名法"，即每个物种的学名由排在第一位的属名和第二位的种名或种加词两部分组成，有时种名后面还有命名者的姓名(可以省略)。第一位的属名(首字母大写)和第二位的种名(首字母小写)要用斜体，但后面的命名者的姓名为正体，如橡胶树为 *Hevea brasiliensis* Muell.。科名是不用斜体的，如大戟科(Euphorbiaceae)。在摘要和正文中第一次出现时用全名，例如，Rubber tree (*Hevea brasiliensis* Muell.) is a perennial plant of the Euphorbiaceae family. 第二次及以后提到学名时，第一位的属名仅用首字母，第二位的种名要写全，如 *H. brasiliensis*。此外，一些拉丁词如 *in vitro*、*in situ* 也要用斜体。

(二) 名词缩写格式

论文中常出现的较长术语或名词可用习惯的缩写形式，但同样要在摘要和正文中第一次出现时用全名，后面用括号标出相应的缩写，第二次及以后提到时只需用缩写形式即可，如 RNA sequencing (RNA-seq)、3-hydroxy-3-metylglutaryl coenzyme A reductase(HMGR)、methyl jasmonate(MeJA)等。

(三) 征引文献的"作者-出版年"格式

在正文中征引文献时，一定要注意只出现作者的姓或家族名，而不是全名。例如，Numerous studies have been performed concerning the flower senescence and many genes associated with petal senescence have been characterized(Shahri & Tahir, 2014), but it is as yet unknown how the onset of petal senescence is regulated(van Doorn & Woltering, 2008).

参考文献对应的是下面两篇：

Shahri, W., & Tahir, I. (2014). Flower senescence: some molecular aspects. *Planta*, 239, 277-297.

van Doorn, W. G.., & Woltering, E. J. (2008). Physiology and molecular biology of petal senescence. *Journal of Experimental Botany*, 59, 453-480.

那么，正文中的(Shahri & Tahir, 2014)就不能写成(Shahri, W., & Tahir, I., 2014)；(van Doorn & Woltering, 2008)不能写成(van Doorn, W. G.., & Woltering, E. J., 2008)。

(四)数字与英语单位的书写格式

还有一个最常见的格式错误是数字与英语单位之间空一格，但是%和℃除外。英语单位和化学物质名称之间也要空一格。例如，30 μLRNase 要改为 30 μL RNase，5 μLRNA 要改为 5 μL RNA，260 nm、280 nm 要改为 260 nm、280 nm，但 4℃ 和 75% 则是正确的。

常见到初学者将转速的单位写错，如 12,000 rpm/min，这其实是错的，rpm 的意思就是 revolution per minute，不能再写作 rpm/min，要么去掉"/min"写成 12,000 rpm，要么写成 12,000 r/min。此外，一般低速离心常以转速"rpm"来表示，高速离心则以"g"表示，例如，The slurry was centrifuged for 10 min at 4℃ (15,000g), the supernatant was filtered through Miracloth, and 0.5 mL of StrepTactin Sepharose(IBA) was added. 注意数字与单位 g 之间没有空格。

使用百分数(%)作单位时，需要注明是质量百分数(w/v)还是体积百分数(v/v)。例如，Small samples(~1.5 mm^2) from at least 12 different leaves were cut on a modeling waxplate in a drop of 2.5% (w/v) paraformaldehyde and 0.5% (v/v) glutar-aldehyde in 0.06 M Sørensen phosphate buffer, pH 7.2. 注意酸碱度(值)pH 不能写成 PH。

使用比率单位(如浓度、速度等)时，可用负号上标表示(例如，a flow rate of 300 nl min^{-1})；也可用斜线表示(例如，5 mg/mL antipain)，但用斜线表示时，要注意斜线与前后两个字母之间没有空格，也不能一次使用多个斜线，如不能用 m/s/s 来表示 m s^{-2}(加速度，米每二次方秒)。使用"per"表示只能在全称中使用，如 50 kilometers per hour，不能写作 50 km per h。

需要指出的是，在很多情况下需要使用负号(注意负号与数字之间没有空格)，例如，−79℃、$P \leq 1 \times 10^{-25}$、3.8 mg l^{-1} KCl，但要注意输入的是负号(−, unicode 代码 2212)而不是连字号(-)，也不是减号(–)。负号输入时在键入 2212 之后按"Alt+X"。

中英文的温度单位符号有所不同，中文的温度单位符号为℃，英文的温度单位符号为°C；一个常见的单位错误是在 SCI 论文中使用中文的温度单位符号℃，而不是使用英文的温度单位符号°C。

SCI 论文中的单位通常用缩写，例如 day(s)简写成 d，hour(s)简写成 h，minute(s)简写成 min，second(s)简写成 s，但 week(s)和 month(s)不简写。

另外，单位要用国际单位，格式要统一规范，同时注意期刊要求。

(五)数字书写形式

数字的书写形式也要注意。10 以下的数字、句首数字通常用英语单词表示，10 以上的数字、有小数点的数字、带单位的数字、表示范围或多个数字一起比较时，用阿拉伯数字表示。例如，

【例句 1】It consists of over 30 different components, called nucleoporins, which form eight identical subunits arranged in a circle. (10 以上的数字一般用阿拉伯数字表示，而 10 以下的数字用英语单词表示)

【例句 2】There are three possible ways by which the cell accomplishes the task. (10 以下的数字一般用英语单词表示)

【例句 3】A hundred thousand Americans didn't need to die. (句首数字通常用英文单词表示)

【例句 4】Fifteen hundred versus a hundred thousand is not a reasonable difference. (句首数字通常用英语单词表示)

【例句 5】Nine of these amino acids have nonpolar R groups and are therefore hydrophobic. (句首数字通常用英语单词表示)

【例句 6】Targeting sequences usually comprise a length of 3-80 amino acids that are recognized by specific receptors that guide the protein to the correct site and make contact with the appropriate translocation machinery. (表示范围或多个数字一起比较时，用阿拉伯数字表示)

【例句 7】After 2 h of exposure, membrane levels of PIN1 had returned to its normal non-salt-stressed level. (带单位的数字用阿拉伯数字表示)

【例句 8】Strikingly, in contrast to the earlier observed large increase in cellular PIN3 levels, membrane levels of PIN3 showed only a 4% transient upregulation. (带单位的数字用阿拉伯数字表示)

【例句 9】Sections were immediately transferred for 1 h to NBT staining solution(0.1% NBT in 10 mM potassium phosphate buffer, pH 7.8). (有小数点的数字和带单位的数字用阿拉伯数字表示)

(六)基因和蛋白质的书写格式

在生物和医学文献中，基因和蛋白质正式符号宜参照 http://www.ncbi.nlm.nih.gov/gene 书写。不同生物的基因符号书写规则略有差异。一般生物的基因和蛋白质命名由罗马字母和阿拉伯数字组成，中间不加标点，数字编号也不用上下标；基因符号

要用斜体，蛋白质符号则要用正体；隐性基因和隐性基因突变体用小写字母斜体表示。以植物为例，文心兰的 *OnELF3* 和 OnELF3 分别表示对应的显性基因和蛋白质，拟南芥的显性基因和野生型 *PIN1* 对应的隐性基因和隐性基因突变体为 *pin1*。小 RNA（small RNA）或微 RNA（microRNA）名称不用斜体，但其基因名称要用斜体，例如，

Since the early stage of discovery of plant small RNAs, *miR165/166* have been characterized as a relatively abundant class of miRNAs. The *Arabidopsis* genome contains seven copies of *miR166* genes and two copies of *miR165* genes.

人类基因和小鼠基因符号虽然都用斜体，但人类基因符号所有字母都大写，而小鼠基因符号中只第一个字母用大写；人类和老鼠蛋白质符号都不用斜体，而是用正体的大写字母书写。

更详细的小鼠/大鼠命名规则参考 http：//www. informatics. jax. org/mgihome/nomen/gene. shtml，人类命名规则参考 http：//www. genenames. org/，斑马鱼命名规则参考 http：//zfin. org/，爪蟾命名规则参考 http：//www. xenbase. org/gene/static/genenamenclature. jsp，果蝇命名规则参考 http：//flybase. org。限制性内切酶和质粒要用标准的名称来规范书写。由于目前不同研究者对同一基因命名存在差异，导致同一个基因有多个别名，而未经批准的或不规范的命名会给读者与研究者带来混乱，因此，人类基因名称使用根据国际人类基因组组织基因命名委员会[Human Genome Organization Gene Nomenclature Committee, H(UGO)GNC]给出的标准命名，而脊椎动物的基因名称（如小鼠的 MGI）使用应根据相关物种特定命名委员会或脊椎动物基因命名委员会（VGNC）批准的基因符号。

二、语法错误

（一）定冠词使用

英语中定冠词使用虽然是初中就学过的基础语法知识，但是，在写作中仍然犯得最多和最普遍的错误。

①论文中前面提到过的人或事物，后面再次提到时就要用定冠词（the）。

【例文】Biophysicists have developed <u>a high-throughput super-resolution microscope</u> to probe nanoscale structures and dynamics of mammalian cells, showing in unprecedented detail the twists and turns of an organelle important for cell division.... <u>The microscope</u>, a super-resolution fluorescence microscope, is not at all the typical optical microscope that one would see in an introductory biology class.

②带有说明或限制性的定语从句或修饰短语的名词前要加定冠词（the）。The extreme limit to which each can increase, the dependency of one organic being on another, the case of a country undergoing some physical change。

③宇宙间独一无二的事物，或江河湖海、山川群岛、海峡海湾等地理名词前面要

加定冠词(the)，如 the sun, the moon, the earth, the world, the Pacific, the Taiwan Straits，但国名、地名、单个岛屿或山名前面不加，如 Asia, China, Beijing, Mount Tai。

④专有名词前面无须加任何冠词，例如论文中提到的某个基因或蛋白的具体名称。

【例文】To investigate this crosstalk function of MYC2 and MYC3 in more detail, we utilized our ChIP-seq data to determine the number of plant hormone TFs that are bound by MYC2 and MYC3.

著作中的某个专用名词，如《论自然选择》(*On Natural Selection*)中的 natural selection，每次提到这个术语时都不用冠词。

【例文1】This preservation of favourable variations and the rejection of injurious variations, I call natural selection.

【例文2】Natural selection will modify the structure of the young in relation to the parent, and of the parent in relation to the young.

【例文3】It may be said that natural selection is daily and hourly scrutinising, throughout the world, every variation, even the slightest; rejecting that which is bad, preserving and adding up all that is good; silently and insensibly working, whenever and wherever opportunity offers, at the improvement of each organic being in relation to its organic and inorganic conditions of life.

(二) 单复数对应

英语中主谓的单复数对应，不是以英语为母语的作者这类错误犯得最多，实际上，即便是以英语为母语(英、美、加、澳、新)的作者也可能因疏忽而出现此类错误。

主句子中主谓的单复数对应问题举例说明如下：

①确定不是单个事物和事项的情况下，一般使用复数名词。

【例文】They determined the personal diets by means of questionnaires in which the participants were asked to fill in how often they had eaten the individual animal products in the last 12 months—from"several times a day"to"never".

注意：有些英语名词没有复数形式，如 evidence, consensus, assitance, advice 等。

②注意区分主语的单复数，并使谓语动词与主语在单复数形式上保持一致。

【例文1】Our people spend time playing video games, and watching television. The latter is the biggest culprit; for some unknown reason, people believe what they see and hear on television. (Our people 和 people 为复数)

【例文2】A recent survey reports that the general public believes they know more than scientists. (the general public 为单数集合名词)

【例文3】I have long maintained that the intelligence quotient of the average American has greatly declined in the last 30 years. (the intelligence quotient 为单数)

【例文 4】Part of the gap between Science and human perception is communication. (Part 为单数)

【例文 5】The percentage of water varies according to your age and gender. (The percentage 为单数)

【例文 6】The vast majority of scientists believe that GMO foods are safe, and that the increased use of pesticides because of genetically modified crops poses no health problems for the people of our nation. (the increased use of pesticides 为单数)

【例文 7】Learning to work with data scientists is a necessary skill for a successful career. (动名词 Learning 为单数)

③定语从句单复数要与所修饰名词单复数形式上保持一致。

【例文 1】This is similar to a priest, who is not allowed to marry, giving counsel to a married couple. (a priest 为单数)

【例文 2】Although he is very thin, he has perseverance and courage which are decisive in becoming a qualified submariner. (perseverance and courage 为复数)

④名词分数的单复数形式与分数后面名词的单复数形式一致，若后面的名词为复数，谓语动词也用复数，若后面名词为单数或不可数名词，谓语动词则用单数。

【例文 1】A vast majority of environmental scientists work for the government, while others work for engineering and oil companies, and some even have their own businesses. (注意 A vast majority of 之后的 environmental scientists 为复数)

【例文 2】The next highest profit margin was 26.4% for financial services, but more than 72% of industry profit margins were single-digits and the median industry profit margin is 6%. (more than 72% of 之后的名词 industry profit margins 为复数)

【例文 3】More than nine-in-ten scientists (93%) favor the use of animals in scientific research, but only about half of the public (52%) agrees. (Scientists 为复数而 the public 是单数)

【例文 4】About 30%-40% of the weight of the human body is the skeleton, but when the bound water is removed, either by chemical desiccation or heat, half the weight is lost. (About 30%-40% of 之后的 the weight of the human body 为单数)

⑤名词全称为复数，其缩写形式也用复数，名词全称为单数，其缩写形式也用单数，但当一个名词修饰另一个名词时，修饰名词要用单数形式。

【例文 1】Transcription factor (TF) DNA sequence preferences direct their regulatory activity, but are currently known for only-1% of eukaryotic TFs. (Transcription factor 为单数，所以 TF 也为单数)

【例文 2】As transcription factors (TFs) play a crucial role in regulating the transcription process through binding on the genome alone or in a combinatorial manner, TF enrichment analysis is an efficient and important procedure to locate the candidate functional TFs. (transcription factors 为复数，所以 TFs 也为复数，但 TF enrichment analysis 中的修饰名词 TF 为单数)

⑥对于一些集合名词如 team，committee，faculty 等，判断是单数还是复数的一个简单原则：当这些词前面使用定冠词 the 时，谓语动词用单数；当这些词前面使用不定冠词 a 时，谓语动词用复数；对于 all，any，none 等一些可以是单数也可以是复数的词来讲，如果用 all of it，any of it，none of it 就用单数谓语动词，如果用 all of them，any of them，none of them 就用复数谓语动词。

(三) 悬垂修饰问题

悬垂修饰语(dangling modifiers)是指非谓语动词短语(如现在分词短语、过去分词短语、不定式短语、动名词短语以及省略主语的从句)做修饰语时，其逻辑主语与句子的主语不一致，即句子的主语不可能是悬垂修饰语的动作发出者。科技写作中悬垂修饰问题极为常见，即使欧美人也经常犯这类错误，主要原因是科技英语中大量使用被动语态所致。

【例文1】Using sarkosyl to induce nuclear run-on, the transcriptionally inactive b-globin gene in mature erythrocytes was demonstrated to harbor high levels of Pol Ⅱ at 5' proximal regulatory regions. (句子为被动句，主语为 the transcriptionally inactive b-globin gene，是无法做现在分词短语 Using sarkosyl to induce nuclear run-on 的逻辑主语的)

可修改为：Using sarkosyl to induce nuclear run-on, we demonstrated that the transcriptionally inactive b-globin gene in mature erythrocytes could harbor high levels of Pol Ⅱ at 5' proximal regulatory regions.

【例文2】Comparing to the Tesla Model 3, which is equipped with a tow eye hook only in the front of the vehicle, Model Y has a cover on the right side of the rear bumper to conceal the second tow eye. (句子主语 Model Y 不可能是现在分词短语 comparing to the Tesla Model 3 主语)

可修改为：Compared to the Tesla Model 3, which is equipped with a tow eye hook only in the front of the vehicle, Model Y has a cover on the right side of the rear bumper to conceal the second tow eye.

【例文3】Based on the primary results, we discarded the original hypothesis. (过去分词短语 based on the primary results 的主语与句子的主语 we 不一致。另外，如果过去分词短语 based on 一般用来修饰某个名词或名词短语时，应该置于被修饰名词的后面，而不是置于句首，如 a new world order based on international co-operation)

可修改为：On the basis of primary results, we discarded the original hypothesis. (修饰句子动词谓语时，使用介词词组 on the basis of)

【例文4】Before adding the compound, it was determined that the solution's pH was

6.4.（it 不可能是动名词 adding the compound 的主语）

可以修改为：Before the addition of the compound, it was determined that the solution's pH was 6.4.（名词+被动语态）

或修改为：Before adding the compound, we determined that the solution's pH was 6.4.（修改主句为主动语态，使句子的主语也是 adding the compound 的主语）

【例文 5】To institute a carbon tax, it is essential first to address the increasing influence of corporate lobbies.（it 不可能当不定式短语 to institute a carbon tax 的逻辑主语）

可修改为：To institute a carbon tax, reforming politicians must first address the increasing influence of corporate lobbies.

【例文 6】To illustrate the effectiveness of the proposed design method, the design of the two-bar structure acted by concentrated load is presented.（the design 不可能当不定式短语 to illustrate the effectiveness of the proposed design method 的逻辑主语）

可修改为：To illustrate the effectiveness of the proposed design method, we presented the design of the two-bar structure acted by concentrated load.

【例文 7】When confronted with the same contingencies later in the day, fewer errors were made.（从句 when confronted with the same contingencies later in the day 中省略的主语与句子的主语 fewer errors 不一致，或者说 fewer errors 不能做分词从句的主语）

可修改为：When confronted with the same contingencies later in the day, these subjects made fewer errors.

但要注意，一些充当插入语的悬垂分词或悬垂不定式已经大量使用并合法化，如 generally/broadly/strictly speaking, considerng, regarding, assuming, concerning, judging, given, provided 等。

（四）平行与并列错误

平行结构要求结构类似，平行单词要求的词性相同（名词对名词、形容词对形容词等）、类型相同（现在分词对现在分词、过去分词对过去分词、不定式对不定式等）。而并列谓语成分需要是同一主语发出的动作。

【例文 1】In this study, our results show that MeRAVs can bind CAACA motif in cassava, which indicates that MeRAVs recognition and binding CAACA motif is a common feature of RAV family in cassava.

该句中的 recognition 应当改为 recognizing，才能与 binding 并列，此外，bind 是不及物动词，后面需要加介词，也就是 binding 应改为 binding to。

【例文 2】To detect the flg22-triggered ROS burst, at least 50 leaf discs were collected and soaked in double distilled water in dark for 12 h, and then placed these leaf discs in a black 96-wells plate and add a mixture of 0.2 μM luminox reagent, 10 μg/mL horseradish peroxidase and 1 μM flg22.

该句中 then placed these leaf discs in a black 96-wells plate 的谓语动词 placed 既不与前面的 collected and soaked 形成并列关系，and 之后谓语动词 add 的时态和语态也是错误的。

可修改为：To detect the flg22-triggered ROS burst, at least 50 leaf discs were collected and soaked in double distilled water in dark for 12 h, and then transferred into a black 96-wells plate added with a mixture of 0.2 μM luminox reagent, 10 μg/mL horseradish peroxidase and 1 μM flg22.

为了避免错误，在稿件完成后，可利用 Word 自带的拼写与语法校对功能进行检查。例如，红色波形下划线表示可能的拼写错误，用绿色波形下划线表示可能的语法错误，或者利用专门的英语语法改错和润色软件 Grammarly(https：//app.grammarly.com)、1Checker(http：//www.1checker.com/)、Ginger Software (https：//www.gingersoftware.com/)、StyleWriter Software(http：//www.stylewriter-usa.com/)、WhiteSmoke (http：//www.whitesmoke.com/)、Virtual Writing Tutor (https：//virtualwritingtutor.com/)、NOUNPLUS(https：//www.nounplus.net/grammarcheck/)、AutoCrit Online Editing (https：//www.autocrit.com/)、lang-8 (http：//lang-8.com/)、Hemingway Editor (http：//www.hemingwayapp.com/)、ProWritingAid (https：//prowritingaid.com/)、Whitesmoke (http：//www.whitesmoke.com)等帮助查找语法错误和修改润色。笔者认为，这些软件虽然有所帮助，但最好是作者对文稿多次阅读，仔细推敲语句，效果较好。另外，写好后放置一段时间再看，最好出声朗读，更容易发现语法错误和句式欠佳之处。有条件的请以英语为母语的人或有 SCI 写作经验的老师批阅一下效果更佳。

三、口语化和歧视语使用问题

（一）口语化问题

SCI 论文是正式文体，因此，要避免口语化的写作风格，例如，使用 good, nice, pretty good, bad 等词来评价人、事或物，也不要使用 a lot, sort of 等口语词。不要使用缩写词如 don't, didn't, haven't, can't 等，而应该写成 do not, did not, have not, cannot(要写成一个单词形式的 cannot，而不是 can not)。

常用的口语化词(如 many, a lot of)可以用更为正式的词(如 numerous, plentiful, a myriad of, a plethora of, a multitude of, an abundance of)来代替。

【例文1】For the bacterial statistics, 10 leaf discs were taken at each sample point and ground thoroughly.

该句中，口语化表达 taken 宜用更正式的词 collected 来代替。

【例文2】These assays alone cannot tell what the protein concentration of a substance is.

该句中，口语化表达 tell what 宜用更正式的词 determine 来代替。

【例文 3】In this study, we found that *MeRAVs* common positively regulates the resistance to *Xanthomonas axonopodis* pv. *manihotis* (*Xam*) and stimulates the innate immune response by regulating the burst of ROS in cassava.

该句中，common 是一个口语化的词，因此，common positively regulates 宜修改为 positively co-regulate。同样，标题"The common modulation of RAV transcription factors in ROS burst and extensive transcriptional reprogramming underlie disease resistance in cassava"中，common modulation 也应修改为 co-modulation。

(二) 歧视语使用问题

在 SCI 论文写作中避免使用 he 或 men 泛指一般个人或男女两性，可以使用包含两性的复数名词(如 person, people, individuals, all 等)、中性名词(如 assistant, worker, technician 等)或复数代词(如 they, their 等)。不同种族和族裔群体为专有名词，需要大写表示(如 Blacks, African-American, Asian 等)，避免使用 the nigger, bagel, Non-White 等种族歧视语。涉及残疾人称呼时，要注意避免使用情绪化或判断性的名词(如 cripple, deformed, retarded 等)，也避免使用直接指残疾状况的名词[如 the disabled(可使用 people with disabilities)、amnesiacs(可使用 people with amnesia)、quadriplegic victim confined to a wheelchair(可使用 person with quadriplegia who uses a wheelchair)等]。

四、其他写作问题

(一) 用语模糊

学术英语写作忌笼统、忌模糊，贵具体、贵精确。用语模糊会影响真实信息的传达，影响读者对文意的理解。

【例文 1】These results suggest that MeRAVs binding CAACA motif may have broad spectrum in cassava, and MeRAVs can regulate cassava disease resistance by regulating the transcription level of disease resistance genes.

【例文 2】MeRAV5 can directly regulate the expression of MeNR1 and MeNR2 to regulate the content of endogenous NO and interact with MeCAT1 to regulate the accumulation of reactive oxygen species(ROS) to regulate disease resistance of cassava.

上述两句中使用的 regulate 就是一个比较模糊的词，因为 regulate 既可以是 positively regulate，也可以是 negatively regulate；既可以是 upregulate，也可以是 downregulate。如果是 upregulate 之意，就可以用 induce, activate, stimulate, trigger, promote, increase, enhance, cause 等来代替，如果是 downregulate，就可以用 inhibit, suppress, block, decrease, induce, prevent 等来代替。学术英语写作要尽可能具体、精确。

(二) 注意替代

英语用词忌重复，贵变化。因此，写作时用词要注意变化，尤其要重视利用同义词或近义词进行替代。注意下面例文中下划线所示的替代词。

【例文1】While some writers and social thinkers saw American's laissez-faire capitalist system as the path to progress, others viewed the new order with profound uneasiness.

【例文2】Kinetin did not change period length but instead modified circadian phase in a dose-dependent manner(Figure 5A; see Supplemental Figure 1 online) for all LUC reporter constructs assayed.

【例文3】At low concentrations, kinetin resulted in a leading phase, whereas higher concentrations caused the phases of the reporters to lag behind those of untreated seedlings.

【例文4】Mutants with altered period length normally display a circadian phase defect: a long-period mutant will show a lagging phase, whereas a short-period mutant will exhibit a leading phase(Dunlap et al., 2004).

【例文5】Existentialism stressed the primacy of the thinking person and of concrete individual experience as the source of knowledge; this philosophy also emphasized the anguish and solitude inherent in the making of choices.

(三) 文风应简洁、清晰

学术语言应简洁、清晰，句型能简则简，选用最简洁、最精练的表述方法，不必要的、多余词能删除则删除。以下以 Knisely 在 *A Student Handbook for Writing in Biology* 几个例句加以说明。

【例文1】There are two protein assays that are often used in research laboratories.

将不必要的复合句修改为单句。

修改为：Two protein assays are often used inn research laboratories.

【例文2】It is interesting to note that some enzymes are stable at temperatures above 60℃.

删除不必要的导语 It is interesting to note that。

修改为：Some enzymes are stable at temperatures above 60℃.

【例文3】We make the recommendation that micropipettors be used to measure volumes less than 1 mL.

将名词短语 make the recommendation 换成动词 recommend。

修改为：We recommend that micropipettors be used to measure volumes less than 1 mL.

【例文4】The analyses were done on the recombinant DNA to determine which piece of foreign DNA was inserted into the vector.

用 The analyses 作主语不够直接、清晰。

修改为：The recombinant DNA was analyzed to determine which piece of foreign DNA was inserted into the vector.

【例文 5】The data show that the longer the enzyme was exposed to the salt solution, the lower the enzyme activity in the assay. This means that the salt changes the conformation of the enzyme, which makes it less reactive with the substance.

过多使用代词，会使指代模糊。

修改为：The data show that the longer the enzyme was exposed to the salt solution, the lower the enzyme activity in the assay. Exposure to the salt solution may change the conformation of the enzyme, resulting in lower enzyme-substance activity.

【例文 6】Catalase is an enzyme that breaks down hydrogen peroxide in both plant and animal cells. Low or high temperature can lower the rate at which the catalase can react with the hydrogen peroxide. In optimal conditions, the enzyme functions at a rate that will prevent any substantial buildup of the toxin. If the temperature is too low, the rate will be too slow, but high temperatures lead to the denaturation of the enzyme.

英语写作要连贯才能清晰。实现连贯的方法有重复主题词或关键词，使用过渡词。这样，句子之间才能过渡自然、文意流畅。

修改为：Catalase is an enzyme that breaks down hydrogen peroxide in both plant and animal cells. One of the factors that affects the rate of this reaction is temperature. At optimal temperatures, the rate is sufficient to prevent substantial buildup of the toxic hydrogen peroxide. If the temperature is too low, however, the rate will be too slow, and hydrogen peroxide accumulates in the cell. On the other hand, high temperatures may denature the enzyme.

下篇 SCI论文阅读技巧

很多以英语为非母语的科学工作者以阅读英语为苦，指望将来母语会取代英语的地位，就不必再费心力阅读英语文献。普林斯顿大学现代史教授迈克尔·戈尔丁（Michael Gordin）在他的著作《科学巴别塔》（*Scientific Babel*）中指出，英语现在是一门全球通用的科学语言，未来仍将如此，不可能有一种语言会取代英语的地位。即使讲英语的科学家突然消失，未来很长一段时间内英语仍将是科学的主导语言。因为每当一个新的领域出现时，它的术语就出现在英语的词汇表上。英语拥有描述几乎所有科学概念和过程的词汇，有那么多的科学知识是用英语写的。看起来，在我们有生之年，阅读英语科技文献仍然是科研的必修课。初学者只有获得必要的SCI论文阅读技巧，才能有利于自己科研事业的进步和发展。

英语读写能力对科研工作者的重要性怎么强调都不过分。因为读不了，就一定写不了；读不好，就一定写不好。古人曾说过，"能读千赋则善赋""能观千剑则晓剑"。在这方面，俄罗斯著名物理学家金兹伯格有切肤之痛，他曾说过："我的切身经历表明，一个人要真正做好工作，取得满意的成就，需要多方面的知识和能力。缺乏语言文字修养，是一件非常糟糕的事情，特别是可能极大地妨碍科学交流。"

第十四章 SCI 论文阅读概述

一、重视普通英语和专业英语的阅读

SCI 论文的阅读（或科技英语阅读）能力有赖于普通英语的阅读能力。北京外国语大学赵德鑫教授说："科技英语不是独立于英语之外的另一种什么英语，只不过是有些英语语法项目在科技文章中出现较多，如动词的被动语态、各种一般时态、非人称的结构和用语等，还有，文章中出现科技词汇或专业词汇较多。"所以，SCI 论文阅读的前提是要有一定的普通英语阅读能力，在此能力的基础上，多识科技词汇，注意科技英语中常用的词汇与句型，以及了解相关的科技文体篇章特点，才能够提高 SCI 论文的阅读能力。

对以英语为非母语的人来说，学习英语是一辈子的事。科技工作者虽然没有太多时间来学习普通英语，但是我建议可以在业余时间尽可能读一点文史哲的英语著作和报纸杂志文章，这对 SCI 论文的阅读和写作大有益处。另外，由于互联网的便利性，我们可以随时随地在网上直接阅读英美著名的报纸杂志文章。英国的著名报纸有：《泰晤士报》(*Times*)、《每日电讯报》(*The Daily Telegraph*)、《卫报》(*The Guardian*)、《金融时报》(*The Financial Times*)等，主要期刊有：《经济学家》(*The Economist*)、《旁观者》(*The Spectator*)、《新政治家》(*The New Statesman*)等；美国的著名报纸有：《纽约时报》(*The New York Times*)、《华盛顿邮报》(*Washington Post*)、《洛杉矶时报》(*The Los Angeles Times*)、《华尔街日报》(*The Wall Street Journal*)等，主要期刊有：《读者文摘》(*Reader's Digest*)、《时代》周刊(*Time*)、《新闻周刊》(*News Week*)、《美国新闻与世界报道》(*U.S. News & World Report*)、《商业周刊》(*Business Week*)、《财富》(*Fortune*)等；英美著名的电台网站有：英国广播公司(British Broadcasting Corporation，BBC)、美国有线电视新闻网(Cable News Network，CNN)、福克斯新闻(Fox News)等。

在专业英语阅读方面，建议初学者先啃几本自身研究领域的英语经典教科书和专著，如果最开始看不懂，可利用汉语译本对照着阅读。科普及科学新闻网站的文章最好每天定时浏览阅读，例如《自然》《科学》《每日科学》(Science Daily)、《科学美国人》(Scientific American)、《新科学家》(New Scientist)、《生活科学》(Live Science)、《科学新闻》(Science News)等。现在很多科学家的个人社交媒体(如推特、博客和微信公众号)推送的文章，也可定时阅读。除此之外，对于自身研究领域的主流期刊文章，每个领域IF值排名靠前的10本或20本期刊文章更是应经常阅读。

以植物分子生物学为例，除需要阅读顶级综合性期刊，如俗称的CNS，也就是《细胞》《自然》和《科学》，以及《美国科学院院刊》《自然通讯》《科学进展》(Science Advances)等外，还要阅读生命科学领域内的重要期刊，如《自然生物技术》(Nature Biotechnology)、《自然遗传学》(Nature Genetics)、《细胞研究》(Cell Research)、《分子细胞》(Molecular Cell)、《核酸研究》(Nucleic Acid Research)、《欧洲分子生物学组织期刊》(EMBO Journal)、《细胞报告》(Cell Reports)、《电子生命》(eLife)、《基因与发育》(Gene & Development)、《基因组生物学》(Genome Biology)、《基因组研究》(Genome Research)等。重点要阅读本领域期刊影响因子(Journal Impact Factor, JIF)排名靠前的期刊文章，如排名前20的期刊(表14-1)。但是，这只是举例，阅读范围并不一定要局限于此，也不一定以影响因子排名论英雄，因为影响因子呈现动态变化，期刊影响因子每年都会上下浮动，且影响因子受到很多因素的影响，是可以人为操纵的。此外，论文的价值和创新不能纯粹以影响因子衡量，如植物科学领域的三大经典期刊《植物细胞》《植物杂志》(The Plant Journal)和《植物生理学》(Plant Physiology)近年来虽然影响因子滑坡，但领域内口碑仍在。

表14-1 2023年植物科学类期刊影响因子(JIF)排名前20

排名	期刊名称与中文名	期刊影响因子
1	Molecular Plant 《分子植物》	27.5
2	Annual Review of Plant Biology 《植物生物学年评》[*]	23.9
3	Trends in Plant Science 《植物科学动态》[*]	20.5
4	Nature Plants 《自然植物》	18.0
5	Plant Biotechnology Journal 《植物生物技术杂志》	13.8
6	Plant Cell 《植物细胞》	11.6
7	Journal of Integrative Plant Biology 《整合植物生物学杂志》	11.4
8	Plant Communications 《植物通讯》	10.5
9	Annual Review of Phytopathology 《植物病理学年评》[*]	10.2
10	Current Opinion in Plant Biology 《当代植物生物学观点》[*]	9.5
11	New Phytologist 《新植物学家》	9.4
12	Horticulture Research 《园艺研究》	8.7

(续)

排名	期刊名称与中文名	期刊影响因子
13	Phytomedicine 《植物药》	7.9
14	Phytochemistry Reviews 《植物化学综述》*	7.7
15	PlantPhysiology 《植物生理学》	7.4
16	Plant Cell and Environment 《植物细胞与环境》	7.3
17	Plant Journal 《植物杂志》	7.2
18	Critical Reviews in Plant Sciences 《植物科学评论》*	6.9
19	Journal of Experimental Botany 《实验植物学杂志》	6.9
20	Crop Journal 《作物学报》	6.6

注：根据科睿唯安发布的 2023 年期刊征引报告（Journal Citation Reports™，JCR）；* 为专门发表综述性论文的期刊。

二、阅读 SCI 论文要养成习惯

读文献应成为科学工作者日常工作的一部分，无论是刚进实验室的研究生，还是资深科学家，都应如此。不读文献，就无法及时了解科学前沿，无法进行实验设计和论文写作。在以往的印刷版时代，期刊论文要到图书馆去查阅和复印，是件很麻烦的事；现在足不出户，就可以将需要的论文下载到电脑和手机上进行阅读。除了有目的地查阅和下载论文外，不少期刊有 RSS 订阅或邮件订阅服务，数据库中可将目标期刊设置提醒服务（content alert），这样在打开 RSS 阅读器（RSS Reader）或打开邮箱时就能看到该期刊最新一期出版的文章。科普及科学新闻网站、专业微信公众号、专业 QQ 群、论坛也会定期推出最新的论文介绍。

强调养成每天阅读论文的习惯，并不意味着研究生到实验室就埋头阅读论文，而是应该在不做实验的时间或其他业余时间阅读论文。对于实验类学科来讲，做实验是主要的工作，读论文或写论文应该安排在不做实验的时间里。在实验室里大白天专注读论文或写论文其实是不明智的或者说是令人讨厌的。多数导师希望学生在实验室里应争分夺秒做实验，而不是成天伏在桌上读论文或写论文。读论文或写论文应在做实验的间歇，在实验室之外的私人时间。1959 年的诺贝尔医学或生理学奖获得者阿瑟·科恩伯格（Arthur Kornberg）在其传记中说："撰写论文是研究工作的组成部分，并且肯定值得花费时间——花费 5% 的时间是恰当的。然而，当我看见学生或同事趴在桌上撰写论文，而不是在实验室里忙碌时，我承认对此感到不快。"

现在已有很多实验室（或研究组）每周定期召开组会或小型研讨会（seminar），每次都会安排研究生利用 PPT 汇报自己本周所读的最新论文或最经典论文，这是个很好的鼓励和督促研究生养成阅读论文的习惯。学生如果论文没有读透，就讲不好。另外，论文讲解后成员之间展开对论文的讨论，导师的点拨，都能加深学生对论文及科研本身的理解。

三、阅读多少论文才足够?

研究生期间应该读多少篇论文才足够?有人建议硕士至少精读 50 篇,泛读 100 篇 SCI 论文,博士阅读 SCI 论文的数量至少是硕士生的 2~3 倍。也有人建议每周至少应精读 1~2 篇 CNS 顶级期刊或本领域内顶级期刊文章。我个人的看法是,阅读论文的数量依据学习阶段、学科性质、研究过程等因素来确定,难以一概而论。刚开始阅读 SCI 论文的硕士研究生,可能 1 周精读 1 篇都很吃力,随着词汇量的增加,学科背景知识的了解,阅读速度会大大提高,最后达到没有语言障碍,跟读汉语文章一样,这时就可根据需要来确定阅读数量。

文献是不是读得越多越好?也不一定。有的科学家担心文献读得太多,怕别人的思想掩盖自己的独创性,或者已知的知识框架限制自己的思维。著名神经生物学家蒲慕明认为,文献不能多看、乱看。他说:"我深深感到新入科研之门的年轻学生最不该做的就是大量下载所有与他领域有关的文献,而且努力去读所有的文献。一个科研新手往往很难判断所得信息的可信度与其意义,已存在的大量信息难免造成不必要的困惑。事实上,科学界泛滥成灾的文献,对年轻科学家富有创造力的心智可能会造成窒息性的伤害。身为一个神经生物学家,我常常在想,大脑处理信息的创造性与大脑已存信息量之间有什么关系,为什么科学上最富有创造性的,尤其是在物理与数学领域,常常是在科学家年轻的时候完成的,为什么大脑的创造力似乎随年龄而衰退,我现在的假说是'信息量'与'创造力'之间可能是成反比的。每一个新存入神经网络的信息,都是对创造性处理信息的一个新的约束。知识累积越多,脑中各式各样的框架也越多,而这些已知的框架正是创新的主要障碍。因此,对知识极谨慎、有'抵制性'地选择吸收,可能是保持创造力的重要一环。"南非分子生物学家、诺贝尔奖获得者悉尼·布伦纳(Syndey Brenner)也强调科学研究上"无知"的重要性。

我个人觉得,目前我国多数研究生读 SCI 文章不是太多,而是严重不足。每年给研究生批改和审阅论文,最大的感受是研究生的论文仅仅格式错误就改不胜改,说明学生论文阅读太少或者阅读不仔细。不少研究生做一些学徒式的或跟风式的("me-too"式的)实验,文献都没读够、没吃透,不看别人如何实验设计和数据处理,而是自己闭门造车,结果是基本的研究"套路"都没学到家,实验结果漏洞百出,数据不规范,分析不到位,辛辛苦苦做了一两年的实验都无法发表像样的文章。因此,研究生对于一般性研究,还是应该多读文献。更不用说,一些专业英语基础较差的学生,更应该多读文献。当一个人读英语文献没有障碍且读了较多的基础性文献后,在转向一个新领域或者开始研究一个经典的难题时,可听从科学大家的建议,在研究初期不要让太多的文献淹没自己的想法。耶鲁大学心理学系教授布莱恩·绍尔(Brian Scholl)的一篇文章《关于学术界的各种思考》(*Miscellaneous Musings on Academia*)建议,当你进入一个新的领域,你不能无视文献,但阅读过早也会有害,因为这会扼杀自己的洞察力。文章还建议，在进入新领域时阅读少数几篇文献（或许综述文章的一节），就可以提出你自己的猜想和进行实验了，等实验有结果后，再详细考察阅读文献。著名理论物理学家、诺贝尔奖获得者杨振宁曾忠告年轻研究者"不要淹在文献的海洋中，而应该追溯问题的源头。"他说，一个问题，"如果我决定去研究它，我就一定从头做起，而且不去看别人的文章。做了一段时间，如果有困难，再去看别人的文章。"

一般而言，研究生应该在力所能及的情况下尽可能多读，但要注意以下几点：

①对于毫无基础的学生而言，要想读懂一篇 SCI 论文，需要很多语言知识和背景信息。为了降低入门的难度，可先看中文论文（尤其是中文综述论文），后看英语论文，以便了解一些基本的术语和背景知识；先看学位论文，后看期刊论文，因为不论是中文的学位论文，还是外国的学位论文，学位论文一般引言部分对研究背景和相关进展综述较为全面和清楚，方法描述也比较详细。

②要多读好文章。鉴于目前科技期刊数量和论文出版数量快速增加，单篇论文篇幅也在增加，科学家无法读遍所有的文章，所以，必须择优阅读，尽可能挑选顶级期刊的文章来阅读。虽然不能单纯以影响因子论期刊文章水平高低，但顶级期刊的文章普遍研究质量和写作水平较高。

③要注意思考。虽然研究生读文章应该"韩信将兵，多多益善"，但读得太多，思考太少，就会导致"贪多嚼不烂"，"消化"不良。因此，研究生应带着自己的问题或课题看文献。主要从两方面着手：一是这个问题的解决方法是什么，此为"纬"；二是这个问题的来源和进展情况如何，此为"经"。经和纬可以相交，也可以相离。以这两个维度来找文献、看文章，根据关切度和重要性确定阅读范围，可以减少盲目性。

④采用批判性阅读方法看文献，重点思考论文采用的方法是否足够，实验设计是否合理，作者所得结果是否论证了论文的结论或解决了引言设定的问题，还有什么问题有待解决，或者自己是否想到更好的方法来解决。以审稿人的眼光来看文献，可以发现每篇文章的优缺点，对于自己学术进步大有好处。

⑤做好阅读笔记，将好的观点、方法和语句记下来，或者对文章进行分类和概述，或者写下阅读心得。"好记性不如烂笔头"，阅读笔记有助于加深记忆，深入理解，积累知识，促进写作。

四、SCI 论文的查阅、下载与管理

如果所在机构购买知名数据库的话，如 SCI 科学引文索引数据库（Web of Science）、Science Direct 电子期刊数据库、Wiley InterScience 电子期刊全文库、Springer Link 电子期刊、IEEE/IET Electronic Library（IEL）数据库等，那么，即可在这些数据库中利用主题词或关键词查阅并下载全文。

很多人直接利用 Google Scholar（谷歌学术）、Google（谷歌）、Yahoo（雅虎）、Bing（必应）等浏览器来搜索 SCI 文章。其中 Google Scholar 是 Google 于 2004 年年底推出

的专门面向学术资源的免费搜索工具，相当于同时对多个数据库资源进行检索，可查找包括期刊论文、学位论文、书籍、预印本、文摘和技术报告在内的学术文献，内容涵盖自然科学、人文科学、社会科学等多种学科。单一关键词可以搜索到包含这一关键词的所有文章。如果想缩小范围，更精准地找到目标文献，可以利用两个或三个关键词组合来搜索。除了用关键词搜索外，还可利用特定作者姓名、出版物名称来搜索。如果想查找所有提及作者或某篇作品的文献，可将作者姓名或某篇作品标题加引号后，输入搜索。单击搜索结果页右侧的"近期文章"链接，则可显示与搜索主题相关的最新研究进展。如果想了解与目标文献相关的文章，则点击多个结果旁边显示的"相关文章"链接，就可以看到按与原始搜索结果相似度大小排列的文章列表。想查找并下载全文时，最简单的方法是将"[PDF]题目或关键词"或"题目或关键词 PDF"键入搜索。

对于生物医学文献，一般使用美国国立生物技术信息中心（National Center for Biotechnology Information，NCBI）网站进行搜索。NCBI 不仅有 PubMed 医学文献检索数据库，还有 GenBank、RefSeq、UniGene、dbSNP 等多种大型生物学数据库。对于查询生物医学文献、人类基因组信息、基因表达、蛋白质结构、肿瘤遗传信息及不同种属遗传信息等都十分有用。查找文献时，可在该网站搜索页面搜索框左栏查找并定位 PubMed，或者直接在浏览器地址栏中输入 http://www.ncbi.nlm.nih.gov/pubmed/后，在右栏输入关键词或主题词搜索即可。例如，寻找"长链非编码 RNA"的论文，就将"long noncoding RNAs"或"lncRNAs"键入搜索即可。如果想缩小搜索范围，就用若干个关键词组合来搜索，例如，要找"植物长链非编码 RNA"，就将"plant long noncoding RNAs"或"plant lncRNAs"键入搜索即可。当然也可用 3 种布尔运算（即是 AND、OR 和 NOT）来提高搜索效率。此外，同 Google Scholar 一样，同样可寻找作者或期刊的文章，只要在搜索框中键入作者姓氏/期刊全称或缩写。当输入关键词后，潜在的目标文献会以每页 20 篇文章呈现。每篇文章标题后面有 Similar Articles（相似文章），点击这个链接可找到类似的文献；如果文章标题下面有 Full Text（免费全文），点击这个链接可免费下载全文。搜索结果页面左侧有 Article Types（文章类型），例如，Clinical Trial（临床试验）和 Review（综述文章），点击可找到包含该关键词的临床试验或综述文章。再下面是文本的可获得性（Text Availability），分只提供摘要（Abstract）和可免费下载全文（Free Full Text）等选项。此外，还有出版日期（Publication Dates）和物种（Species）的限定项。

除利用上述工具搜索目的文献外，还可根据综述文章或研究性论文后面的参考文献（References）来回溯相关文献，或者直接到期刊的官方网站检索，在论文的网络版还可找到引用本文献的文献（Citations 或 Citing Articles）。这样，就可通过文献的互引来搜索目标文献。对于化学领域的参考文献，可以利用 Chemistry Reference Resolver（http://chemsearch.kovsky.net/），将不同格式的科学引文复制粘贴，就可定向找到期刊官网的目标论文。

　　Google Scholar 和 NCBI 的 PubMed 检索到的文献并不能保证免费下载全文（PDF 版本）。下载不到全文时，可通过高校的图书馆网站服务，也可请国内外各大学的朋友帮助下载，或者直接给文献通讯作者发 Email 索取。此外，利用 Sci-Hub 等文献资源下载工具也可免费下载到全文。实在不行，可到科研社交网络服务网站 ResearchGate，丁香园、小木虫等网络论坛或者各种文献互助小组帮助获取。

　　当下载较多文献时，可利用文件夹分组储存管理，也可借助 EndNote、Mendeley、Zotero、JabRef、Noteexpress、papers、E-study 等软件来管理。以 EndNote 为例，它是一个基于 Web of Science 平台，用于科技文章中管理参考文献数据库的软件。网络版 EndNote 与 Web of Science 无缝链接，可保存需要收藏的参考文献，并可按主题建立自己的数据库，随时分类、标签、检索、更新、编辑自己收集到的文献。同样，为了提高论文阅读效率，可以养成写作阅读笔记的习惯，对文献的主题、类型、作者名、论文发表时间、重要方法（结果或结论）、论文结构、好的措辞和句子等加以记录和分类。当然，阅读笔记也可以在文献管理软件中撰写和保存。

第十五章　为什么阅读 SCI 论文如此重要

对于初学者而言，阅读 SCI 论文在科研的多个方面都十分重要，以下就科研选题、实验设计、结果分析、亮点提炼和论文写作几个方面介绍阅读 SCI 论文的重要性。

一、了解学术前沿和科研选题需要阅读 SCI 论文

阅读论文是科学家终身应该保持的活动，不阅读科技论文（主要指 SCI 论文），就不能了解学术前沿，无法跟上学术进展，科研思想很快就会落伍。科学家如此，期刊编辑也如此。不止一位科学家和编辑如此说：他们每天都会习惯性地关注相关领域重要期刊的上线论文，并且浏览或阅读自己感兴趣的论文。

研究生不单是接受旧知识，还应以创造新知识为目标，创造新知识必须了解学术前沿。鉴于教材和专著的内容往往是科学研究较为充分的领域，新出现的领域和正在快速取得进展的知识都无法及时写入教材与专著，因此，教材和专著的出版周期与期刊相差较大。有人估计，教材和专著与期刊文章在内容新颖方面至少相差 10 年以上，因此，研究生学习应以论文阅读为主。

科研选题，即选择和确定具体研究课题，是科研工作必不可少的前期准备工作。一个好的选题对科研工作的开展和科研成果的获得十分重要。爱因斯坦说："提出问题比解决问题更重要。"海森堡说："提出正确的问题，往往等于解决了问题的大半。"科研选题除根据国家或地区经济、文化及社会发展的需要，以及行业、产业和生产实践调研产生的关键问题外，一个重要的方式就是在阅读文献。当然，着眼于科研选题的阅读需要有问题意识和批判意识。以科研选题为目的阅读，应该重点关注某领域的研究热点、经典问题、研究空白、科研文献结果之间的不一致、论文中讨论和结论中提出的未解决问题。具体来说，分为以下 4 种。

①多读 SCI 论文，尤其是最新的 SCI 论文，其效果与多听学术报告一样，可以了解到当前领域的研究热点、最新的研究技术和研究方法。从研究热点中可以寻找自己最感兴趣的问题，或者利用这些新技术来解决自己已有的问题，往往是一个好的课题

的切入点。

②平时注意扩大阅读 SCI 论文的领域范围,借鉴自己领域之外的东西,主动促进学科交叉与融合,产生新的研究课题切入点。

③多读与某一问题相关的 SCI 论文,可以了解前人对该问题的解决程度,已经完全解决,还是尚有疑问。如果完全解决,是否还可用最新的技术进行验证;如果尚有疑问,是否有好的办法(如最新的研究手段或多学科合作研究)来加以解决。

④对于一篇 SCI 论文,利用批判性阅读方法,找出论文的破绽和漏洞,然后自己设计新的实验来加以解决。其实,每篇论文都会在讨论部分指出其自身研究工作的不足和局限,以及提出在部分证据基础之上的假说。那么针对这些问题,提出全面的解决之道,或者证实或证伪其提出的假说,也可以形成自己的研究课题。

对于一个此前从未涉足的领域,利用新的研究方法来解决该领域的老问题是个不错的切入点。因为未解决的经典问题对于该领域的资深科学家和新进入的行外人而言,起跑线基本上都是一样的。大家都在暗中摸索,谁都有可能取得突破。而新的研究方法一定能获得新的洞见。例如,橡胶树(*Hevea brasiliensis*)是一种重要的热带经济林树种,由其产生的天然橡胶是重要的工业原料和战略物资,但我在 2013 年之前,从未研究过橡胶树。2013 年在一个课题的资助下,我决定研究一下橡胶树。切入点在哪里呢?当时我唯一知道的是,橡胶树死皮(tapping panel dryness,TPD)是天然橡胶产业的一个世界性难题,也是天然橡胶单产提高的主要限制因子之一。据估算,全世界每年因橡胶树死皮病而损失的干胶产量为 5×10^5 t,价值相当于 4 亿美元。对于橡胶树死皮病的研究不仅在理论上,而且在生产实践中都有着重要的意义。死皮病作为橡胶树的"百年顽症",研究者曾从病理、生理、遗传、土壤和生化等方面进行了探索与研究,但其发生机制仍不清楚。当时我很早就注意到基于新一代测序技术的转录组测序(RNA-seq),该方法是大规模研究转录组的一种新的且更为有效的方法,能够大规模进行基因差异表达分析,在很多生物学研究方面取得了很大的成绩,但橡胶树尚没有人做过转录组测序。我就利用转录组测序技术对橡胶树死皮病基因差异表达模式进行研究,最后以"Transcriptome sequencing and analysis of rubber tree(*Hevea brasiliensis* Muell.)to discover putative genes associated with tapping panel dryness(TPD)"为题,发表在 2015 年 16 期的《BMC 基因组学》(*BMC Genomics*)上。该文成为橡胶树转录组测序研究的第一篇文章。当时的选题就是得益于我大量阅读了其他植物研究方面的转录组测序文章。

二、实验设计需要阅读 SCI 论文

对于初学者来说,不仅 SCI 论文写作需要模仿,相关的实验设计也需要模仿。初学者在选题后,通过查询类似题目的论文,挑选最接近的或相关题目中最好的 SCI 论文,仔细阅读其实验设计和所用方法,加以借鉴。

多读 SCI 论文可以对某类研究加以总结，了解其基本的研究套路。对于一个生手而言，如果阅读的 SCI 论文少或者读了但没弄明白，不按套路来进行实验设计，那么得出的数据结果就可能是不完整的或有缺陷的。例如，在一般的组学(转录组、蛋白质或代谢组)研究文章中，通常会有表型分析(如生理测定或解剖分析)，然后是组学分析，最后是组学数据的常规方法验证(如 qPCR 验证转录组学数据、Western Blot 验证蛋白质组学数据等)。缺少这些环节，在实验设计上就是有缺陷的。并且，组学数据应该能从分子水平上解释或说明前面的表型数据，组学数据的常规方法验证能证明组学数据是一致的和可靠的。

阅读 SCI 论文能够学习成熟的和合理的实验设计，这样得出的实验结果可与前人的数据进行比较分析，避免不看论文或看而不懂盲目进行实验设计，结果闭门造车，产生的实验数据都是无效(用)数据。例如，某学生写了一篇关于植物内参基因筛选的文章，通过与已经发表的相关文章比较阅读发现，该学生的文章有若干硬伤：理论上，不同处理应该有不同的最稳定内参基因，因此，需要对不同处理分别分析其最稳定表达的内参基因种类及个数，但学生利用 GeNorm、Norm-Finder 和 BestKeeper 3 个软件对候选的内参基因表达稳定性分析中，均没有分处理进行，而是放在一起分析，且没有对不同处理最适内参基因个数进行分析。此外，几种方法分析的结果肯定是不一致的，最后需要 RefFinder 或别的分析方法对几种分析软件结果进行综合排序，但该学生也没有做到。目的基因的表达验证结果未进行统计学处理，难以在表达结果上验证文章得出的最稳定与最不稳定基因是正确的。这些都是该学生在实验设计前没有看 SCI 文章，导致实验设计有缺陷及数据处理不当造成的。

三、实验结果分析与组织需要阅读 SCI 论文

学生不看论文，论文看得少或者没有看近 10 年的文献，以至于论文不知道要做哪些内容，分析到什么深度，需要些什么样的图表才能达到发表 SCI 论文的要求。例如，有学生做了一篇某植物细菌性叶枯病病原菌——黄单胞菌属细菌菌株的鉴定和测序的文章，我看了一下，感觉文章的前半部分，也就是菌株的分离和鉴定属常规方法，所拍照片不专业，达不到发表 SCI 论文的标准；后半部分菌株的测序是重头戏，但可惜分析深度不够，分析结果和图表都是测序公司提供的初步分析结果，同样也达不到发表 SCI 论文的标准。

我们看一下近 10 年细菌测序的两篇 SCI 论文是怎么做的。

第一篇是 2011 年发表在《分子植物病理学》(*Molecular Plant Pathology*) 12 卷第 6 期期刊上的一篇文章"Genome sequencing and comparative analysis of the carrot bacterial blight pathogen, *Xanthomonas hortorum* pv. *carotae* M081"，该论文的结果分下面 5 部分：

Isolation and preliminary typing of Xhc M081

Sequencing and assembly of an improved, high-quality draft genome sequence

Comparative and phylogenomic analyses

Candidate virulence genes of Xhc M081

Development of molecular markers for Xhc

该研究不仅做了高精度测序，还进行与其他菌株的比较基因组分析和系统基因组分析，筛选其毒性基因或致病基因，开发分子标记以便加以鉴定。

这篇文章的前面3个图的标题分别为：

Fig. 1 Circular representation of the improved, high-quality draft genome sequence of *Xanthomonas hortorum* pv. *carotae*(Xhc)M081

Fig. 2 Synteny plots comparing the genome structure of *Xanthomonas hortorum* pv. *carotae*(Xhc)M081 with the genomes of other *Xanthomonas* species

Fig. 3 Isolate M081 groups with *Xanthomonas hortorum*. (a) Unrooted phylogenomic tree of 10 *Xanthomonas* isolates based on a superalignment of 1776 translated sequences. (b) Neighbour-joining tree of concatenated nucleotide sequences for partial *dnaK*, *fyuA*, *gyrB* and *rpoD* genes from *Xanthomonas* strains.

第二篇是2005年发表在《核酸研究》(*Nucleic Acids Research*)第33卷第2期的文章"The genome sequence of *Xanthomonas oryzae* pathovar *oryzae* KACC10331, the bacterial blight pathogen of rice"，该论文做的东西比第一篇还要多，分析也比第一篇深入，结果和讨论分下面7部分：

General features

Comparative genomics

Mobile elements

Metabolic characteristics and RM systems

Extracellular polysaccharides, lipopolysaccharide and surface-borne features

Potential pathogenicity and virulence determinants

Hypersensitive reaction and pathogenicity(*hrp*) and avirulence(*avr*) genes

这篇文章的前面3个图的标题与第一篇类似，分别为：

Figure 1. Circular genome map of *X. oryzae* pv. *oryzae* str. KACC10331

Figure 2. Nucleotide alignments of *Xoo*(x-axis) versus *Xac*(y-axis), left; and *Xoo*(x-axis) versus *Xcc*(y-axis), right

Figure 3. Linear genomic comparisons of *X. oryzae* pv. *oryzae* with *X. axonopodis* pv. *citri* and *X. campestris* pv. *campestris*

由此可见，细菌基因组测序文章至少应该包含环形基因组图谱及与其他菌株的比较基因组分析图。而这些必要的图片在该学生的文章中一个都没有。事实上，不仅是细菌基因组测序，其他植物、动物基因组测序也是如此，必要的内容一定要有，该有的图片一定要有。如果不看近期的文献，闭门造车，结果就达不到发表

SCI 论文的要求。

以笔者对转录组学分析的经验，如果事先未进行大量的文献阅读，面对公司提供的大量转录组学初步分析数据，就无从下手深入分析。因为你不知道哪些数据跟你的研究目的挂钩，哪些数据最能达到研究目的及分析出最好的结果。以我们 2016 年在《BMC 基因组学》第 17 卷第 1 期上发表论文"Molecular mechanism of ethylene stimulation of latex yield in rubber tree(*Hevea brasiliensis*) revealed by *de novo* sequencing and transcriptome analysis"为例来说明这个问题。由于乙烯刺激橡胶树增产机制在分子水平可能有多个分析角度或方面，但由于我们事先通过阅读文献了解到，一直以来没有鉴定出乙烯刺激影响的特定代谢途径，因此乙烯刺激橡胶树增产机制一直是个谜。而更令人困惑的是，乙烯刺激后并不影响天然橡胶生物合成途径，甚至还有抑制作用。由于橡胶合成途径包括碳固定或加尔文循环、糖酵解、天然橡胶生物合成前体异戊烯基焦磷酸（IPP）生物合成及橡胶链合成几个阶段，我们以这几个代谢途径作为考察重点，发现异戊烯基焦磷酸（IPP）的生物合成途径差异基因并未显著富集，甚至 MVA 途径中的限速酶基因 HMGR 表达略有下降。但是作为 IPP 与橡胶生物合成前体物的来源——糖酵解途径中的限速酶和关键酶基因显著上调表达，此外，乙酰辅酶 A 转化为乙醇的代谢途径中的关键酶基因表达下调，因此，糖酵解途径加速运行以提供充足的 IPP 和天然橡胶生物合成前体，同时抑制乙酰辅酶 A 流向乙醇合成，而不是影响橡胶生物合成途径本身，是乙烯刺激橡胶树胶乳增产的主要原因。另外，在橡胶树皮内碳固定（加尔文循环）途径中的很多限速酶和关键酶基因也显著上调。因此，树皮加尔文循环通量提高会源源不断地提供碳水化合物以供胶乳再生，从而促进胶乳再生，增强乙烯刺激效果的耐久性。

四、SCI 论文写作中结果提炼和突出亮点需要阅读 SCI 论文

论文研究越深入，结论越具有多方面的潜在应用价值，论文的重要性和价值也就越高。在实验设计和论文撰写时要注意，应尽可能使结论或技术具有范围更广的适用性，而不是很狭隘地进行有限应用，这样会提高论文发表的成功率，在高水平期刊上发表更是如此。实验设计要保证能得出应用性较广的结论，在论文构思和写作时，也要挖掘实验结果得出的结论在本领域及其他领域或交叉领域的普适性或应用价值，并加以突出强调。期刊编辑和审稿人很看重这一点。要做到这一点，就需要广泛阅读 SCI 论文，一方面学习高水平期刊论文在提炼结论与突出亮点方面的经验；另一方面，也只有了解自己的领域和相关领域的情况，才能深入理解自己的实验结果，才有利于概括出普适性的结论。

目前，学生做基因克隆的文章非常多，但基因克隆的文章重头戏在于基因功能鉴定。如果没有做必要的功能鉴定，只是序列分析和表达分析，就很难发表在高水平的 SCI 期刊上。即使实验做出来了，若 SCI 文章看得不够，也不能对自己的实验结果有正

确的评估，看不到实验结果的创新性所在，因此，文章写出来就没有亮点。例如，学生做了一篇橡胶树 *HbHMGS* 基因启动子调控元件分析的文章。文章按部就班对 *HbHMGS* 基因启动子的顺式元件进行生物信息学分析，对各缺失片段转化拟南芥进行表达分析，全然没有意识到 *HbHMGS* 基因-454 bp 缺失启动子是一个比 CaMV 35S 启动子还要强的超强组成性启动子（为 CaMV 35S 启动子的 2.19 倍），而这在植物转化研究中具有很大的应用潜力。我们抓住这个亮点，在文章中给予强调，以"Identification of cis-regulatory regions responsible for developmental and hormonal regulation of *HbHMGS1* in transgenic *Arabidopsis thaliana*"为题在 *Biotechnology Letters* 期刊上发表。

例如，学生写了一篇《木薯叶肉原生质体制备及目标基因瞬时表达体系的建立》的文章，不仅引言部分对植物原生质体瞬时表达体系的意义写得不够，题目也不吸引人（原题目为：Isolation of mesophyll protoplast and establishment of gene transient expression system in cassava）。因此，通过查阅大量的文献，重写了引言部分。此外，由于这是一篇方法论文，需要对方法的优势和重要性进行强调，并在题目上加以表现，因此将题目改写为："Highly efficient mesophyll protoplast isolation and PEG-mediated transient gene expression for rapid and large-scale gene characterization in cassava (*Manihot esculenta* Crantz)"。

五、SCI 论文写作中发展写作技巧需要阅读 SCI 论文

国内一些机构规定硕士生毕业需要发表 SCI 论文，但是，由于学生普通英语的写作能力本身就较差，再加上阅读 SCI 论文的数量有限，因此，让学生独自写一篇 SCI 论文简直是一种不可能完成的任务。这种情况有多严重呢？国内一位著名教授说："学生写了一个 SCI 初稿，不要说一句话不能用，甚至连一个短语都没有能用的。搞得我从头到尾自己重新写，费时费力，出力不讨好。"这种情况显然不是个例。学生写不了 SCI 论文的最根本原因就是 SCI 论文读得少。

英语写作能力主要包括措辞、造句和段落发展 3 方面的能力，这 3 方面能力的提高都需要大量阅读。学习英语写作就是一个模仿的过程，阅读的东西越多，可模仿借鉴的范本和表达方法知道的也就越多，写作时所能调用的表达方法也就越丰富。俗话说："读书破万卷，下笔如有神""熟读唐诗三百首，不会作诗也会吟"其实就是说在"输出（写作）"之前要有大量的"输入（阅读）"才行。另外，多阅读、多模仿的意义还在于，学会用英语思维来表达思想，所写出来的东西是地道的英语表达，而不是生造出来的中式英语。

对于初学者而言，平时需要进行大量的精读与泛读，熟知 SCI 论文的结构与写作要求，熟知论文不同部分的常用表述方法，常用词汇和句子有一定的积累；具体写作时，可找若干篇内容类似的高水平论文作为范本，从内容组织到遣词造句都可以进行参考和模仿。但是，模仿不是直接拷贝，除了用模范论文中的词汇和句型表达自己论

文的内容外，必要时可用同义词替换和句型转换对相同内容的句子加以改写。

阅读本专业相关的文章可以学习一些地道的英语表达。例如，常用的表达方法"如上所述"的英语表达为 as described above 或 as previously mentioned；"如图1所示"的英语表达为 as indicated in Figure 1 或 as shown in Figure 1；"除非另有说明，否则本书中T只表示温度"的英语表达为 T will represent temperature alone in this book unless otherwise stated。

育种与组织培养文章中，"目标性状"一般用 desired characteristics 表示，也可用 desired traits 或 characteristics of interest 等来表示，但"目标基因"一般用 gene of interest 表示。"与母株（或亲本）性状一致（或相似）的"地道英语表达为 true-to-type：*In vitro* propagation methodologies can be used to vegetatively propagate (*via* micropropagation) large number of true-to-type clones of plants exhibiting especially desirable characteristics。

在拟南芥雌蕊特化方面，"顶-基格式形成依赖于雌蕊原基内从上至下的生长素浓度梯度；生长素水平在顶端区域最高，向基部逐步降低。"最精练的表达为：The apical-basal patterning is dependent on an auxin gradient spanning the gynoecial primordium with peak levels in the apical regions and descending levels basally。

表达"与……同时发生的，伴随的"可用 accompanying 和 concomitant。

【例文1】Anti-NGF therapy profoundly reduces bone cancer pain and the accompanying increase in markers of peripheral and central sensitization.

【例文2】According to 1 study, dietary supplementation of the leucine metabolite beta-hydroxy-beta-methylbutyrate (HMB) 3 g/day to humans undertaking intensive resistance training exercise resulted in an increased deposition of fat-free mass and an accompanying increase in strength.

【例文3】Here, it is shown that GRF5 also stimulates chloroplast division, resulting in a higher chloroplast number per cell with a concomitant increase in chlorophyll levels in 35S: GRF5 leaves, which can sustain higher rates of photosynthesis.

【例文4】Later during leaf development, cell proliferation ceases with the arrest of the mitotic cell cycle, and cell expansion starts, concomitant with the onset of endoreduplication.

表达"阐明、揭示、有助于了解"可用 clarify, shed/throw new light on 或 provide new/key insights into。

【例文1】Study of 500,000 people clarifies the risks of obesity.

【例文2】Research published in the open access journal Microbiome sheds new light on how gut bacteria may influence anxiety-like behaviors.

【例文3】By assessing when these rock environments became habitable, and in some cases when they may have been buried and sterilized again, the study provides new insights into the evolutionary aspect of the deep biosphere.

有时，为了找到一个确切的表达，需要阅读和查找大量的论文。例如，在一篇论文中，需要用英语来描述"基因表达模式转变（就是由上调转变为下调，或由下调转变为上调）"，上调基因和下调基因可用 up-regulated genes 和 down-regulated genes 来表示，但"基因表达模式转变"的"转变"用什么单词更合适呢？change 和 vary 显然不合适，因为其意义太一般化了（数量和质量的变化都可用这两个单词来表达）。通过阅读大量文献，才找到"基因表达模式转变"的确切英语表述为：shifts in gene expression patterns。此外，switch 和 convert (conversion) 也可以用来表达同样的意思，up-regulated genes 和 down-regulated genes 表述为 on-switch genes 和 off-switch genes 也不可以。

六、提高自己学术鉴赏力和学术水平需要阅读高水平 SCI 论文

粗略地说，学术鉴赏力就是指对学术工作做出评价的能力。只有具备一定的学术鉴赏力才能理解好的科研工作是什么，不好的科研工作是什么，并且能说出好的科研工作之所以好的原因与所在。学术水平是指科研工作者研究和解决学术问题的能力。

初学者有多种途径可以提高学术鉴赏力和学术水平，例如，导师的指导、与同学和师友的切磋、听学术讲座等，但阅读高水平的 SCI 论文则是其中最重要的一条途径。

好的科研工作首先应该基于一个十分重要的科学问题，解决这个问题能增加人类对自然的认识，能解决一个重大（或/和普遍）的理论或生产实践问题，能改善人类生存环境和提高人类福祉，并且这个问题是可以利用现有的方法解决的，如果这个问题虽然很重要，但现有的方法不能解决，那也没有什么用。其次，一个好的研究是在一个重要领域有新突破，提出了新的概念和理论，发现或产生了新的物质和材料，提出了新的技术和方法，开创了一个新的研究领域或提供了一个理解事物或现象的独特视角与维度等。最后，研究结果可以重复，有坚实的证据（例如正反证据或多重证据）来证实研究结论，不至于今天发表，明天就被人推翻或证伪。

不少著名的科学家提倡学生定时阅读 CNS 文章，这个建议是很好的，但是，阅读者自己某个领域的主流期刊文章也不能放过。因为不是所有的好文章能都发表到 CNS，正如诺贝尔奖的得奖之作也不全来自 CNS。在阅读论文以了解本领域及相关领域的重大发现、研究进展及最新动态的同时，也要发展批判阅读（critical reading）能力。所谓批判阅读能力，就是不会对论文结果和结论盲从盲信，而是基于较广的跨学科知识背景，对文章提出自己的问题，分析论文所用的方法和证据，评估论文结果和结论的可靠性和重要性。简而言之，就是能分析研究工作的优势与局限，不仅知道论文的成就和长处，也能发现论文的漏洞和不足，能客观地认识研究工作的内容和实质。只有这样，才能够在不断提高自己 SCI 论文阅读能力的同时，不断提高自己的学术鉴赏力和学术水平。

第十六章　SCI论文阅读的主要文字障碍

初学者在开始阅读SCI论文时，除了缺乏相关专业背景和专业基础知识外，生词过多、长句和复杂句理解困难、不清楚下文重复和指代的含义都是影响阅读的主要障碍。以下就SCI论文阅读的主要文字障碍进行说明。

一、生词

词汇是构成文章大厦的砖瓦。没有掌握大量的英语词汇，是很难顺利阅读文章的。因此，生词是初学者阅读SCI论文的首先遇到的文字障碍。

记单词有很多方法，其中最主要的方法是在大量的阅读中将生词记下来，查阅英汉词典或英英词典等工具书，记住相应的词义，并连同包含该词的句子也记下来。一个生词见一次可能记不住，但通过大量阅读，在不同阅读材料和上下文中遇见多了，就能将生词记住，并能从不同的使用环境中加深对词汇的理解。孤立地记背生词由于脱离使用环境，往往枯燥而效率低下。第二个重要的记单词方法是了解最主要的构词法——派生法(derivation)或词缀法(affixation)。派生法指词干(stem)通过附加前缀(prefix)或后缀(suffix)的构词方式。例如，specialization(特长)和purification(净化)分别是由形容词special和pure分别加上动词后缀-ize(意思为make，表示"使成……状态""使……化"等意思，英式英语中也使用-ise)和-fy(意思为"to make..."或"to become..."，表示"使成为……，使……化"或"成为……")。衍生演变为动词specialize和purify，然后加上名词形式的后缀-tion(来源于古法语、法语或拉丁语，表示"行为"。引申意有"行为的过程、结果、情况、性质、状态、动作")，才变成名词形式specialization和purification。利用字根法和词缀法来记单词，也就是来将某些单词(尤其是较长的科技单词)进行分解，根据其字根和词缀(前缀和后缀)意义来记忆单词的意义。例如，我们知道词根chron是time(时间)的意思，那么就有助于我们记忆与之相关的一组单词：chronic(长期的，慢性的)、chronicle(编年史，年代史)、chronograph(计时器，秒表)、chronology(年代学)、chronometer(精密计时器，航行表)、synchronal(同时的、同步的)、synchronize(同步化,将钟表拨至相同的时间,校准)和 synchronous(同时存在的,同步发生的,同步的)等。如果知道"aqu"是 water(水)的意思,那么,有助于记忆如下单词:aquarium(水族馆,养鱼缸)、aquatic(水生的,水产的,水栖的,水中的)、aqueduct(沟渠,引水渠,导水管)、subaqueous(水中的,水下的)、superaqueous(水上的)。如果我们知道前缀"anti-"有 against(反,抗,阻,排斥)、opposite(对立,相反)之意,那么,就有助于忘记以"anti-"为前缀的一系列词汇,如 antibody(抗体)、antiwar(反战的)、antiracist(反种族的,反种族歧视的)、antiquark(反夸克)、antisocial(反社会的)、antiserum(抗血清)、anticancer(抗癌的)、antipathy(反感)、antibacterial(抗菌的,抗菌剂)、antibiotic(抗生素、抗菌素、抗菌的)、antiseptic(杀菌剂,防腐的)等。如果知道前缀"a/an"有 not 或 without(无,非,不)之意,则 achromatic(无色的,色盲的)、anachronism(过时的人,不合时宜的)、atypical(非典型的)、anemia(贫血)、asexual(无性的,性冷淡的)、asymmetric(不对称的)就更好记忆。此外,前缀"de"有 negative of 或 removal of(负的,负面的,无,脱去,除去)之意,前缀"pseudo"有 not authentic, false or pretended(不真实的,假的或伪的)之意,前缀"homo"有 same(同,同样的)之意,前缀"hetero"有 other, different(异,不同的)之意,等等。其他的构词法还包括转类法(conversion)、首字母缩略法(acronym)、截短法(clipping)、拼缀法(blending)、合并法(compounding)等。转类法指词形不变,但改变词性或词类功能的方法(如名词作动词,形容词作动词等),如 interest(名词:兴趣)转类为 interest(动词:使……感兴趣),cool(形容词:凉的)转类为 cool(动词:使凉爽),empty(形容词:空的)转类为 empty(动词:倒空)。首字母缩略法指提取主要单词(一般为实词)的首字母组成新词的方法,如 CAD 为 Computer Assisted Design(计算机辅助设计)的缩略,WHO 为 World Health Organization(世界卫生组织)的缩略。截短法指截取较长单词的一部分作为新词,如 refrigerator(冰箱)截短为 fridge, influenza(感冒)截短为 flu, department(系,部)截短为 dept。拼缀法指将两个词同时进行裁剪后拼合而成的新词,如 science fiction(科学幻想小说)拼缀为 sci-fi, smoke(烟雾)和 fog(雾)拼缀为 smog(雾霾,烟雾)。合并法指两个或两个以上的单词组合而成新词,如 snow(雪)和 white(白色)合并为 snowwhite(雪白的),air(空气)和 conditioning(调节)合并为 air-conditioning(空调)。了解这些构词法对于掌握生词,增进阅读和理解能力将大有裨益。

另外要注意的一点是,科技英语词汇在特定专业领域内具有语义单一性特征,但很多普通词汇和半科技词汇具有多义性。对于这种单词,初学者如果只知其一,不知其二,就会影响理解。例如,我们都知道 student 的意思是"学生",但在下面的句子中,其意思是"研究者,学者"。

【例文 1】Dunsterville was the most notable of recent students of South American orchids.(邓斯特维尔曾是近期最著名的南美洲兰花研究

【例文 2】Let the climate and vegetation change, let other competing rodents or new beasts of prey immigrate, or <u>old</u> ones become modified, and all <u>analogy</u> would lead us to believe that some at least of the squirrels would decrease in numbers or become exterminated, unless they also became modified and improved in structure in a corresponding manner. (假若气候和植被发生变化, 与其相互竞争的啮齿动物或新的捕食动物迁移至此, 或者原有的此类物种发生变化, 所有此类情况都会使我们相信, 至少有一些松鼠数量会减少或灭绝, 除非它们也相应地在结构上进行变化和改进)

在上句中, old 不是"老的", 而是"原有的, 原来存在的", analogy 不是"类比或比喻", 而是"类似情况"。strength 有"强度"之意, 但也有"浓度、数量"之意。

【例文3】To study the effect of different <u>strength</u> of MS media, the explants were cultured onto three different <u>strength</u> of MS medium(full, half and quarter)[full <u>strength</u> MS medium(4.4 mg/L MS), half <u>strength</u> MS medium(2.2 mg/L MS)and quarter <u>strength</u> MS medium(1.1 mg/L MS)]. [为了研究不同浓度的 MS 培养基对外植体的影响, 将外植体培养在3种不同浓度的 MS 培养基(全量 MS 培养基 4.4 mg/L MS、半量 MS 培养基 2.2 mg/L MS 和 1/4 量 MS 培养基 1.1 mg/L MS)上]

还有一种情况是, 有些单词看起来是普通词汇, 但在特定的领域内是专业术语, 有其规范的中文译名。这类单词如果没有掌握其专业含义, 同样会影响对相关文章的准确理解。

【例文1】Generally the <u>component</u> shape is produced in machine tools by two different techniques, namely <u>generating</u> and <u>forming</u>. (通常, 机床加工零件的外形有两种不同的技术方法, 即加工和成形)

上例中的 component、generating、forming 就不能理解或翻译为"成分、产生、形成"。

【例文2】Although it is not yet known how recognition occurs, <u>chaperones</u> are likely to play a significant role. (虽然还不知道识别是如何发生的, 但分子伴侣很可能扮演重要的角色)

上例中的 chaperone, 并不是一般意义上的"年长女伴、陪护人、保护人、监护人", 而是专业术语"分子伴侣"。

二、长句和复杂句

SCI 论文通常句式简单, 但是也会遇到一些长句和复杂句的情况。对于初学者来说, 长句和复杂句通常难以理解, 因而也是一个重要的文字障碍。

碰到长句和复杂句时, 要进行语法分析。首先分析句子的主语是什么, 谓语是什么, 宾语是什么。在弄清楚句子的主干(主谓结构或主谓宾结构)后, 再分析介词结构、非谓语成分、同位语结构及各种从句(主要是定语从句)与主谓宾之间的修饰关系。一种较为复杂的情况是, 在从句中还可再嵌套从句。这种层层嵌套的结构会使初学者对句子的理解更加困难。但不论句子如何复杂, 对语法关系进行分析, 弄清句子结构之间的语义关系，在适当的地方断句，对于正确理解是必要的。

【例文 1】The presumably miR165/166-resistant version of *PHB* mRNA that is encoded by the gain-of-function *phb-1d* allele is not restricted to the adaxial domains of developing cotyledons, but is also found abaxially. （获得功能突变等位基因 *phb-1d* 编码的 *PHB* mRNA，推测其 miR165/166 抗性版本并不局限于发育中子叶的近轴区域，在子叶背面也有表达）

说明：该句的总体上为系表结构，主语为 The presumably miR165/166-resistant version of *PHB* mRNA，后面有两个表语：is not restricted to the adaxial domains of developing cotyledons，but is also found abaxially。在 *PHB* mRNA 后面有一个 that 引导的省掉主语的定语从句：is encoded by the gain-of-function *phb-1d* allele。

【例文 2】These reporter constructs and the *qrt* mutation can be introduced into a mutant background such that plants are heterozygous for one or two reporter constructs, enabling sister chromatids (both carrying the same reporter) to be distinguished from non-sister chromatids (carrying different reporters) based on the fluorescence of pollen grains. [突变体背景引入这些报告基因构件和 *qrt* 突变，植物就具有杂合的一个或两个报告基因构件，从而能基于花粉粒荧光，将姐妹染色单体（都携带相同的报告基因）与非姐妹染色单体（携带不同的报告基因）区分开来]

说明：这个句子的主句是 These reporter constructs and the *qrt* mutation can be introduced into a mutant background，后面是 such that 引导的结果状语从句。在后面的结果状语从句中，句子主体为 plants are heterozygous for one or two reporter constructs，后面紧跟一个现在分词结构 enabling sister chromatids (both carrying the same reporter) to be distinguished from non-sister chromatids (carrying different reporters) based on the fluorescence of pollen grains.

【例文 3】The discovery that two related miRNAs, miR165 and miR166, display complementarity to the very sequence that is mutated in the gain-of-function alleles of *PHB* and *PHV* prompted speculation that these alleles are freed from miRNA-directed negative regulation. （发现 miR165 和 miR166 这两个相关的 miRNAs 与 *PHB* 和 *PHV* 的获得功能等位基因突变的序列显示互补性，这促使人们推测，这些等位基因不受 miRNA 指导的负调控）

说明：这个句子中，主干结构为 The discovery...prompted speculation...。主语 The discovery 后面接有定语从句 that two related miRNAs, miR165 and miR166, display complementarity to the very sequence that is mutated in the gain-of-function alleles of *PHB* and *PHV*，这个定语从句还嵌套一个定语从句，嵌套的定语从句 that is mutated in the gain-of-function alleles of PHB and PHV 是修饰前面 the very sequence。此外，宾语 speculation 后面接有定语从句 that these alleles are freed from miRNA-directed negative regulation。

【例文 4】Moreover, expressing a *REV* mRNA in which the miRNA complementarity site contains 2-nt changes that decrease the complementarity between miR165/166 and *REV* phenocopies a gain-of-function *rev* allele, even though the protein encoded by the gene is not altered. (此外，REV mRNA 中 miRNA 互补位置包含 2 个核苷酸变化，这降低了 miR165/166 和 REV 之间的互补性，因此，即使 REV 基因编码的蛋白质并没有改变，REV mRNA 的表达也与 rev 等位基因的获得功能突变表型类似)

说明：该句主句主语为 expressing a REV mRNA，后面有一个定语从句 in which the miRNA complementarity site contains 2-nt changes that decrease the complementarity between miR165/166 and REV，其中，该定语从句又嵌套一个定语从句 that decrease the complementarity between miR165/166 and REV，修饰前面的 2-nt changes。该句的主句谓语为 phenocopy，表型模写(phenocopy)又称表型模拟或拟表型，是指因环境条件的改变所引起的表型改变类似于某基因型改变引起的表现型变化的现象。该句主句的宾语为 a gain-of-function rev allele。句子最后的 even though the protein encoded by the gene is not altered 为一个 even though(尽管)引导的让步状语从句。

【例文 5】The last decades have seen the development of a large number of crops whose inherent posttranscriptional gene silencing mechanism has been exploited to target essential viral genes through the production of dsRNA that triggers an endogenous RNA-induced silencing complex(RISC), leading to gene silencing in susceptible viruses conferring them with resistance even before the onset of infection. [近几十年来，已经培育了大量(RNA 干涉介导的转基因抗病毒)农作物。其方法通过产生触发内源性 RNA 诱导的沉默复合物(RNA-induced silencing complex, RISC)的 dsRNA，利用农作物固有的转录后基因沉默机制来靶向基本病毒基因，使易感病毒基因沉默，从而赋予这些作物(病毒)抗性(甚至在病毒感染开始前就出现的抗性)]

说明：该句上一句是 RNA interference(RNAi) has emerged as a leading technology in designing genetically modified crops engineered to resist viral infection。该句的主句很简单，为"The last decades have seen the development of a large number of crops"，但句子后面修饰 a large number of crops 的定语从句过长，从而导致难以理解。定语从句是一个被动句，whose inherent posttranscriptional gene silencing mechanism has been exploited 为句子的主体，to target essential viral genes 为不定式结构的宾语补足语，through the production of dsRNA that triggers an endogenous RNA-induced silencing complex(RISC)为介词结构作状语，而这个介词结构中，还包含一个修饰 dsRNA 的定语从句 that triggers an endogenous RNA-induced silencing complex(RISC)。句子最后为现在分词短语 leading to gene silencing in susceptible viruses conferring them with resistance even before the onset of infection 作状语。

三、重复和指代

英语学术论文中，通常利用重复关键词语或利用代词来实现句子与句子之间的衔接和照应。重复关键词语有时可采用完全重复、缩略重复、同义词重复、范畴词或关系非常密切的相关名词重复，当然，也可采用代词来指代前面提到的关键词语。这些不同的重复和指代手段一定要熟悉，要弄清重复和指代的是上文提到的哪个词语，否则就会造成误解。

【例文1】The findings, published in Nature Communications on May 14, 2020, hold promise for future treatment and prevention of obesity, diabetes, and especially nonalcoholic steatohepatitis(NASH), a type of fatty liver disease that is characterized by inflammation and fat accumulation in the liver. In the next few years, the condition is expected to become the leading cause of liver transplants in the United States. [发表在2020年5月14日的《自然通讯》杂志上这一发现，有望在未来帮助治疗和预防肥胖、糖尿病，特别是以肝脏炎症和脂肪堆积为特征的非酒精性脂肪性肝炎(nonalcoholic steatohepatitis, NASH)。几年后，非酒精性脂肪性肝炎有望成为美国肝移植的主要原因]

说明：第二句的 the condition 指 nonalcoholic steatohepatitis(NASH)。

【例文2】Santos and his colleagues have recently identified a small mitochondrial uncoupler, named BAM15, that decreases the body fat mass of mice without affecting food intake and muscle mass or increasing body temperature. Additionally, the molecule decreases insulin resistance and has beneficial effects on oxidative stress and inflammation. (弗吉尼亚理工学院桑托斯和他的同事最近发现了一种叫作BAM15的线粒体解偶联剂，它可以在不影响食物摄入和肌肉质量，也不增加体温的情况下，减少小鼠的体脂质量。此外，BAM15还可降低胰岛素抵抗，并对氧化应激和炎症有有益作用)

说明：第二句的 the molecule 是指 BAM15。

【例文3】Here, as on the other occasions, I lie under a heavy disadvantage, for out of the the many striking cases which I have collected, I can give only one or two instances of transitional habits and structures in closely allied species of the same genus; and of diversified habits, either constant or occasional, in the same species. And it seems to me that nothing less than a long list of such cases is sufficient to lessen the difficulty in any particular case like that of the bat. (和其他情况一样，面对这个问题，我处于严重的不利局面，因为在我收集的许多引人注目的例子中，我只能举出一两个例子来说明同一属的近缘物种有过渡性习性和结构；以及同一物种中存在多样化习性，无论这种习性是稳定存在的还是偶然存在的。在我看来，只有列出一长串这样的例子，才足以减少解释像蝙蝠这样特殊例子的困难)

说明：第二句的 such cases 是指 instances of transitional habits and structures in closely allied species of the same genus; and of diversified habits, either constant or occasional, in the same species。

【例文 4】 We have seen that it is the common, the widely-diffused, and widely-ranging species, belonging to the larger genera, which vary most; and these will tend to transmit to their modified offspring that superiority which now makes them dominant in their own countries. (我们已经看到，变异最大正是较大的属中常见的、广泛传播的、分布广泛的物种，并且这些物种往往会将现今使其在本地占优势的优越性传递给它们的改良后代)

说明：第二个句的 these 是指 the common, the widely-diffused, and widely-ranging species。

关于更多的阅读理解技巧，读者可阅读刘进平编著的《英语阅读理解科技英语翻译和 SCI 论文写作技巧》。

第十七章　SCI论文阅读法之精读法

一、概述

精读主要是指选择与自己专业最相关的典型文献进行仔细阅读。精读不仅要了解文章内容，而且要在了解内容的基础上，分析文章的结构和写法，学习英语措辞和造句。泛读只是根据自己的阅读目的，选择最感兴趣的内容进行快速阅读或浏览，并不会对文章进行全面和详细的阅读与分析，主要目的是快速、精准地获得相关的专业内容（如专业进展、技术方法、问题和不足等）。精读不是以获得专业内容为唯一目的，而是以所读文章为样板或示范，对文献从内容到结构进行全面系统地学习，小到一个单词和术语的用法，大到文章结构和脉络的把握，都要了然于胸。精读是泛读的基础，没有相当数量的文献精读，就无法做到自如地泛读。因此，精读是初学者最基础的和最主要的文献阅读方法。

初学者在最开始阅读SCI文献时，会感到特别吃力，很多专业术语不了解，生词一大堆，有些论文的句子较长且结构复杂，再加上专业背景不熟悉，几天都无法读完一篇。这种情况下不要着急，因为每个人都是这样过来的，即便是普通英语学得比较好，也不可能一开始就能很自如地阅读专业英语文献。精读不要放过每一个词和每一个句子，要确切理解其意思，不能满足于一知半解，不能囫囵吞枣，必须发挥"蚂蚁啃骨头"的精神，耐着性子一篇接着一篇"啃"下来，三五十篇之后，英语阅读能力就会明显地提高。

对于初学者而言，尝试对文章进行英汉翻译也是一种不错的方法。因为翻译成功与否，既取决于对原文的理解，也取决于用汉语怎么表达。实际上翻译最大的困难还是在于理解，如果能透彻理解原文，表达就相对容易一些。因此，翻译是能精确衡量一个人是否吃透原文的试金石。

此外，不少研究小组或实验室会定期组织学生进行文献研讨，由学生轮流阅读最新的SCI论文，并做成PPT上台讲解，然后大家对文章加以讨论学习。这不仅是一种良好的科研训练方式,也是一种非常有效的文献精读方式。因为没有读懂,没有吃透原文,是很难讲清楚的。

二、精读的第一步

精读的第一步是通读全文,消灭生词难句,精确了解文章的意思和内容。

初学者阅读 SCI 论文最大的障碍可能是词汇量不足,因此,精读的重要任务就是消灭生词。只有通过大量精读,才能扩大词汇量。记单词除了在精读过程中利用标注法和摘抄法进行记忆外,将单词分解成词素(词根和词干),以及利用构词法(如派生、复合、缩略、词类转化等)来记忆科技英语单词也相当有效。

通读时,从标题和摘要到讨论和结论按顺序阅读。遇到生词,甚至是虽然认识,但词义没有精确掌握的单词,或者发音困难、对应的中文术语模糊的单词,也要查一下大型的普通词典及专业词典,将其释意和音标在文章空白处。如果是利用中文搜索引擎和网上词典,则要对多条解释详细比勘,选择最恰当的释义或对应的中文术语。在释义感觉不妥帖时,可通过英英词典和英语搜索引擎,查找权威的源语解释,来确定中文释义是否恰当。遇到难句,要对句子的语法进行分析,把握主句结构(找出主谓宾),了解分句与分句之间的语义关系,主句与从句的语法修饰关系。同时,要能识别英语中的比较、倒装、省略、强调等特定结构,弄清其修辞功能。

对于英语基础较差的读者,生词太多,语法不懂,可以通过谷歌浏览器、搜狗浏览器、有道词典、百度翻译、CNKI 翻译助手(知网在线辅助翻译系统)、Lingoes Translator(灵格斯词霸)、SCI Translate、Copy Translator、DocTranslator、DeepL 翻译器、全文整篇翻译(Onlinedoctranslator)、Word、WPS、翻译狗和知云文献翻译软件等对 SCI 论文加以翻译对照,以辅助自己理解原文。随着人工智能(artificial intelligence,AI)的崛起,以 AI 工具为基础的 SCI 论文阅读工具应运而生,如 SciSpace、Paper Digest、Explainpaper、ChatDOC、New Bing、RESOOMER、ChatGPT 等。但是,这些方法只是在初学者基础较差的情况下辅助使用,只要阅读水平允许,读者应该尽可能阅读原文。原因是利用翻译软件目前还无法精确翻译原文,对于普通词语与专业术语、同义词或近义词的分辨,以及复杂句子的理解和翻译都做得不是很好。此外,在某些句子中,对定语从句的修饰关系和代词的指向还不能很精确地识别。需要强调的是,这些翻译软件或插件只能作为刚开始阅读文献时的辅助工具,绝对不能完全依赖,否则 SCI 论文阅读水平永远得不到提高。也有人建议初学者应该从阅读中国作者发表的 SCI 论文开始。阅读中国作者 SCI 论文的便利之处在于,有些 SCI 论文相关的内容可能在中文期刊发表过,阅读这些中文论文对理解其英语论文直接帮助很大。甚至有些 SCI 论文就是从学位论文(硕士论文或博士论文)整理后发表的,那么利用中国知网搜索下载到其中文版的学位论文,对照着阅读其 SCI 论文,会更容易理解。

很多情况下,对论文选题背景和技术缺乏了解也是重要的阅读障碍。因此,阅读研究性论文之前，大量阅读综述文章和专著，了解基本的术语和专业背景至关重要。此外，很多不错的期刊，如《当代生物学》和《分子植物》等，每期都有跟论文同时配发的评论文章，同时阅读相关的评论文章显然有助于对论文本身的理解。对于英语较差的初学者，可以预先阅读中文综述文章或者相关中文专著和教材，并注意专业术语的英语与汉语对应名称；有条件的，还可以将英语原版图书与对应的汉语翻译版对照阅读，在精确把握英语术语对应的汉语术语的同时，可帮助深入理解相关的专业知识和英语表达。

在互联网环境下的阅读要比以往没有互联网环境的阅读便利许多，难理解的词语或事物可以通过网络搜索（网页、图片和视频搜索）来查证和了解。除英汉和英英网络词典外，网络百科（如百度百科、互动百科、维基百科等）也是很方便的查证资源。对于新出现的词汇和术语，其含义可以通过网络搜索和文献研读加以确定。SCI论文一般涉及前沿的和最新的知识，往往会使用一些尚未进入教科书的术语和知识，因此，初学者要读懂一篇SCI论文常需要查阅大量的SCI论文和网络资源。对于中文网上解释不清的词语，应多查英文网络。例如，在一篇综述文章"The plant circadian clock: From a simple timekeeper to a complex developmental manager"中读到一句这样的话：Supporting this idea, exogenous sucrose has the ability to shorten the period in wild-type plants grown under free-running conditions. 这句话中的free-running是什么意思呢？查一下网络，解释为"不同步的；自由振荡的；自激的；易流动的；易流动的"。这样的解释仍然无法明白其确切含义。搜索英文浏览器，则可知晓free-running指的是：Circadian rhythms are detected as oscillations in behavior or physiology, with periods of approximately 24 h that persist in the absence of external cues（在没有外部信号的情况下，昼夜节律或生物钟仍检测到在行为或生理上持续按大约24小时的节律振荡）。对于很多新出现的术语，中文网络上并无详细的解释和说明，这时候，查英文网络就尤为必要。比如retrograde signal或retrograde signaling，这个意思是什么呢？中文网络对retrograde的解释为"倒退的；退化的；退步的"，但仍然说明不了任何问题。查英文浏览器，则可知道其确定定义：The term retrograde signaling refers to the fact that chloroplasts and mitochondria utilize specific signaling molecules to convey information on their developmental and physiological states to the nucleus and modulate the expression of nuclear genes accordingly.（逆行信号转导是指叶绿体和线粒体利用特异的信号转导分子，将其发育和生理状态的信息传递到细胞核，并相应地调控核基因的表达）。

三、精读的第二步

精读的第二步是分析文章的结构和写法，把握文章的选题思路和研究策略。

标准化SCI论文具有IMRD或IMRaD的结构形式，这些不同部分都有其结构和写作要求。怎样分析文章的结构和写法呢？具体方法如下。

①题目方面。除了弄清其意思外，还要分析其结构是名词性词组还是句子。关键词是否出现？是哪（几）个？如果是名词性词组，哪个名词突显其创新性？如果是句子，是什么句型？所用时态和动词是什么？这个题目的好处在哪儿？

②摘要方面。除了弄清其意思外，还要分别指出包含背景（Background）、目的（Objective）、方法（Methods）、结果（Results）和结论（Conclusion）等要素的句子，可用彩色笔划出来或标出来。摘要各部分或每个句子所用时态、句型（主动或被动）是什么？主动语句中人称为第几人称？

③引言方面。除了弄清其意思外，还要分析其逻辑层次，哪几句是"起、承、转、合"部分，或者说大小背景、综述、空白（问题）、论文研究的目的和意义层次，文献征引采用作者突显式引用还是作者非突显式引用，引言各部分所用时态等。

④方法方面。简要说明各标题的意义，指出哪些句子保证了方法的科学性（如重复、对照、统计处理等），这部分写作所用的句型和时态等。

⑤结果方面。除了弄清其意思外，还要分别说明叙述架构、逻辑层次、结果每个段落的论述先后顺序、所用时态和人称、图（表）的类型、图（表）与文字的关系等。指出方法写作常用的典型句型及经常使用的动词等。

⑥讨论方面。除了弄清其意思外，还要分别说明讨论的重点"叙述顺序"句型和时态，结果中哪些与前人的结果一致，哪些不一致，原因可能是什么，推出了什么样的结论，有什么普遍意义，研究结果是否符合预期，是否达到研究目的，实验中是否存在某些不足和局限，未解决的问题还有什么，最后的结论是什么。

⑦参考文献部分。要了解参考文献为著者-出版年制还是顺序编码制。

科技论文采用 IMRD 或 IMRaD 结构形式本身就直观地反映科学发现的过程。引言（Introduction）要回答"研究的是什么问题（What was the problem）"，材料和方法（Materials and Methods）要回答"怎样研究这个问题（How did you study it）"，结果（Results）要回答"发现了什么（What did you find）"，讨论（Discussion）要回答"这些发现意味着什么（What do these findings mean）"。此外，科技论文的每一部分都有各自的写作思路：引言一般从宽到窄地描述论文相关的主题或领域，说明哪些是已知的，还有什么是未知的，然后描述作者为什么会选择某个未知或不足作为拟研究的问题，作者对这个问题的解决有什么设想或猜想，最后是对论文采用的主要方法与取得的成果及其重要性预览；材料和方法通常会写出各种方法的研究目的；结果的各个小标题指明了利用证据论证的几个主要步骤或环节，结果的每一个小节或段落，其典型的结构也是先介绍实验的目的和动机，或者先介绍问题的背景，然后叙述用什么方法获得什么结果，最后会一个简短总结，说明这些实验结果证明了什么；讨论要阐明论文工作取得的核心成果及其意义，通过引用参考文献，论证成果的可靠性与创新性，叙述并解释为什么与别人的结果相同或不同，最后说明论文成果为什么重要，还有什么不足之处。在理解整个论文结构，详细阅读各论文的各部分后，文章的选题思路和研究策略也就明白了。

在前述基础上，读者还可进一步对论文进行批判性阅读。批判性阅读是一种积极主动的阅读方式，在这种阅读方式中，读者和作者的地位是相对平等的，读者不对作者仰望和膜拜，读者不是被动地接受作者所说的东西，而是要经过读者自己的思考和评价，得出自己的独立判断，与作者的思想进行互动和交流，更深入地理解所读材料。具体而言，就是要带着问题阅读，而不是简单接受文本所反映的事实和判断，被作者的想法牵着鼻子走，而是与文本保持一定的距离，运用自己的思维去独立评价。就论文阅读而言，不是被动地接受论文的结论，而是要对其假设、方法和结果进行思考和评估，分析作者的假设是否可行，方法是否合理，所获得的结果是否足以支持论文的结论，作者对结果的解释和推论是否准确可靠等；也可以对论文的写法进行评判，例如，评判作者的写作思路是否恰当，表达方式是否完美等。除了带着问题阅读外，还可以采用挑错式阅读，就是在文章中找错、找碴儿，或者先假定作者是错的，然后通过阅读，根据文本所提供的证据来判断是否足够改变这种假定。一般而言，决定科技论文结论是否可靠的最重要的部分就是材料与方法，许多论文结论经不起检验，就是因为材料不合适、样本选择不当、样本量不够大、没有设置重复、无法进行统计学处理或者没有设置（阴性和阳性）对照等。当然，最重要的是方法和材料足以让其他作者重复或再现论文结果。从结果来讲，图像有可能是出于伪造或者仅仅是赝像（这在显微照片中较常见）而已，证据全是间接证据而无直接证据，对图像或实物解读错误，没有完全排除其他可能的解释（如考古学、古生物学中的化石）等。坚实的结论需要采用尽可能多的方法、从尽可能多的角度和方面来证明。

四、精读的第三步

精读的第三步是学习文章的措辞、造句和段落发展技巧，记下相关的用法和例句，以便写作时为我所用。

由于英语写作能力主要包括措辞、造句和段落发展3方面的能力，所以，这一步主要是为发展写作能力而进行的。

"书到用时方恨少"，写作也是这样。写作最能让人感受英语表达能力的不足。词汇相当于建筑材料（砖瓦），而段落和文章则相当于建筑物。没有相当数量的有效词汇（不只是认识，而且会使用），就是无米而炊。而不了解各种句型，就无法有效遣词造句。在词汇和句型学习方面，郑孝通教授提出了"三点法"，也就是：第一，要密切注意某些单词的特殊功能；第二，要不断扩大对词组的识别能力和运用能力；第三，要大量积累英语的各种句型。在学习造句方面，斯坦利·费什（Stanley Fish）在《如何遣词造句》（*How to Write a Sentence And How to Read One*）中指出，要重视对句子的理解和鉴赏能力培养，在此基础上，对句子进行分析和模仿。模仿造句要先从结构形式入手。"在学习如何写句子的过程中，最好从形式开始，不要关注内容。""你必须先接受形式的束缚，然后形式会让你重获自由。"

学习专业术语主要针对名词，而学习英语造句则主要抓住动词。专业术语学习要注意记忆和辨析相同或相近的名词，避免在写作中用错。学习英语造句的重点和难点在动词，因为动词除有很多同义词、近义词需要区分外，其时态和语态变化也相当复杂，因此，在精读过程中要十分注意学习动词的用法。

我国学者在英语写作中经常会犯"中式英语"的问题，也就是在措辞和造句中习惯于用母语（汉语）思维。问题的根源仍然在于英语文章读得少，没有注意英语在词语组合、主谓搭配、造句习惯方面的独特性，或者说没有学会用英语思维。

初学者在这一步可以将有参考或借鉴价值的用词和句子记下来，从摘要、引言、方法、结果与讨论中摘出哪些可作为模板句使用的典型句子，以及经常使用的动词等，以便在将来写作中加以利用。很多写作书会给读者归纳一些 SCI 论文写作高频词或常用句式，但如果你自己在阅读本专业文献中记下一些常用的表达法，会更有用。

总之，对于一篇写得好的论文，精读时就是要多方面吸取其营养，"食其肉、啖其血、敲其骨、吸其髓"，而后已。

五、举例说明

以《自然植物》的一篇长论文为例说明精读的方法。之所以举例这篇文章，是因为目前组学研究正成为领域内的主流，此外，组学研究文章既难读也难写，不论是阅读还是写作都需要大量的知识储备和资源查证。

案例全文

（一）标题

【原文】Integrated multi-omics framework of the plant response to jasmonic acid（图 17-1）。

【参考译文】植物对茉莉酸响应的多组学整合框架。

图 17-1　例文标题

说明：标题是一个名词结构，其中多组学（multi-omics）手段是随着高通量技术的发展而出现的一种将基因组学（genomic）、表观基因组学（epigenomics）、转录组学（transcriptomic）、蛋白质组学（proteomic）、代谢组学（metabolomic）等组学手段整合在一起的分析方法。多组学手段可以在不同的水平上量化分子的变化，能提供对组成细胞、组织和有机体的分子变化的全面或整体的理解，是一种能比单一组学手段提供更多生物信息的革命性的数据分析方法。如果相关概念不熟悉，可阅读维基百科（Wikipedia）的词条（Multiomics）（en. wikipedia. org/wiki/Multiomics），或者阅读下面这篇综述文章：Hasin Y, Seldin M, Lusis A. Multi-omics approaches to disease. Genome Biology, 2017, 18：83。Framework 是个多义词，基本含义有两个：①基础性的观念或概念结构[a basic conceptional structure (as of ideas)]；②骨架、支架、框架（a skeletal, openwork, or structural frame）。译成中文时可根据不同语境译为"框架""结构""机制""体制""体系""观点"等，但都很难译出其真正的英语含义：A framework is a genuine or conceptual structure expected to serve as a support or guide for the working of something that extends the structure into something useful. In technical term, a framework is frequently a layered structure showing what sort of projects can be build and how they would interrelate. 我们在理解了其英语含义后，就可在将来的写作中加以使用。

（二）摘要

【原文】

Abstract

Understanding the systems-level actions of transcriptional responses to hormones provides insight into how the genome is reprogrammed in response to environmental stimuli. Here, we investigated the signalling pathway of the hormone jasmonic acid (JA), which controls a plethora of critically important processes in plants and is orchestrated by the transcription factor MYC2 and its closest relatives in *Arabidopsis thaliana*. We generated an integrated framework of the response to JA, which spans from the activity of master and secondary regulatory transcription factors, through gene expression outputs and alternative splicing, to protein abundance changes, protein phosphorylation and chromatin remodelling. We integrated time-series transcriptome analysis with (phospho)proteomic data to reconstruct gene regulatory network models. These enabled us to predict previously unknown points of crosstalk of JA to other signalling pathways and to identify new components of the JA regulatory mechanism, which we validated through targeted mutant analysis. These results provide a comprehensive understanding of how a plant hormone remodels cellular functions and plant behaviour, the general principles of which provide a framework for analyses of cross-regulation between other hormone and stress signalling pathways.

【译文】
摘要

了解植物对激素的转录反应系统级作用,有助于深入了解基因组是如何响应环境刺激而重编程的。本论文中,我们研究了茉莉酸激素(jasmonic acid, JA)的信号传导通路。JA 信号传导途径控制着植物中过多的至关重要的过程,并由拟南芥转录因子 MYC2 及其最近的同源物调控。我们确定了一个 JA 反应(应答)的综合系统,这个系统整合了主调控转录因子和次(级)调控转录因子的活性、基因表达输出和选择性剪接、蛋白质丰度变化、蛋白质磷酸化和染色质重塑等过程。我们将时间序列转录组分析和(磷酸)蛋白质组数据整合在一起重建基因调控网络模型。这使我们能够预测 JA 与其他信号通路串扰的未知节点,并鉴定 JA 调控机制的新组成部分,这些预测结果我们通过靶向突变分析进行了验证。本文结果有助于全面理解植物激素如何重塑细胞功能和植物行为,其一般原则为其他激素和胁迫信号转导通路之间的交叉调控提供了分析框架。

说明:初学者在读 SCI 论文时遇到的第一个问题是专业知识背景不熟悉和语言上的生词难句。其中尤以专业知识背景不熟悉为影响 SCI 论文理解的最大障碍。就以上述摘要为例,如果想理解其意思,不仅需要理解文章所涉及的多组学方法,也就是转录组学(transcriptomic)、(磷酸)蛋白质组学[(phospho)proteomic]、表观基因组学(epigenomics)等组学方法,还要了解相关的知识内容,如茉莉酸的信号转导、植物激素信号转导串扰和互作等。如果读者在阅读该篇文章之前,能够熟悉如下综述文献,将有助于对本文的理解:

1. 茉莉酸的信号转导综述文章

Wasternack C, Hause B, 2013. Jasmonates: Biosynthesis, perception, signal trans duction and action in plant stress response, growth and development. An update to the 2007 review in Annals of Botany[J]. Ann Bot, 111(6): 1021-1058.

Wasternack C, 2015. How jasmonates earned their laurels: Past and present[J]. J Plant Growth Regul, 34: 761-794.

Browse J, 2009. Jasmonate passes muster: A receptor and targets for the defense hormone. Annu Rev Plant Biol, 60: 183-205.

Yan Y, Borrego E, Kolomiets M V, 2013. Chap. 16 Jasmonate biosynthesis, perception and function in plant development and stress response[M]//Baez R V ed. Lipid Metabolism. Rijeka: InTech, pp. 393-442.

Santino A, Taurino M, de Domenico S, Flors V et al., 2013. Jasmonate signaling in plant development and defense response to multiple (a)biotic stresses[J]. Plant Cell Rep, 32(7): 1085-98.

Kazan K, Manners J M, 2013. MYC2: The master in action[J]. Mol Plant, 6: 686-703.

Goossens J, Mertens J, Goossens A, 2017. Role and functioning of bHLH transcription factors in jasmonate signalling[J]. J Exp Bot, 68(6): 1333-1347.

Chini A, Gimenez-Ibanez S, Goossens A, et al., 2016. Redundancy and specificity in jasmonate signalling[J]. Curr Opin Plant Biol, 33: 147-156.

2. 植物激素信号转导串扰和互作综述文章

Depuydt S, Hardtke C S, 2011. Hormone signalling crosstalk in plant growth regulation [J]. Curr Bioi, 21(9): 365-373.

Robert-Seilaniantz A, Grant M, Jones J D, 2011. Hormone crosstalk in plant disease and defense: More than just jasmonate-salicylate antagonism. Annu Rev Phytopathol, 49: 317-343.

Song S, Qi T, Wasternack C, et al., 2014 Jasmonate signaling and crosstalk with gibberellin and ethylene[J]. Curr Opin Plant Biol, 21: 112-119.

Zhu Z, 2014. Molecular basis for jasmonate and ethylene signal interactions in Arabidopsis[J]. J Exp Bot, 65: 5743-5748.

Hoffmann M, Hentrich M, Pollmann S, 2011. Auxin-oxylipin crosstalk: Relationship of antagonists[J]. J. Integr. Plant Biol, 53: 29-445.

当然，为了理解摘要，先阅读论文的正文及其所引的参考文献，当然是可以的，但是仍然不够。初学者应该多读一点综述文章，来为阅读研究性论文打底。如果英语综述文章阅读还存在困难，就从中文综述文章阅读开始。

接下来我们看一下一些术语的释意。一般的专业术语，例如，基因表达(gene expression)、转录因子(transcription factor, TF)、选择性剪接(alternative splicing)、蛋白质丰度(protein abundance)、蛋白质磷酸化(protein phosphorylation)、染色质重塑(chromatin remodelling)等可以在分子生物学或分子遗传学的教科书中找到，此处不再赘述。关键是那些尚未进入教科书的术语或半术语(介于专业术语与普通名词之间)，这需要查询网络与论文。"激素转录反应系统级作用"(systems-level actions of transcriptional responses to hormones)指植物在感知激素信号后，引起转录组学、(磷酸)蛋白质组学、表观基因组学等不同系统水平上的作用。接下来说的"基因组被重编程"(the genome is reprogrammed)是什么意思呢？细胞或有机体的 DNA 序列或基因组就像编好的计算机程序一样，按顺序在什么时间执行什么程序，或者说发育过程被编程，在适当的时间表达某些基因。原来指可通过表观遗传修饰(如 DNA 甲基化、组蛋白修饰和非组蛋白结合染色质等)加以调控，也就是所谓"表观遗传重编程"(epigenetic reprogramming)，尤其是指已分化的细胞在特定的条件下被逆转后恢复到全能或多能干细胞(干细胞可以分化为任何细胞类型)。现在又出现利用基因编辑(如 CRISPR/Cas9)和合成生物学手段对基因组进行"遗传重编程"(genetic reprogramming)。重编程在本文中泛化使用，指基因组在响应环境刺激而改变原有的基因表达水平或表达模式。MYC2 and its closest relatives 又是什么意思呢？这里的 relative 相当于 homolog(同源蛋白,同源基因,同源染色体),具体来讲,就是指 MYC3 和 MYC4。

最后我们重点讲一下 master and secondary regulatory transcription factors。就像一个大公司管理等级或层次(hierarchy)一样,生物体也存在调控等级或层次(regulatory hierarchy)。主调控因子(master regulator)或主调控基因(master regulatory gene)或者主调控转录因子(master regulatory transcription factor)是描述占据调控层次顶端的转录因子蛋白,它通过直接作用或通过基因表达变化的级联(a cascade of gene expression changes)来调控多个下游基因(downstream genes)。如果读者事先不了解这个术语,可阅读维基百科的词条或者阅读下面这两篇文章:①Chan SS, Kyba M. What is a master regulator? J. Stem Cell Res Ther, 2013, 3: 114. ② Fournier et al. FOXA and master transcription factors recruit Mediator and Cohesin to the core transcriptional regulatory circuitry of cancer cells. Scientific Reports, 2016, 6: 34962.

与主调控转录因子和次(级)调控转录因子(secondary regulatory transcription factor)相类似的一对术语是全局调控因子(global regulator)是与局部调控因子(local regulator)或专用调控因子(dedicated regulator)。可阅读下面这两篇综述文章:①Gottesman S. Bacterial regulation: global regulatory networks. Annu Rev Genet, 1984, 18: 415-441. ② Martínez-Antonio A, Collado-Vides J. Identifying global regulators in transcriptional regulatory networks in bacteria. Current Opinion in Microbiology, 2003, 6(5): 482-489. Gottesman(1984)将根据全局调控因子(global regulator)定义为具有多型性表型(pleiotropic phenotype)及能调控不同代谢途径操纵子能力的转录因子。Martínez-Antonio 和 Collado-Vides(2003)针对所调控基因的数目、辅调控因子(co-regulator)的数目和类型、启动子的不同西格玛(sigma)类型、调控的转录因子数目、进化家族(evolutionary family)的大小和种类对这个概念进行修正(图 17-2)。

按照前面的精读步骤,接下来对摘要进行结构分析。摘要的字数一般限制在 250 个单词以内,本文摘要为 180 个单词。摘要一般包括如下 4 方面内容:①陈述研究的主要目标和范围(States the main objectives and scope of the research);②描述使用的方法(Describes the methods used);③总结结果(Summarizes the results);④陈述主要结论(States the principal conclusions)。该摘要的第一句话"Understanding the systems-level actions of transcriptional responses to hormones provides insight into how the genome is reprogrammed in response to environmental stimuli."为研究目的或论文研究的逻辑依据(rationale)。在"Here, we investigated the signalling pathway of the hormone jasmonic acid (JA), which controls a plethora of critically important processes in plants and is orchestrated by the transcription factor MYC2 and its closest relatives in *Arabidopsis thaliana*"句中,前面的主句介绍主要研究活动或工作范围,后面 which 引导的非限制性定语从句"which controls a plethora of critically important processes in plants and is orchestrated by the transcription factor MYC2 and its closest relatives in *Arabidopsis thaliana*"介绍研究的背景

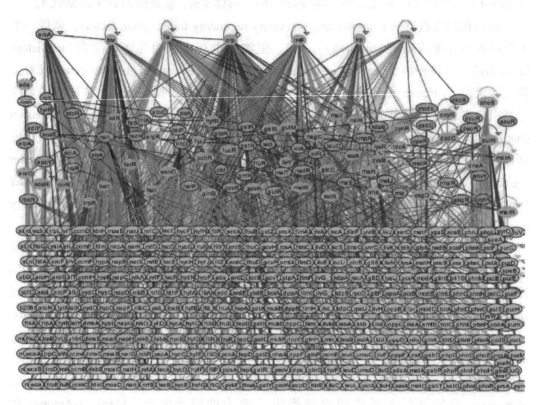

下层椭圆小圈表示被调控的基因，中层椭圆形小圈表示转录因子(TFs)，最上层的椭圆形小圈表示 TFs 中的全局调控因子。线条由浅到深分别表示激活、抑制和双重调节(激活和抑制)。

图 17-2　大肠杆菌($E.\ coli$)转录调控网络概览图

信息。后面的"We generated an integrated framework of the response to JA, which spans from the activity of master and secondary regulatory transcription factors, through gene expression outputs and alternative splicing, to protein abundance changes, protein phosphorylation and chromatin remodelling. We integrated time-series transcriptome analysis with (phospho) proteomic data to reconstruct gene regulatory network models. These enabled us to predict previously unknown points of crosstalk of JA to other signalling pathways and to identify new components of the JA regulatory mechanism, which we validated through targeted mutant analysis"为研究结果，最后一句话"These results provide a comprehensive understanding of how a plant hormone remodels cellular functions and plant behaviour, the general principles of which provide a framework for analyses of cross-regulation between other hormone and stress signalling pathways"为研究结论和意义。注意，这只是大体区分。事实上，结果部分完全可以与所用的主要方法结合在一起介绍。例如，"We integrated time-series transcriptome analysis with (phospho) proteomic data to reconstruct gene regulatory network models. These enabled us to predict previously unknown points of crosstalk of JA to other signalling pathways and to identify new components of the JA regulatory mechanism, which we validated through targeted mutant analysis",这两句则是结果与方法在同一句中体现。

最后,我们学习一下本篇论文摘要的一些词语和句子,以便在今后的写作中使用。介绍研究目的的第一句话"Understanding the systems-level actions of transcriptional responses to hormones provides insight into how the genome is reprogrammed in response to environmental stimuli",以动名词结构 Understanding the systems-level actions of transcriptional responses to hormones 作主语,动词谓语为 provides insight into,由于句子的内容为不受时间影响的普遍事实,所以使用现在时,又因为动名词作主语,为第三人称单数形式。insight 的意思是"洞察力,洞悉,深入了解"(the ability to have) a clear, deep, and sometimes sudden understanding of a complicated problem or situation)。provide insight into / provide an insight into / provide insights into 都可以使用,意思是"有助于深入了解……"。这个词组经常在科技论文中使用,但主语一般为名词或动名词结构,不能是人。例如,①Yet understanding the savant will help provide insight into the whole neurophysiological underpinning of human behavior. ②The new data provide insight into the ways that stars like the Sun end their lives. ③The algorithm used in the program may provide insight into how the brain controls behavior. 有时,还可在论文标题中使用,例如,Large-scale ruminant genome sequencing provides insights into their evolution and distinct traits.

接下来介绍主要研究活动和主要研究成果,前三句都使用第一人称(作者自己)和主动语态:"Here, we investigated..." "We generated..." "We integrated...with...to reconstruct...",第四句"These enabled us to predict...and to identify..."用第三人称作主语。由于叙述的是过去进行的实验或动作,而不是论文中呈现或描述了什么结果,因此这四句的主句都用一般过去时。最后一句"These results provide a comprehensive understanding of..., the general principles of which provide a framework for..."是对论文发现的结论和意义的描述,动词用一般现在时。目前,许多国际知名科技期刊论文摘要普遍使用第一人称和主动语态造句,要注意学习应用。

(三)引言

以下为这篇例文的引言(Introduction)或背景(Background)部分,原文没有 Introduction 或 Background 这样的标题。

【原文 1】Plant hormones are structurally unrelated, small signalling molecules that play pivotal roles in a wide range of fundamental processes of plants, including growth, development and responses to environmental stimuli[1]. Hormone perception by plants stimulates a cascade of transcriptional reprogramming that ultimately modifies cellular function and plant behaviour[2,3,4,5]. This is initiated by one or a family of high-affinity receptors, followed by signal transduction through protein-protein interactions, post-translational modification events and regulation of transcription factor (TF) activity that ultimately drive changes in gene expression[2,3,6].

【参考译文1】植物激素是结构上不相关的、小的信号分子，在各种不同的植物基础过程(包括生长、发育和对环境刺激的反应)中发挥关键作用[1]。植物对激素的感知刺激一系列连续的转录重编程，最终改变细胞功能和植物行为[2,3,4,5]。这个过程由一个或一个家族的高亲和力受体启动，随后通过蛋白质-蛋白质互作、翻译后修饰事件和转录因子(TF)活性调控进行信号转导，最终驱动基因表达的变化[2,3,6]。

【原文2】One of the key plant hormones is jasmonic acid (JA), which regulates crucial processes, including fertility, seedling emergence, the response to wounding and the growth-defence balance[7]. Jasmonates are perceived as jasmonoyl-isoleucine by a complex comprising the co-receptors CORONATINE INSENSITIVE1 (COI1) and JASMONATE ZIM DOMAIN (JAZ)[8,9,10,11]. COI1 is an F-box protein and part of a Skp-Cullin-F-box E3 ubiquitin ligase complex (SCF^{COI1})[12] that targets JAZ proteins for proteasomal degradation after JA perception. JAZ proteins are transcriptional repressors that inhibit the activity of key TFs of the JA pathway such as the basic helix-loop-helix (bHLH) TF MYC2 and its closest homologues MYC3, MYC4 and MYC5 (refs. [13,14,15]) in the absence of JA. The SCF^{COI1}-JAZ complex tightly controls the level of free non-repressed MYCs in a JA-dependent manner, thereby determining the transcriptional output of the entire JA response[8,9,16]. The key regulatory step in the JA pathway is the hormone-triggered formation of a complex between the E3 ligase SCF^{COI1} and JAZ repressors that are bound to the master regulatory TF MYC2. This results in the degradation of JAZ repressors and permits the activity of MYC2, accompanied by MYC3, MYC4, MYC5 and numerous other TFs, all of which have distinct but overlapping roles in driving JA-responsive gene expression[13,14,15,16,17,18,19,20]. The result is a cascade of JA-induced genome reprogramming to modulate plant behaviour such as plant immune responses[4,19,21]. However, our knowledge of the JA-responsive genome regulatory programme and, more broadly, in the general response of plants to environmental stimuli is currently limited by assessments of only one or a small number of components.

【参考译文2】茉莉酸(jasmonic acid，JA)是一种重要的植物激素，它调控包括繁殖、出苗、伤害反应和生长防御平衡等关键过程。植物对茉莉酸(盐)感知是由共受体CORONATINE INSENSITIVE1(COI1)和茉莉酸ZIM DOMAIN(JAZ)组成的复合体与茉莉单酰异亮氨酸(jasmonoyl-isoleucine)形式结合进行的[8,9,10,11]。COI1是一种F-box蛋白，是Skp-Cullin-F-box E3泛素连接酶复合物(SCF^{COI1})[12]的一部分，JA感知后SCF^{COI1}将靶蛋白JAZ进行蛋白酶体降解。在没有JA的情况下，JAZ蛋白是抑制JA

途径的关键转录因子(TF)——如碱性螺旋-环-螺旋(basic helix-loop-helix, bHLH)转录因子 MYC2 及其最近的同源蛋白 MYC3、MYC4 和 MYC5——活性的转录抑制因子(参考文献[13,14,15])。SCF^{COI1}-JAZ 复合体以 JA 依赖的方式严格控制游离的、未受到抑制的 MYCs 水平,从而决定整个 JA 反应的转录输出[8,9,16]。JA 途径中的关键调控步骤是在 E3 连接酶 SCF^{COI1} 和 JAZ 抑制因子之间结合形成一个复合体(该复合体与主调控因子 MYC2 结合),SCF^{COI1} 与 JAZ 结合导致 JAZ 抑制因子降解,从而允许 MYC2 发挥作用,并伴随 MYC3、MYC4、MYC5 和许多其他转录因子(所有这些转录因子都在驱动 JA 反应的基因表达中发挥明显但重叠的作用)发挥其功能[13,14,15,16,17,18,19,20]。其结果是 JA 诱导基因组重编程,以调控植物行为(如植物免疫反应)[4,19,21]。然而,我们对 JA 响应的基因组调控程序的了解,以及更广泛地说,我们对植物对环境刺激的一般响应的了解,目前仅限于对其中一种或少数成分的评估。

【原文 3】Here, we aimed to decipher the MYC2-MYC3-driven regulatory network using a multi-omics analysis that includes the direct targets of key TFs, chromatin modifications, global protein abundance and protein phosphorylation. Our analysis was conducted with etiolated seedlings, for which the JA regulatory network is poorly characterized even though MYC2 is active[21,22,23]. We discovered that MYC2 and MYC3 directly target hundreds of TFs, resulting in a large gene regulatory network that not only amplifies the transcriptional JA response but also facilitates extensive crosstalk with other signalling pathways. Furthermore, we found that MYC2 has a profound impact on the JA-dependent epigenome, proteome and phosphoproteome. We also generated a network model that predicted new components of the JA signalling pathway, which we validated by targeted genetic analyses, thus demonstrating the power of our integrated multi-omics approach to yield fundamental biological insight into plant hormone responses.

【参考译文 3】在本论文中,我们的目的是通过多组学手段对包括关键转录因子(TFs)调控的直接靶基因、染色质修饰、总蛋白质丰度和蛋白质磷酸化进行分析,来破译 MYC2-MYC3 驱动的调控网络。我们的分析是用黄化幼苗进行的,因为尽管黄化幼苗中 MYC2 有活性,但其 JA 调控网络尚未得到很好的鉴定[21,22,23]。我们发现 MYC2 和 MYC3 直接靶向作用于数百个 TFs,形成一个庞大的基因调控网络,这不仅放大了 JA 的转录反应,还促进了与其他信号转导通路的广泛串扰。此外,我们发现 MYC2 对依赖于 JA 的表观基因组、蛋白质组和磷酸蛋白质组有着深刻的影响。我们还建立了一个预测 JA 信号转导通路新成分的网络模型,并通过靶向遗传分析进行验证,从而证明我们的多组分整合手段有助于深入理解植物激素反应中的基础生物学。

说明:精读的第一步是消灭生词难句,了解专业知识背景。Cascade 这个词在生物医学中一般译为"级联"(something arranged or occurring in a series or in a succession of stages so that each stage derives from or acts upon the product of the preceding），尤指血液凝固过程中所发生的、连续的顺序激活反应，或者酶与激素的连续顺序激活反应。此处a cascade of（transcriptional reprogramming）相当于 a series of 或 a succession of，意思是"一系列连续的"。泛素化作用（ubiquitination）和蛋白酶体降解（proteasomal degradation）虽然在一般的分子生物学教科书中都有，但茉莉酸（JA）信号转导机制则需借助图片才易于理解。因此，可预先阅读下面这篇文章：Wasternack C, Hause B. Jasmonates: Biosynthesis, perception, signal transduction and action in plant stress response, growth and development. An update to the 2007 review in Annals of Botany. Ann Bot, 2013, 111: 1021-1058. 读者通过对 Wasternack 和 Hause（2013）综述文章中的茉莉酸（JA）信号感知诱导基因表达机制示意图（图 17-3）的分析，可帮助了解论文的引言内容。

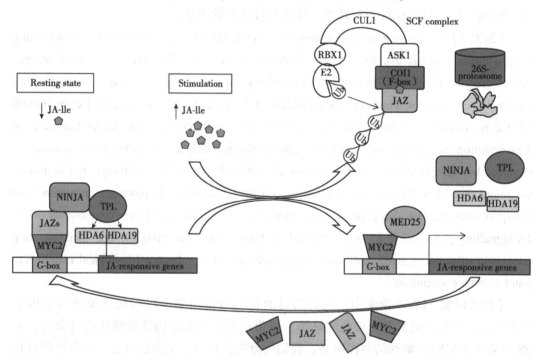

当 JA-Ile 水平较低时，基因表达处于静息状态（图左），这是由于 JAZs 蛋白与 MYC2 结合，使得 MYC2 与 JA 应答基因启动子内 G-box 结合，不能激活基因转录；共抑制蛋白 NINJA 与 JAZs 和 TPL 蛋白结合，通过 HDA6 和 HDA19 来阻遏转录。当 JA 刺激后，JA-Ile 水平较高时（图右），COI1 招募 JAZs 蛋白，启动泛素化作用，然后 JAZs 蛋白 26S 蛋白酶体降解。随后 MYC2 激活 JA 早期反应基因（如编码 JAZ 和 MYC2 的基因）的转录（由 MED25 介导）。

图 17-3 茉莉酸（JA）信号感知诱导基因表达机制示意图

精读的第二步是分析结构。引言为读者理解该文提供必要的背景信息，为研究工作提供理据。引言总体上应该是"倒三角形"或"漏斗形"结构，也就是说，首先应从宽到窄介绍所研究的问题及其重要性，简要回顾该问题先前的相关研究，指出当前研究的知识空白和不足，然后在结尾部分陈述本研究的具体目标，利用何种方法解决此问题，做了哪些工作，取得了什么结果，要重点突出论文的创新和发现。

这篇文章的引言是典型的、相对较短的三段式引言。第一段较宽泛地介绍一般的植物激素感知后引发一系列转录重编程，驱动基因表达改变，并最终改变细胞功能和植物行为。第二段缩窄到茉莉酸的情况。首先说明茉莉酸的重要作用，然后通过文献综述，介绍当前对茉莉酸（JA）信号感知诱导基因表达机制的了解，最后用"然而（However）"引出转折句，也就是识别出当前研究中的空白或不足——our knowledge of the JA-responsive genome regulatory programme and, more broadly, in the general response of plants to environmental stimuli is currently limited by assessments of only one or a small number of components（我们对JA反应的基因组调控程序的了解，以及更广泛地说，我们对植物对环境刺激的一般反应的了解，目前仅限于对其中一种或少数成分的评估）。第三段首先介绍所用的研究手段和研究目标，然后介绍论文的重要发现、创新成果以及核心结论。

精读的第三步是学习一些写作方面的知识。首先可以学习引言的这种最简单的"三段式结构"，对研究主题和研究进展的介绍简明扼要、富有层次感。征引参考文献的方式为"非作者突显式引用"，就是将参考文献序号标在所引述内容的句子后面，而不是突出作者（例如，张三做了什么，李四做了什么），这样使行文更简洁，也更有逻辑性。前两段叙述的内容为不受时间影响的普遍事实和研究结论，用一般现在时，最后一段介绍作者所做的工作，用一般过去时。第三段对论文的主要发现进行概括或预览，全部使用第一人称（we或our）和主动语态，但语言表达与摘要并不完全相同，是有所变化的。表达研究目的时，可用"we aimed to...using..."；表达所做的分析工作和所用的材料时，可用被动句"our analysis was conducted with..."；表达论文的发现或结果时，可用"we discovered that..."或"we found that..."或"we also generated a network model that..."。

（四）结果

【原文1】

Results

MYC2 and MYC3 target a large proportion of JA-responsive genes

To decipher the JA-governed regulatory network with its high degree of dynamic interconnectivity with other signalling pathways, we applied a multi-omics network approach that comprised five newly generated high-quality large-scale datasets (Fig. 1a, b; Extended Data Figs. 1a-i and 2a-d; Supplementary Tables 1 and 2). MYC2 is the master regulatory TF of JA responses, and plants with a null mutation of this TF have a clear decrease in JA sensitivity[15]. Thus, we included the *myc2* (*jin1-8* SALK_ 061267) mutant[15] in our analyses (Fig. 1b). MYC2 is responsible for strong JA-responsive gene activation and acts additively with MYC3 and MYC4(refs. [13,15,16,17,18,19,20]). *myc3* and *myc4* single mutants behave like wild-type (WT) plants with regards to JA-induced root growth inhibition. However, in combination with the *myc2* mutant, *myc2 myc3* double mutants exhibit an increased JA hyposensitivity, almost as pronounced as in *myc2 myc3 myc4* triple mutants[13]. We consequently selected MYC3 for an in-depth analysis. To better understand how the master TFs MYC2 and MYC3 control the JA-induced transcriptional cascade, we determined their genome-wide binding sites using chromatin immunoprecipitation (ChIP) with sequencing (ChIP-seq). Four biological replicates of JA-treated (2 h) 3-day-old etiolated *Arabidopsis* seedlings that express a native promoter-driven and epitope (YPet)-tagged version of MYC2 and three biological replicates of MYC3 (Col-0 *MYC2*::*MYC2-YPet*, Col-0 *MYC3*::*MYC3-YPet*) were used[24]. The rationale behind dissecting jasmonate signalling in etiolated seedlings is that although MYC2 is highly expressed in etiolated seedlings and regulates important processes such as photomorphogenesis and apical hook formation[21,22,23], a comprehensive characterization of this special developmental stage is still missing.

【参考译文1】

结果

MYC2 和 MYC3 靶向大部分 JA 应答基因

为了破译 JA 控制的调控网络及其与其他信号通路的高度动态互连，我们采用由 5 个新生成的高质量大规模数据集组成的多组学网络手段（图 1a，b；扩展数据图 1a-i 和 2a-d；补充表 1 和 2）。MYC2 是 JA 反应的主调控转录因子，该转录因子的无效突变（null mutation）植株 JA 敏感性明显降低[15]。因此，我们将 *myc2*（*jin1-8* SALK_061267）突变体[15]纳入我们的分析中（图 1b）。MYC2 对 JA 应答基因具有很强的激活起作用，其作用与 MYC3 和 MYC4 作用具有加性效应（参考文献[13,15,16,17,18,19,20]）。*myc3* 和 *myc4* 单突变体与野生型一样，JA 诱导可使根系生长受到抑制。然而，与 *myc2* 突变体组合的双突变体 *myc2 myc3* 表现 JA 低敏感性（hyposensitivity）有所增加，几乎与 *myc2 myc3 myc4* 三突变体一样明显[13]。因此，我们选择 MYC3 进行深入分析。为了更好地了解主转录因子 MYC2 和 MYC3 如何控制 JA 诱导的转录级联，我们使用染色质免疫沉淀（chromatin immunoprecipitation，ChIP）及测序（ChIP seq）鉴定它们的全基因组结合位点。取表达天然启动子驱动的、具有表位（YPet）标签版本的 MYC2 的 3 日龄黄化拟南芥实生苗，经 JA 处理（2 h）后的 4 个生物学重复和同样的 3 个 MYC3 生物学重复（Col-0 *MYC2*::*MYC2-YPet*, Col-0 *MYC3*::*MYC3-YPet*）[24]作为实验材料。在黄化幼苗中分析 JA 信号转导的理据是：尽管 MYC2 在黄化幼苗中高度表达，并调控诸如光形态发生和顶端钩形成[21,22,23]这样的重要过程，但尚未对这一特殊发育阶段进行过全面鉴定。

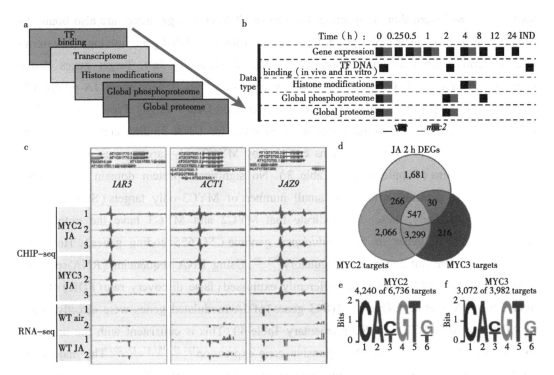

Fig. 1 | Design of our study and key datasets utilized. a, b, Overview of profiled regulatory layers (a) and detailed description of collected samples (b). IND, indefinite. **c,** AnnoJ genome browser screenshot visualizing the binding of MYC2 and MYC3 to three example genes: *IAR3* (also known as *JR3*), *ACT1* and *JAZ9* (also known as *TIFY7*). MYC2 and MYC3 binding was determined by ChIP-seq using JA-treated (2 h) Col-0 *MYC2∷MYC2-YPet* and Col-0 *MYC3∷MYC3-YPet* seedlings. Three independent biological ChIP-seq replicates are shown. In addition, mRNA expression of the three example genes and WT seedlings [with or without (that is, air) 2 h of JA treatment] is shown. Expression data were derived from RNA-seq analysis. **d,** Venn diagram illustrating the overlap between MYC2, MYC3 target genes and differentially expressed genes (DEGs) after 2 h of JA treatment (JA 2 h DEGs). **e, f,** The top-ranked motif in MYC2(e) and MYC3(f) ChIP-seq data was the G-box (CAC/TGTG) motif. Motifs were determined by MEME analysis using the top-ranked peaks that were identified using the GEM tool.

图1. 我们的研究设计和使用的关键数据集。**a，b，** 分析的调控层概观(a)和收集样品的详细说明(b)。IND，不确定时间。**c，** AnnoJ 基因组浏览器屏幕截图显示 MYC2 和 MYC3 与3个示例基因的结合：*IAR3*(也称为 *JR3*)、*ACT1* 和 *JAZ9*(也称为 *TIFY7*)。通过对 JA 处理(2 h)的 Col-0 *MYC2∷MYC2-YPet* 和 Col-0 *MYC3∷MYC3-YPet* 实生苗 ChIP 测序，来测定 MYC2 和 MYC3 结合。图中所示为3个独立的生物学 ChIP 测序重复。此外，还显示3个示例基因和野生型(WT)实生苗(用 JA 或不用 JA(用空气)处理 2 h)的 mRNA 表达。表达数据来自 RNA 测序分析。**d，** 维恩图显示 MYC2、MYC3 的靶基因和 JA 处理 2 h 后差异表达基因(DEGs)(JA 2 h DEGs)之间的重叠。**e，f，** 在 MYC2(e)和 MYC3(f) ChIP 测序数据中，顶级基序是 G-盒(CAC/TGTG)基序。利用 GEM 工具鉴定出的顶级峰的 MEME 分析来确定基序。

【原文2】We identified 6,736 MYC2 and 3,982 MYC3 high-confidence binding sites ($P \leq 1 \times 10^{-25}$ and conserved in at least two independent biological replicates), equating to 6,178 MYC2 and 4,092 MYC3 target genes (within 500 nucleotides of a binding site centre or nearest neighbouring gene) (Fig. 1c, d; Supplementary Table 1). Of the target genes identified, 3,847 were shared, meaning that almost all MYC3 target genes are also bound by MYC2(Fig. 1c, d). Their target genes were enriched for JA-related gene ontology(GO) terms and for terms related to other hormones (Extended Data Fig. 3a). Target genes shared between MYC2 and MYC3 were significantly enriched ($P<0.05$) for more JA-related GO terms than for target genes unique to either TF(Extended Data Fig. 3b). Proteins encoded by shared MYC2 and MYC3 target genes were enriched for DNA binding and transcriptional regulatory domains; in contrast, proteins encoded by MYC2-only target genes were enriched for kinase domains (Supplementary Table 3). No significant protein domain or GO term enrichment was detected among the small number of MYC3-only targets (Supplementary Table 3). Collectively, these data indicate that MYC2 and MYC3 have the potential to regulate 23.2% of genes in the *Arabidopsis* genome (27,655 coding genes). However, binding events are not necessarily regulatory[2,3,25]. Using RNA sequencing (RNA-seq), we determined that 2,522 genes were differently expressed (false discovery rate (FDR) <0.05) after 2 h of JA treatment. One-third(843 genes) of JA-modulated genes were directly bound by MYC2 or MYC3(Fig. 1d; Supplementary Table 4). This is consistent with the important role of MYC2 and MYC3 in JA-responsive gene expression[13,15,16,17,19,20]. The majority of JA-responsive genes that are directly targeted by MYC2 and MYC3 were transcriptionally upregulated after JA application, which indicates that MYC2 and MYC3 predominantly act as transcriptional activators(Extended Data Fig. 3c).

【参考译文 2】我们鉴定了 6736 个 MYC2 和 3982 个 MYC3 高保真（或高置信度, high-confidence）结合位点（$P \leqslant 1 \times 10^{-25}$，并且至少在两个独立的生物重复中保守），相当于 6178 个 MYC2 靶基因和 4092 个 MYC3 靶基因（靶基因指位于结合位点中心 500 个核苷酸内的基因或最近的相邻基因）（图 1c, d；补充表 1）。在所鉴定的靶基因中，共有 3847 个为 MYC2 和 MYC3 共同的靶基因，这意味着几乎所有的 MYC3 靶基因也都被 MYC2 所结合（图 1c, d）。它们的靶基因被富集为 JA 相关的基因属性分类（gene ontology, GO）类名（term）和其他激素相关类名（扩展数据图 3a）。MYC2 和 MYC3 之间共同的靶基因富集于与 JA 相关的 GO 类名显著（$P<0.05$）多于富集于各自独有的转录因子类名（扩展数据图 3b）。MYC2 和 MYC3 共同靶基因编码的蛋白质富集为 DNA 结合和转录调控域；相反，只是 MYC2 的靶基因编码的蛋白质富集为激酶域（补充表 3）。在少量只是 MYC3 的靶基因中未检测到显著的蛋白质结构域或 GO 类名富集（补充表 3）。总之，这些数据表明 MYC2 和 MYC3 有可能调控拟南芥基因组中 23.2% 的基因（27655 个编码基因）。然而，结合事件不一定具有调控功能[2,3,25]。采用 RNA 测序分析（RNA-seq）方法，检测到经 2 h JA 处理后 2522 个基因差异表达[假发现率（false discovery rate, FDR）<0.05]。JA 调控基因的 1/3（843 个基因）直接被 MYC2 或 MYC3 结合（图 1d；补充表 4）。这与 MYC2 和 MYC3 在 JA 应答基因表达中发挥重要功

能一致[13,15,16,17,19,20]。大多数被 MYC2 和 MYC3 直接靶向的 JA 应答基因在 JA 处理后转录上调，表明 MYC2 和 MYC3 主要作为转录激活因子发挥作用（扩展数据图 3c）。

【原文 3】The G-box(CA[C/T]GT[G/T])motif was the most common DNA sequence motif found at MYC2 or MYC3 binding sites, which is concordant with the observation that they shared a large proportion of their binding sites(Fig. 1e, f). This motif was also similar to a motif sequence bound by MYC2 that was determined in vitro[26]. The majority of MYC2 and MYC3 binding sites contained the G-box motif(4,240 out of 6,736 for MYC2, and 3,072 out of 3,982 for MYC3)(Fig. 1e, f; Supplementary Table 5). However, the absence of the motif from a substantial number of MYC2 and MYC3 binding sites suggests that the TFs may bind indirectly to some sites through a partner protein (or proteins). We identified putative partner TFs by determining DNA motifs enriched in MYC2 binding sites that did not contain a G-box motif. The most strongly enriched motifs were CACG[A/C]G[286 sites, statistical significance estimate of a motif(E)=2×10^{-52}], which may correspond to the TFs CAMTA1(also known as AT5G09410)or FAR1(also known as AT4G15090), and AT[A/T][A/T][A/T]ATA(714 sites, E=8.9×10^{-35}), which may correspond to the ARID family TFs AT2G17410 and AT1G04880 (Extended Data Fig. 3d, e). Molecular investigations of these TFs would be required to determine whether they bind cooperatively with MYC2 to DNA.

【参考译文 3】G-盒（CA[C/T]GT[G/T]）基序是在 MYC2 或 MYC3 结合位点发现的最常见的 DNA 序列基序，这与它们共有大部分结合位点的观察结果一致（图 1e, f）。G-盒基序也与体外测定的 MYC2 结合的基序序列相似[26]。大多数 MYC2 和 MYC3 结合位点（MYC2 的 6736 位点中有 4240 位点，MYC3 的 3982 位点中有 3072 位点）都含有 G-盒基序（图 1e, f；补充表 5）。然而，有相当一部分 MYC2 和 MYC3 结合位点不存在该基序，表明转录因子（TFs）可能通过一个或多个伙伴蛋白（partner protein）间接结合到某些位点。我们通过测定富集在 MYC2 结合位点（不含 G-盒基序）的 DNA 基序来鉴定可能的伙伴转录因子。富集最多的基序是 CACG[A/C]G[286 个位点，基序的统计显著性估计（E）=2×10^{-52}]，该基序对应于转录因子 CAMTA1（也称为 AT5G09410）或 FAR1（也称为 AT4G15090），以及[A/T][A/T][A/T]ATA（714 个位点，E=8.9×10^{-35}），该基序对应于 ARID 家族转录因子 AT2G17410 和 AT1G04880（扩展数据图 3d, e）。需要对这些转录因子进行分子研究，以确定它们是否与 MYC2 协同结合到 DNA 上。

【原文 4】Master TFs directly target the majority of signalling components in their respective pathway, a phenomenon that has already been observed for the ethylene, abscisic acid(ABA)and cytokinin signalling pathways[2,3,27]. This pattern also holds true for the JA signalling pathway. Our MYC2 and MYC3 ChIP-seq analyses determined that approximately two-thirds of the genes encoding for known JA pathway components(112 out of 168 genes for MYC2, and 96 out of 168 genes for MYC3) were bound by MYC2 and MYC3 (Extended Data Fig. 4a, b; Supplementary Table 6). Interestingly, the majority of all known JA genes that were differentially expressed following JA treatment were bound by MYC2 or MYC3, whereas fewer non-differentially expressed known JA genes were directly targeted (Extended Data Fig. 4b; Supplementary Table 6). MYCs initiate various feedforward loops that enable rapid activation of the transcriptional JA response[19,28]. Our ChIP-seq approach revealed that beyond the autoregulation of MYC2 and MYC3, these TFs also regulate JA biosynthesis either directly by targeting the JA biosynthesis genes *LOX2*, *LOX3*, *LOX4*, *LOX6* and *AOS* or indirectly through binding to the AP2-ERF TF gene *ORA47* (Supplementary Tables 1 and 6). In addition, MYCs simultaneously target various negative regulators, enabling MYCs to efficiently dampen the JA response pattern (Extended Data Fig. 4c). Key negative regulators of JA signalling are the JAZ repressors, a gene family of 13 members in *Arabidopsis*[29], which can interact with the adaptor protein NINJA to confer TOPLESS-mediated gene repression[30]. Strikingly, all JAZ members and NINJA are directly bound by MYC2 and MYC3 (Extended Data Fig. 4c), which probably leads to a dampening of the JA response and thereby preventing excessive activation of JA signalling.

【参考译文4】植物激素信号转导通路中的主转录因子直接靶向其通路中的大多数信号转导成分，这一现象已经在乙烯（ethylene）、脱落酸（abscisic acid，ABA）和细胞分裂素（cytokinin）信号转导通路中观察到[2,3,27]。这种模式也适用于 JA 信号转导通路。我们对 MYC2 和 MYC3 的 ChIP 测序分析确定，编码已知 JA 信号转导通路成分的基因中，约 2/3 与 MYC2 和 MYC3 结合（168 个基因中与 MYC2 结合的有 112 个，与 MYC3 结合的基因中有 96 个）（扩展数据图 4a，b；补充表 6）。有意思的是，JA 处理后差异表达的所有已知 JA 基因中的绝大多数被 MYC2 或 MYC3 结合，而非差异表达的已知 JA 基因较少被 MYC2 或 MYC3 直接靶向结合（扩展数据图 4b；补充表 6）。MYCs 启动各种前馈回路（feedforward loop），使转录水平上的 JA 响应快速激活[19,28]。我们的 ChIP 测序方法揭示，除 MYC2 和 MYC3 的自我调控外，这些转录因子还通过直接靶向结合 JA 生物合成基因 *LOX2*、*LOX3*、*LOX4*、*LOX6* 和 *AOS* 或通过与 AP2-ERF 转录因子基因 *ORA47* 间接结合来调控 JA 生物合成（补充表 1 和表 6）。此外，MYCs 同时靶向各种负调控因子，使 MYCs 能够有效地抑制 JA 响应模式（扩展数据图 4c）。JA 信号转导的关键负调控因子是 JAZ 抑制因子，拟南芥 JAZ 基因家族有 13 个成员[29]，能与适配体（adaptor）蛋白 NINJA 互作，产生 TOPLESS 介导的基因抑制[30]。值得注意的是，MYC2 和 MYC3 能与所有 JAZ 成员和 NINJA 直接接合（扩展数据图 4c），这可能会导致 JA 响应减弱，从而防止 JA 信号转导过度激活。

【原文5】**MYC2 and MYC3 activate the JA response through a large TF network**

To study the MYC2 and MYC3-governed transcriptional regulatory network in more detail, we investigated the relationship between MYC2-bound and MYC3-bound TF-encoding genes and their transcriptional responsiveness to JA treatment. We conducted a JA time-course experiment(time points of 0, 0.25, 0.5, 1, 2, 4, 8, 12 and 24 h post JA treatment) and identified a total of 7,377 differentially expressed genes at one or more time points within 24 h of JA treatment(Supplementary Table 4). Differentially expressed genes were categorized into clusters with similar expression trends over time to facilitate the visualization of complex expression dynamics and enriched functional annotations (Extended Data Fig. 5a; Supplementary Table 7). The largest upregulated cluster was the "JA cluster", which was enriched for GO terms associated with JA responses (Fig. 2a). In contrast, the "Cell wall cluster" was the largest cluster of downregulated genes and enriched for GO terms associated with cell wall organization, development and differentiation (Fig. 2b). These two main clusters illustrate the defence-growth trade-off when defence pathways are activated[31].

【参考译文5】MYC2 和 MYC3 通过一个大型转录因子网络激活 JA 响应

为了更详细地研究 MYC2 和 MYC3 控制的转录调控网络，我们研究了 MYC2 和 MYC3 结合的转录因子编码基因及其对 JA 处理的转录响应性之间的关系。我们进行了 JA 时间效应实验（JA 处理后 0、0.25、0.5、1、2、4、8、12 和 24 h 的时间点），在 JA 处理后 24 h 内的一个或多个时间点共鉴定了 7377 个差异表达基因（补充表 4）。随着时间的推移，差异表达基因被分类为具有相似表达趋势的簇，以便于对复杂的表达动态变化和富集功能注释进行可视化呈现（扩展数据图 5a；补充表 7）。最大上调的簇是"JA 簇"，它富集与 JA 应答相关的 GO 类名（图 2a）。相反，最大的下调的簇是"细胞壁簇"，富集与细胞壁组织、发育和分化相关的 GO 类名（图 2b）。这两个主簇显示当防御通路激活时的防御-生长协调[31]。

【原文6】Our MYC2 and MYC3 ChIP-seq dataset derived from a 2-h-long JA treatment revealed that up to 63% (0.5 h JA treatment) of differentially expressed genes at any given time point were potentially directly bound by MYC2 and/or MYC3 (Fig. 2c), which highlights the important role of MYCs in transcriptionally regulating JA responses. Our analysis also determined that 522 out of 1,717 known or predicted TFs were differentially expressed within 24 h of JA treatment (Extended Data Fig. 5b). Half of these (268), representing 36 out of 58 TF families, were also direct MYC2 or MYC3 targets (Fig. 2d; Extended Data Fig. 5b), which indicates that MYC2 and MYC3 cooperatively control a massive TF network. The three most numerous families (ERFs, bHLHs and MYBs) in the *Arabidopsis* genome had the most JA-responsive members targeting MYC2 or MYC3, which is concordant with their previously annotated roles in JA responses[32] (Fig. 2d). Plant hormone crosstalk is critical for deploying an appropriate cellular response to environmental stimuli, and numerous reports describe that MYC2 connects the JA pathway to other major plant

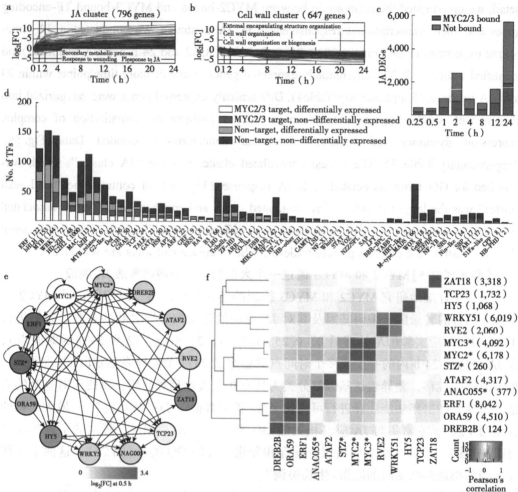

Fig. 2 | MYC2 and MYC3 target a large proportion of JA-responsive genes that encode TFs. a, b, A cluster analysis revealed two main clusters in the JA time-course experiment. The JA cluster (**a**), with 796 genes, reflects the majority of JA-induced genes and the cell wall cluster (**b**), with 647 genes, represents the largest cluster of JA-repressed genes. Clusters visualize the log2 fold-change (log2[FC]) expression dynamics over the indicated 24-h time period. The three strongest enriched GO terms for each cluster are also shown. Clusters were identified by STEM clustering (Pearson's correlation, minimum correlation of 0.7, and up to 50 permutations; significant clusters were Bonferroni-corrected at $P< 0.05$). For each of the indicated time points, the expression of three independent samples ($n=3$) was measured using RNA-seq. **c,** Bar plots illustrating the potential of MYC2 and/or MYC3 (MYC2/3) to bind to a portion of JA DEGs at the indicated time points. JA DEGs for all time points were identified by RNA-seq. MYC2 and MYC3 targets were derived from ChIP-seq analysis using Col-0 *MYC2*::*MYC2-YPet* and Col-0 *MYC3*::*MYC3-YPet* seedlings that were treated for 2 h with JA. **d,** MYC2 and MYC3 target genes from a wide range of TF families. TF families are classified into the following four different groups: MYC2 and MYC3 targets and differentially expressed after JA treatment; MYC2 and MYC3 targets and not differentially expressed; not bound by MYC2 or MYC3 but differentially expressed; and not bound by MYC2 or MYC3 but not differentially expressed. **e,** Nodes represent JA TFs for which direct binding data were generated. ChIP-seq data are indicated by asterisks; all other data are DAP-seq. Edges represent binding events and are directed. Self-loops indicate that the TF binds to its own locus, which is indicative of potential autoregulation. Expression of the TF at 0.5 h after JA treatment is represented by the coloured scale. **f,** Pearson's correlation of TF target sets of genes. Numerals in parentheses indicate the total number of target genes. ChIP-seq data are indicated by asterisks, all other data were generated by DAP-seq. ChIP-seq data were derived from at least three independent experiments: MYC2(JA, $n=4$), MYC3(JA, $n=3$), STZ(air, $n=3$; JA, $n=2$), ANAC055(JA, $n=3$). DAP-seq data were derived from a single experiment($n=1$).

图 2. MYC2 和 MYC3 靶基因大部分是编码 TFs 的 JA 应答基因。**a, b,** 在 JA 时间效应实验中，聚类分析(cluster analysis)揭示两个主要的簇。JA 基因簇(**a**)包含 796 个基因，大多数为 JA 诱导的基因，而细胞壁簇(**b**)包含 647 个基因，为 JA 所抑制的基因的最大簇。簇可视化呈现在所示的 24 小时时间段内 log2 倍数变化(log2[FC])的表达动力学。还显示每个簇的 3 个富集最强的 GO 类名。用 STEM 聚类法(Pearson 相关，最小相关为 0.7，最多 50 次置换，显著性簇经 Bonferroni 校正，$P<0.05$)。对于每个所示的时间点，使用 RNA 测序测定 3 个独立样本($n=3$)的表达。**c,** 条形图说明 MYC2 和/或 MYC3(MYC2/3)在所示时间点结合到一部分 JA DEGs 的能力。用 RNA 测序鉴定所有时间点的 JA-DEGs。用 JA 处理 2 h 的 Col-0 *MYC2*∷*MYC2-YPet* 和 Col-0 *MYC3*∷*MYC3-YPet* 实生苗 ChIP 测序来分析 MYC2 和 MYC3 靶基因。**d,** MYC2 和 MYC3 靶基因来自各种 TF 家族。TF 家族分为以下 4 个不同的组：MYC2 和 MYC3 靶基因并且经 JA 处理后差异表达；MYC2 和 MYC3 靶基因但不差异表达；不被 MYC2 或 MYC3 结合但差异表达；不被 MYC2 或 MYC3 结合也不差异表达。**e,** 节点表示为直接结合数据产生的 JA TFs. ChIP 测序数据用星号表示；其他数据都是 DAP 测序数据。边线表示结合事件与结合取向。自环(self-loop)表示 TF 与自身的位点结合，这可能表示自我调控。JA 处理 0.5 h 后的 TF 表达水平用色阶表示。**f,** TF 靶基因集的 Pearson 相关。括号中的数字表示靶基因的总数。ChIP 测序数据用星号表示，其他数据都由 DAP 测序产生。ChIP 测序数据来自至少 3 个独立实验：MYC2(JA, $n=4$), MYC3(JA, $n=3$), STZ(空气, $n=3$; JA, $n=2$), ANAC055(JA, $n=3$). DAP 测序数据来自单个实验($n=1$).

hormone pathways[23,33]. To investigate this crosstalk function of MYC2 and MYC3 in more detail, we utilized our ChIP-seq data to determine the number of plant hormone TFs that are bound by MYC2 and MYC3. We found that 37%-59% of annotated hormone pathway genes are bound by MYC2 and MYC3 and that their expression changes in response to 24 h of JA treatment(Extended Data Fig. 5c). In addition, we discovered 122 annotated hormone TFs, with representatives from all hormone pathways, that are bound by MYC2 and MYC3, and 118 of these were differentially expressed(Extended Data Fig. 5d; Supplementary Table 1).

【参考译文 6】我们对 MYC2 和 MYC3 的 ChIP 测序数据集是由 JA 处理 2 h 后获得的，数据显示在任何给定时间点，高达 63%(0.5 h JA 处理)的差异表达基因可能被 MYC2 和/或 MYC3 直接结合(图 2c)，这突显了 MYCs 在转录水平上调控 JA 响应中的重要作用。我们的分析还显示，在 1717 个已知或预测为转录因子(TFs)的基因中，522 个基因在 JA 处理后 24 h 内差异表达(扩展数据图 5b)。其中一半(268 个基因)——代表 58 个转录因子家族中的 36 个——是 MYC2 或 MYC3 的直接靶基因(图 2d; 扩展数据图 5b)，这表明 MYC2 和 MYC3 协同控制着一个巨大的转录因子网络。拟南芥基因组中数量最多的 3 个转录因子家族(ERFs、bHLHs 和 MYBs)中拥有最多的靶向 MYC2 或 MYC3 的 JA 应答成员，这与它们之前在 JA 响应中的注释功能一致[32]

（图2d）。植物激素串扰对于植物对环境刺激调动适当的细胞响应至关重要，许多报告描述MYC2将JA信号转导通路连接到其他主要植物激素信号转导通路上[23,33]。为了更详细地研究MYC2和MYC3的这种串扰功能，利用我们的ChIP测序数据来确定MYC2和MYC3结合的植物激素转录因子（TFs）的数量。我们发现，注释为激素通路基因的37%~59%被MYC2和MYC3结合，并且它们的表达在JA处理24 h后发生改变（扩展数据图5c）。此外，我们还发现122个注释为激素的转录因子（代表来自所有的激素通路）被MYC2和MYC3结合，其中118个差异表达（扩展数据图5d；补充表1）。

【原文7】We next set out to better understand the target genes of the network of TFs downstream of MYC2 and MYC3. To do so we conducted ChIP-seq or DNA affinity purification (DAP) with sequencing (DAP-seq) on a subset of TFs [(DREB2B (also known as AT3G11020), ATAF2, HY5 (also known as AT5G11260), RVE2 (also known as AT5G37260) and ZAT18 (also known as AT3G53600)] that were direct MYC2 or MYC3 targets and rapidly upregulated (within 0.5 h) by JA treatment (Fig. 2e) or were members of the upregulated "JA cluster" (TCP23 (also known as AT1G35560) (Fig. 2a). We also included the following TFs with known roles in JA signalling: ERF1 (also known as AT3G23240, ERF1B and AtERF092); ORA59 (also known as AT1G06160); ANAC055 (also known as NAC3); WRKY51 (also known as AT5G64810); and STZ (also known as ZAT10)[34,35,36,37,38]. These TFs formed a highly connected network, with all TFs except DREB2B targeting at least two TFs in the network and these two in turn targeted by two TFs (Fig. 2e; Supplementary Table 8). Autoregulation was common, with seven TFs targeting their own loci (Fig. 2e). The target genes of STZ, ANAC055 and ATAF2 were most similar to those of MYC2 and MYC3 (Fig. 2f). Consistent with this, their target genes shared several significantly enriched GO terms (adjusted $P<0.05$), which suggests that there are related functions in jasmonate signalling (Extended Data Fig. 6a). ORA59 and ERF1, along with DREB2B, formed a distinct group that targeted a related set of genes (Extended Data Fig. 6a). Notably, ERF1 and ORA59 also shared significant enrichment of a separate set of GO terms with one another, but these were not enriched among MYC2 and MYC3 targets (Extended Data Fig. 6a). This is consistent with the joint role of ERF1 and ORA59 in controlling a pathogen defence arm of JA signalling[34,35]. No GO terms were enriched among the targets of DREB2B. WRKY51 and RVE2 had relatively few enriched GO terms but shared most of these with one another (Extended Data Fig. 6a). Most of the terms related to anti-insect defence and were a subset of the enriched MYC2 and MCY3-STZ-ANAC055-ATAF2 GO terms (Extended Data Fig. 6a). STZ and ANAC055 are known regulators of anti-insect defence and our results suggest that WRKY51 and RVE2 may also be involved in this component of jasmonate responses[39]. Interestingly, *STZ* belongs to a group of genes that is inducible by the JA precursor 12-oxo-phytodienoic acid (OPDA) and not by JA[40]. We found that approximately one-third of OPDA-specific response genes (45 genes) are targeted by MYC2 (Supplementary Table 3). Taken together, our analyses determine that MYC2 and MYC3 shape the dynamic JA response through the activation of a large TF network that includes various potentially coupled feedforward and feedback loops and allows extensive cross-communication with other signalling pathways.

【参考译文 7】 接下来我们进一步分析 MYC2 和 MYC3 下游转录因子(TFs)网络的靶基因。为此，我们对包括 DREB2B(也称为 AT3G11020)、ATAF2、HY5(也称为 AT5G11260)、RVE2(也称为 AT5G37260)和 ZAT18(也称为 AT3G53600)的一组转录因子进行 ChIP 测序或 DNA 亲和纯化(DNA affinity purification, DAP)测序(DAP-seq)，这组转录因子是 MYC2 或 MYC3 的直接靶基因，并且经 JA 处理后(在 0.5 h 内)迅速上调(图 2e)或者是上调的"JA 簇"成员(TCP23，也称为 AT1G35560)(图 2a)。此外，我们还对 JA 信号转导中功能已知的转录因子进行了 ChIP 测序或 DAP 测序：ERF1(也称为 AT3G23240、ERF1B 和 AtERF092)、ORA59(也称为 AT1G06160)、ANAC055(也称为 NAC3)、WRKY51(也称为 AT5G64810)和 STZ(也称为 ZAT10)[34,35,36,37,38]。这些转录因子(但不包括 DREB2B)在网络中至少有两个转录因子作为靶基因，而这两个转录因子又依次是另外两个转录因子的靶基因，这样就形成一个高度连接的网络(图 2e；补充表 8)。这些转录因子自我调控也很常见，有 7 个转录因子靶向它们自身位点(图 2e)。STZ、ANAC055 和 ATAF2 的靶基因与 MYC2 和 MYC3 的靶基因最相似(图 2f)。与此一致的是，它们的靶基因共同拥有几个显著富集的 GO 类名(根据 $P<0.05$ 加以调整)，这表明 JA 信号转导有相关的功能(扩展数据图 6a)。ORA59 和 ERF1 与 DREB2B 一起形成独特的一组，它靶向结合相关的一组基因(扩展数据图 6a)。值得注意的是，ERF1 和 ORA59 还彼此共同拥有显著富集的一组单独的 GO 类名，但这些 GO 类名并不是 MYC2 和 MYC3 靶基因富集的类名(扩展数据图 6a)。这与 ERF1 和 ORA59 在控制 JA 信号转导在病原体防御方面的联合作用[34,35]一致。DREB2B 靶基因并没有富集 GO 类名。WRKY51 和 RVE2 的靶基因富集的 GO 类名相对较少，但它们彼此共同拥有大部分的 GO 类名(扩展数据图 6a)。大多数这部分 GO 类名与抗虫防御有关，是一组富集于 MYC2 和 MCY3-STZ-ANAC055-ATAF2 的 GO 类名(扩展数据图 6a)。STZ 和 ANAC055 是已知的抗虫防御调控因子，我们的结果表明 WRKY51 和 RVE2 也可能涉及 JA 响应的这一组分[39]。有意思的是，STZ 属于一组由 JA 前体 12-氧-植物二烯酸(12-oxo-phytodienoic acid, OPDA)而非 JA 诱导的基因[40]。我们发现约 1/3 的 OPDA 特异性应答基因(45 个基因)被 MYC2 靶向结合(补充表 3)。综上所述，我们的分析确定，大型转录因子网络包含各种潜在耦合的前馈和反馈回路，并容许与其他信号转导通路进行广泛的交叉通讯，而 MYC2 和 MYC3 通过激活这个大型转录因子网络来形成动态的 JA 响应。

【原文8】We examined the effect of removing MYC2 activity on JA-responsive transcriptional regulation by generating transcriptomes from a *myc2* null mutant(*jin1-8*)in an early JA response time-series experiment(0, 0.5, 1 and 4 h). The response of *myc2* mutants to JA differed from that of WT plants. There were 2,905 unique genes differentially expressed between *myc2* and WT plants across the time-series(pairwise comparisons between genotypes at each time point; Supplementary Table 9). JA-responsive gene expression occurred in *myc2* plants, which is consistent with the partially redundant function of MYC2, MYC3 and MYC4(ref.[13]). However, JA-responsive genes were upregulated more highly in WT than *myc2* plants(Supplementary Table 9). The *JAZ* genes illustrate this, with 9 out of the 12 genes upregulated more highly in WT than *myc2* plants, as well as reaching peak expression at earlier time points in WT plants(0.5 or 1 h; (Extended Data Fig. 7a). Overall, a majority of the MYC2 target genes differentially expressed between *myc2* and WT plants were more highly expressed in WT, which indicates that loss of MYC2 function reduces the JA responsiveness of these genes(Extended Data Fig. 7b). A total of 130 TFs targeted by MYC2 were differentially expressed in *myc2* mutants compared with WT seedlings, including the TFs ATAF2, ERF1, ANAC055 and STZ, whose targets we had determined by DAP-seq or ChIP-seq(Supplementary Table 10). The *myc2* mutation also affected the expression of secondary, indirect MYC2 target genes(that is, genes targeted by MYC2-regulated TFs, but not by MYC2 itself). Between 23.6% and 26.3% of the genes each targeted by ATAF2, ERF1, ANAC055 or STZ, and not by MYC2, were differentially expressed in *myc2* plants compared with WT(Extended Data Fig. 7c; Supplementary Table 11). Taken together, these data demonstrate that MYC2 regulates gene expression through a large network of downstream TFs during responses to a JA stimulus.

【参考译文8】我们通过*myc2*无效突变体(*jin1-8*)在JA响应时间效应实验早期时间点(0、0.5、1和4h)产生的转录组数据来研究去除MYC2活性对JA响应转录调控的影响。*myc2*突变体对JA的响应与野生型(WT)植株不同。在整个时间序列中，*myc2*和WT植株之间有2905个单一基因差异表达(每个时间点基因型之间成对比较；补充表9)。JA应答基因在*myc2*植株中表达，这与MYC2、MYC3和MYC4的部分功能冗余一致(参考文献[13])。然而，与*myc2*植株相比，野生型植株中JA应答基因上调更高(补充表9)。JAZ基因说明了这一点，12个基因中有9个在WT中的上调幅度高于*myc2*植株，并且在WT植株的早期表达时间点(0.5或1h)达到高峰(扩展数据图7a)。总体而言，*myc2*和WT植株间差异表达的MYC2靶基因大部分在WT中表达更高，这表明MYC2功能的丧失降低了这些基因的JA响应性(扩展数据图7b)。与WT实生苗相比，MYC2靶向结合的130个转录因子(TFs)在*myc2*突变体中差异表达，包括转录因子ATAF2、ERF1、ANAC055和STZ(我们通过DAP测序或ChIP测序确定了它们的靶基因，补充表 10）。*myc2* 突变也影响次级靶基因，也就是 MYC2 的间接靶基因（即 MYC2 调控的转录因子的靶基因，而不是 MYC2 本身的靶基因）的表达。与 WT 相比，ATAF2、ERF1、ANAC055 或 STZ 的靶基因（而非 MYC2 的靶基因）在 *myc2* 植株中的差异表达率在 23.6%~26.3%（扩展数据图 7c；补充表 11）。综上所述，这些数据表明 MYC2 在 JA 刺激响应中通过下游转录因子大型网络调控基因表达。

【原文 9】MYC2 controls JA-induced epigenomic reprogramming

Reprogramming of the epigenome is an integral part of development and environmental stimulus-induced gene expression[41]. For example, activation of the transcriptional JA response requires the formation of MYC2-MED25-mediated chromatin looping[42]. To investigate the extent of JA-induced changes in chromatin architecture and the regulatory importance of MYC2 in this response, we conducted ChIP-seq assays to profile the genome-wide occupancy of the histone modification H3K4me3 (trimethylation of lysine 4 on histone H3) and the histone variant H2A.Z in untreated and in JA-treated (4 h) WT and *myc2* seedlings. H3K4me3 marks active and poised genes whereas the histone variant H2A.Z confers gene responsiveness to environmental stimuli[43, 44]. mRNA expression was monitored in parallel using RNA-seq. JA treatment led to a reprogrammed chromatin landscape, with several thousand differentially enriched H3K4me3 and H2A.Z domains (Extended Data Fig. 8a-c; Supplementary Table 12). We identified 826 differentially expressed genes (675 induced, 151 repressed; WT control versus JA treated) in that experiment. In line with the predominantly activating function of MYC2 (Extended Data Fig. 3c), the JA-induced genes had a stronger promoter enrichment of MYC2 than the JA-repressed genes (Fig. 3a). H3K4me3 levels were increased in JA-induced genes, whereas JA-repressed genes did not exhibit any dynamic change in H3K4me3 levels (Fig. 3b, d). Strikingly, *myc2* mutants only displayed a compromised increase in H3K4me3 levels after JA treatment, which suggests that the JA-induced H3K4me3 depends on functional MYC2 (Fig. 3b-d; Extended Data Fig. 8a). The impact of the *myc2* mutation on JA-induced H3K4me3 changes was also observed in JA-induced genes that are not directly targeted by MYC2 (Extended Data Fig. 8e, f), which is potentially caused by the decreased expression of MYC2-targeted TFs. The scenario of a direct MYC2 regulation network is illustrated by two JA-induced genes, *JAZ2* and *GRX480*, which are directly targeted by MYC2. Their expression depends on MYC2, and their JA-induced increase in gene-body-localized H3K4me3 partially depended on MYC2 (Fig. 3d; Extended Data Fig. 8d). However, whether the MYC2-dependent changes in H3K4me3 levels precede transcription or rather reflect increased transcriptional activity cannot be addressed by these experiments. In contrast, JA-induced changes in H2A.Z occupancy were only slightly affected in *myc2* mutants (Extended Data Fig. 8a, g, h), which suggests that JA-induced H2A.Z dynamics are either independent of MYC2 or precede MYC2 binding. Alternatively, other MYCs such as MYC3, MYC4 and MYC5 are functionally redundant in regulating H2A.Z dynamics.

【参考译文9】MYC2 控制 JA 诱导的表观基因组重编程

表观基因组(epigenome)的重编程是发育和环境刺激诱导的基因表达的一个组成部分[41]。例如，激活转录(水平上)的 JA 响应需要 MYC2-MED25 介导的染色质环形成[42]。为了研究 JA 诱导的染色质架构(chromatin architecture)变化的范围以及 MYC2 在这种响应中的调控重要性，我们进行了 ChIP 测序分析，以确定组蛋白修饰 H3K4me3(组蛋白 H3 上赖氨酸 4 的三甲基化)和组蛋白变体 H2A.Z 在经 JA 处理(4 h)和未经 JA 处理的野生型(WT)和 myc2 实生苗中的全基因组占有率。H3K4me3 标记活跃的和准备表达的基因，而组蛋白变体 H2A.Z 则赋予基因对环境刺激的响应性[43,44]。用 RNA 测序同步监测 mRNA 的表达。JA 处理导致染色质格局(chromatin landscape)重编程，有数千个差异富集的 H3K4me3 和 H2A.Z 结构域(扩展数据图 8a-c；补充表 12)。在该实验中，我们鉴定出 826 个差异表达基因(675 个诱导基因，151 个抑制基因；WT 对照与 JA 处理相比)。与 MYC2 发挥主要激活功能(扩展数据图 3c)一致的是，JA 诱导的基因比 JA 抑制的基因具有更强的 MYC2 启动子富集(图 3a)。JA 诱导基因中 H3K4me3 水平增加，而 JA 抑制的基因中 H3K4me3 水平没有任何动态变化(图 3b, d)。值得注意的是，经 JA 处理后，myc2 突变体仅显示 H3K4me3 水平微弱增加，这表明 JA 诱导的 H3K4me3 增加依赖于有功能的 MYC2(图 3b-d；扩展数据图 8a)。在 JA 诱导但未被 MYC2 直接靶向结合的基因(扩展数据图 8e, f)中也观察到 myc2 突变对 JA 诱导的 H3K4me3 变化的影响，这可能是由 MYC2 靶向结合的转录因子(TFs)表达减少引起的。两个 JA 诱导的基因 JAZ2 和 GRX480(都是 MYC2 直接靶基因)说明 MYC2 直接调控网络的情况。它们的表达依赖于 MYC2，它们的 JA 诱导的基因本体(gene-body)定位的 H3K4me3 增加部分依赖于 MYC2(图 3d；扩展数据图 8d)。然而，这些实验不能解决 H3K4me3 水平依赖于 MYC2 的变化是否先于转录或者只是反映转录活性的增加。相比之下，JA 诱导的 H2A.Z 占有率变化仅在 myc2 突变体中受到微弱的影响(扩展数据图 8a, g, h)，这表明 JA 诱导的 H2A.Z 动态变化要么独立于 MYC2，要么先于 MYC2 结合。或者，其他 MYCs 如 MYC3、MYC4 和 MYC5 在调控 H2A.Z 动态变化方面是功能冗余的。

【原文10】JA extensively remodels the (phospho) proteome

We next explored how JA remodels the proteome and phosphoproteome of etiolated seedlings. Hormone signal transduction typically modifies the phosphorylation of downstream proteins, changing their activity independent of transcript abundance[6]. Transcript abundance is also frequently weakly correlated with protein abundance[45,46]. Consequently, proteomic and

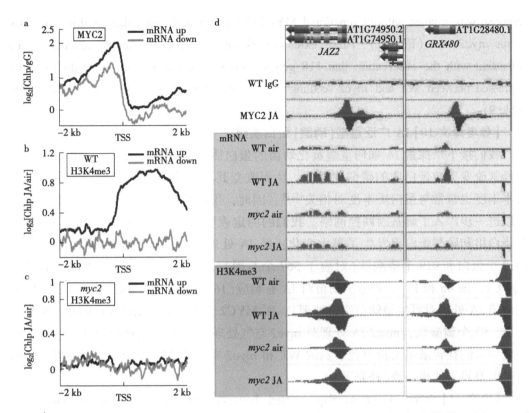

Fig. 3 | The JA-responsive epigenome. a-c, Aggregated profiles showing the log2 [FC] enrichment of MYC2(**a**), H3K4me3 WT(**b**) and H3K4me3 *myc2* (**c**) from 2-kb upstream to 2-kb downstream of the transcriptional start site(TSS) at JA-induced and JA-repressed genes. The profile of MYC2 is shown for Col-0 *MYC2*::*MYC2-YPet* seedlings(**a**) and H3K4me3 profiles are shown are shown for WT(**b**) and *myc2* (**c**) seedlings. **d,** AnnoJ genome browser screenshot visualizing MYC2 binding, mRNA expression and H3K4me3 occupancy at two example genes (*JAZ2* and *GRX480*) in WT and *myc2* seedlings. All tracks were normalized to the respective sequencing depth.

图3. **JA 响应的表观基因组**。**a-c,** 汇总分析(Aggregated profiles)显示 MYC2(**a**)、H3K4me3 WT(**b**) 和 H3K4me3 *myc2*(**c**)从 JA 诱导基因和 JA 抑制基因的转录起始位点(transcriptional start site, TSS) 上游的 2-kb 到下游的 2-kb 的 log2 [FC] 富集。MYC2 分析为 Col-0 *MYC2*::*MYC2-YPet* 实生苗 (**a**), H3K4me3 分析为 WT(**b**) 和 *myc2*(**c**) 实生苗。**d,** AnnoJ 基因组浏览器截图显示 WT 和 *myc2* 实生苗中两个示例基因(*JAZ2* 和 *GRX480*)的 MYC2 结合、mRNA 表达和 H3K4me3 占有率。所有的监测数据都根据各样本的测序深度进行标准化。

phosphoproteomic analyses yield additional insight into gene regulatory networks. We determined that the loss of MYC2 caused substantial changes to the JA-responsive proteome and phosphoproteome; 1,432 proteins and 939 phosphopeptides (corresponding to 567 genes) were significantly differentially abundant in WT seedlings relative to *myc2* seedlings after 2 h of JA treatment ($q < 0.1$; Fig. 4a; Supplementary Tables 13 and 14). WT seedlings responded to JA (161 proteins, 443 phosphopeptides, WT JA versus WT air), and the response was smaller without functional MYC2 (79 proteins, 93 phosphopeptides, myc2 JA versus myc2 air) (Fig. 4a). These extensive changes in phosphopeptide abundance are consistent with the observation that 118 genes encoding protein kinases were differentially expressed between WT and myc2 seedlings in our transcriptome experiments (Supplementary Table 9).

【参考译文10】JA 广泛重塑（磷酸）蛋白质组

我们接下来探索 JA 如何重塑黄化幼苗的蛋白质组和磷酸蛋白质组。激素信号转导经常改变下游蛋白质的磷酸化状态，从而改变其不依赖于转录本丰度的活性[6]。转录本丰度也常常与蛋白质丰度弱相关[45,46]。因此，蛋白质组学和磷酸蛋白质组学分析可以进一步深入了解基因调控网络。我们的测定表明，MYC2 功能丧失导致 JA 响应的蛋白组和磷酸蛋白组发生了重大变化；经 JA 处理 2 h 后，野生型（WT）幼苗中有1432 个蛋白和 939 个磷酸肽（对应于 567 个基因），与 myc2 幼苗相比丰度差异显著（$q<0.1$；图 4a 和 14）。野生型幼苗对 JA 有响应（161 个蛋白质，443 个磷酸肽，野生型幼苗 JA 处理对野生型幼苗空气处理），而 MYC2 没有功能的幼苗反应较小（79 个蛋白质，93 个磷酸肽，myc2 JA 处理对 myc2 空气处理）（图 4a。这些磷酸肽丰度的广泛变化与我们在转录组实验中观察到的 WT 和 myc2 实生苗之间有 118 个编码蛋白激酶的基因差异表达相一致（补充表 9）。

【原文11】Some direct overlap existed between proteins or phosphopeptides and transcripts responsive to JA treatment (Fig. 4b). Both transcripts and proteins encoded by 28 genes were differentially expressed in JA-treated WT seedlings relative to air controls (Fig. 4b). A further 33 differentially expressed proteins in JA-treated WT seedlings had no corresponding differentially expressed transcript, but were encoded by genes that are targeted by MYC2 and MYC3 (Fig. 4b). Differentially abundant phosphopeptides were detected that corresponded to 15 differentially expressed transcripts (Fig. 4b). Transcript and protein abundance was weakly positively correlated (Pearson's correlation value of 0.40341) in JA-treated WT seedlings (Fig. 4c), which is in agreement with previous studies[45,46]. The protein of only one known JA pathway component was differentially abundant in JA-treated WT seedlings relative to controls, and none were differentially phosphorylated. The fact that only a single JA-regulated protein and no phosphoproteins were annotated as JA pathway components may indicate that existing annotations are overly dependent on transcriptome data and that consideration of (phospho) proteome data deepens our understanding of JA responses.

【参考译文11】JA 处理应答蛋白质或磷酸肽与转录本之间存在一些直接的重叠（图 4b）。由 28 个基因编码的转录本和蛋白质在经 JA 处理的野生型（WT）幼苗（与空气处理对照幼苗相比）中均有差异表达（图 4b）。另外 33 个差异表达蛋白在 JA 处理的

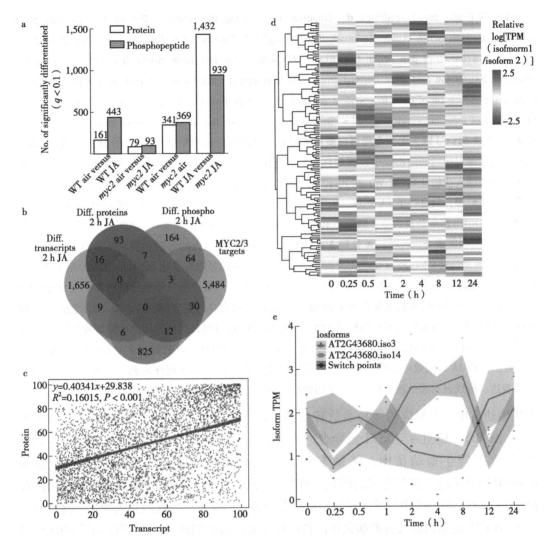

Fig. 4 | Loss of functional MYC2 affects the global proteome and phosphoproteome. a, Total number of significantly differentially abundant (FDR $q < 0.1$; estimated using a modified permutation plug-in method) proteins and phosphopeptides detected in comparisons between JA-treated (2 h) WT and *myc2* seedlings and air controls. Three independent experiments (with or without 2 h of JA treatment; $n = 3$) were conducted for WT and *myc2* seedlings. For the third experiment, only the JA treatment was conducted. **b,** Venn diagram showing the overlap between significantly differentially (Diff.) abundant proteins, transcripts and differentially phosphorylated proteins (Diff. phospho) in JA-treated WT seedlings compared with mock-treated WT controls. Also shown is the overlap with MYC2/3 target genes. **c,** Correlation between rank-normalized log2 fragments per kilobase of transcript per million (FPKM) values of detected proteins and transcripts in WT seedlings treated with JA for 2 h (P value cut-off was < 0.05 using paired Student's t-tests). Scatter plot of lg2[FC] in WT JA-regulated transcript levels versus lg2[FC] in levels of corresponding proteins. Protein and transcript data were derived from three independent experiments ($n =$

3) using WT and *myc2* seedlings. **d**, Heatmap representing the relative TPM of 137 isoform pairs exhibiting isoform switch events. Ratio calculated as log[TPM(isoform 1/isoform 2)]. **e**, Plot showing an example of a transcript pair originating from *AT2G43680* that had isoform-switch events following JA treatment. Expression data were derived from a JA time-course experiment. For each of the indicated time points, the expression of three independent samples ($n=3$) was measured using RNA-seq. Lines indicate the mean TPM of three independent samples. Shaded regions indicate the standard error of these data.

图4. 功能性MYC2缺失影响全局蛋白质组和磷酸蛋白质组。**a**，JA处理(2 h)的WT和*myc2*幼苗及与空气处理对照之间的比较中检测到有显著性差异富集的蛋白质和磷酸肽总数(FDR $q<0.1$；使用改进的置换插入法估计)。对WT和*myc2*幼苗进行了3次独立试验(JA处理或不处理2 h；$n=3$)。在第三次实验中，只进行了JA处理。**b**，维恩图显示JA处理的WT幼苗与对照处理的WT相比差异显著性(Diff.)富集的蛋白质、转录本和差异磷酸化蛋白质(Diff. phospho)之间的重叠。还显示与MYC2/3靶基因的重叠。**c**，经JA处理2 h的野生型幼苗中检测到的蛋白和转录本每百万转录本平均1000个碱基(per kilobase of transcript per million，FPKM)的等级标准化lg2片段之间的相关性(用t检验，P值控制值<0.05)。WT-JA调节转录水平中lg2[FC]的散点图与相应蛋白质水平中log2[FC]的散点图。蛋白质和转录数据来自WT和*myc2*幼苗的3次独立的实验($n=3$)。**d**，显示同源异构体转换事件的137对同源异构体对的相对TPM的热图。以log[TPM(同源异构体1/同源异构体2)]计算比率。**e**，显示源自JA处理后具有同源异构体转换事件的AT2G43680的转录本对(示例)的折线图。表达数据来自JA时间效应实验。对于每个指定的时间点，使用RNA测序来测定3个独立样本($n=3$)的表达。折线表示3个独立样本的平均TPM。阴影区域表示这些数据的标准误差。

野生型幼苗中没有对应的差异表达转录本，这些蛋白是由MYC2和MYC3靶基因编码的(图4b)。检测到与15个差异表达转录本对应的丰度差异的磷酸肽(图4b)。在经JA处理的野生型幼苗中，转录本和蛋白质丰度呈弱正相关(Pearson相关值为0.40341)(图4c)，这与先前的研究一致[45,46]。只有一个已知的JA通路组分的蛋白质在JA处理后野生型幼苗中与对照相比丰度存在差异，但没有一个被差异磷酸化。这种只有一个JA调控的蛋白而没有磷酸化蛋白被注释为JA通路组分的事实表明，现有的注释过度依赖于转录组数据，而将(磷酸化)蛋白质组数据考虑在内会加深我们对JA响应的理解。

【原文12】Alternative splicing can rapidly occur in response to environmental stimuli, contributing to transcriptome reprogramming and potentially fine-tuning physiological responses[47]. It is central to the JA-mediated regulation of transcription, with an alternative isoform of the repressor JAZ10 creating a negative feedback loop that desensitizes cells to a JA stimulus[48,49]. However, the extent of alternative splicing in JA signalling beyond the JAZ repressors is poorly characterized. We observed that phosphorylation of proteins involved in RNA recognition and nucleotide binding was disrupted in JA-treated *myc2* mutants compared with WT seedlings. The spliceosome was the only pathway significantly enriched among these differentially phosphorylated proteins ($P<0.05$, 18 genes matched), which suggests that

MYC2 may influence JA-responsive alternative splicing. Furthermore, 18 genes with splicing-related annotations were differentially expressed between *myc2* and WT seedlings in our transcriptome experiments (Supplementary Table 9). None of the differentially phosphorylated spliceosome components was differentially expressed.

【参考译文12】选择性剪接在对环境刺激的响应中能迅速发生，这有助于转录组重编程，并可能有助于对生理响应做出微调[47]。抑制因子JAZ10的一个选择性剪接的同源蛋白异构体(alternative isoform)产生了一个负反馈环路，使细胞对JA刺激失去敏感性，这对JA介导的转录调控十分重要[48,49]。然而，除JAZ抑制因子之外的JA信号转导成分选择性剪接并未得到充分鉴定。我们观察到，与野生型(WT)幼苗相比，JA处理的 *myc2* 突变体中参与RNA识别和核苷酸结合的蛋白质磷酸化被破坏。剪接体(spliceosome)是这些差异富集的磷酸化蛋白中唯一显著富集的通路($P<0.05$，18个基因匹配)，这表明MYC2可能影响JA响应的选择性剪接。此外，在我们的转录组实验中，*myc2* 和WT幼苗之间18个与剪接相关的注释基因差异表达(补充表9)。但是所有差异磷酸化的剪接体组分均无差异表达。

【原文13】We examined isoform-switch events across our JA transcriptome time-series, for which the most abundant of two isoforms from a single gene changes, to determine the extent of JA-responsive alternative splicing (Fig. 4d, e; Supplementary Table 15). There were 151 switch events, corresponding to 137 isoform pairs from 120 genes, within 24 h of JA treatment. These were identified from 30,547 total individual transcripts detected (average transcript per million (TPM) >1; Supplementary Table 16). Two of the genes exhibiting isoform switches had prior JA annotations [*RVE8* (also known as *AT3G09600*) and *SEN1* (also known as *AT4G35770*); Supplementary Table 15], and others were annotated to a variety of processes (including auxin, ABA, light signalling, disease response, among many others), but there was no significant enrichment of any GO terms or pathways. This indicates that MYC2 influences alternative splicing that diversifies the transcriptome in response to a JA stimulus.

【参考译文13】我们考查了JA转录组时间序列中的同源蛋白异构体转换事件，以确定JA响应的选择性剪接发生的范围，其中，来自单个基因的两个同源蛋白异构体中丰度最高的一个发生了变化(图4d, e)。JA处理后24小时内共发生151个转换事件，对应于120个基因的137对同源蛋白异构体。这些是从检测到的全部30 547个单个转录本中鉴定出来的(TPM>1；补充表16)。其中表现出同源蛋白异构体转换的两个基因，先前注释为JA响应过程[RVE8(也被称为AT3G09600)和SEN1(也被称为AT4G35770)；补充表15]，其他的则被注释为多种过程(包括生长素、ABA、光信号转导、疾病响应等)，但是没有显著富集于任何GO类名或通路。这表明MYC2影响那些在JA刺激下使转录组多样化的选择性剪接。

【原文 14】**Multi-omics modelling of the JA-response regulatory programme**

We then wanted to characterize the broader JA-response genome regulatory programme so that we could increase our understanding of the roles of known JA TFs within this and to identify new potential regulatory interactions. To do so, we generated a gene regulatory network model encompassing the (phospho) proteomic and time-series transcriptomics data (Extended Data Fig. 9a; Supplementary Table 17). Inclusion of the (phospho) proteomic data expanded the network by an additional 957 nodes (genes) compared with a transcript-only network (3,409 versus 4,366 nodes, 28% larger) (Supplementary Table 17). The (phospho) proteomics and transcript data shared 217 nodes within the network, a relatively small proportion, which indicates that these datasets complement one another when attempting to characterize the JA-response genome regulatory programme.

【参考译文 14】**JA 响应调控程序的多组学建模**

然后，我们想鉴定更广泛的 JA 响应基因组调控程序，以便我们能够加深对已知 JA 转录因子（TFs）在其中作用的理解，并确定新的潜在调控互作。为此，我们生成了涵盖（磷酸化）蛋白质组和时间效应转录组学数据（扩展数据图 9a；补充表 17）的基因调控网络模型。与纯转录网络相比，包含（磷蛋白）蛋白质组数据使网络增加了 957 个节点（基因）（3409 对 4366，增加 28%）（补充表 17）。（磷酸化）蛋白质组学和转录本数据在网络中共有 217 个节点，比例相对较小，这表明这些数据集在用来鉴定 JA 响应基因组调控程序时可相互补充。

【原文 15】Many known JA signalling components were present in the 100 most important predicted components of the network (for example, MYC2, ERF1, JAZ1, JAZ2, JAZ5, JAZ10 and ATAF2, among others, within the top 100 of 4,366 components assessed using a normalized motif score) (Supplementary Table 17). MYC2 was predicted to regulate a subnetwork of 26 components, 23 of which were validated as directly bound by MYC2 in ChIP-seq assays (88.5%; Extended Data Fig. 10a; Supplementary Tables 1 and 17). We further validated the network by comparing the ChIP-seq and DAP-seq data previously collected for the remaining 12 JA TFs to their targets in the gene regulatory network (Fig. 2e, f; Extended Data Fig. 10b; Supplementary Table 18). The gene regulatory network identified all of these TFs as components of the JA response, except MYC3 (Supplementary Table 17). It is probable that MYC3 was not considered part of the network because it was only modestly differentially expressed following JA treatment and was not detected in the (phospho) proteome analyses (Supplementary Tables 4, 13 and 14). The wider validation of targets was less strong than for MYC2, ranging from 0% to 33.3%. This could reflect the possibility that interactions predicted by the gene regulatory network may not identify all intermediate components. Last, we examined known genetic interactions. The MYC2 subnetwork included activation of JAZ10 within 0.5 h of a JA stimulus, with JAZ10 reciprocally repressing MYC2(Extended Data Fig. 10a, b). This is consistent with the known role of JAZ10 in establishing negative feedback to attenuate JA signalling[49]. MYC2 was also predicted to activate ABA-INDUCIBLE BHLH-TYPE TRANSCRIPTION FACTOR(AIB; also known as JAM1, bHLH017 and AT2G46510) (Extended Data Fig. 10a, b), which establishes a negative feedback loop in which AIB negatively regulates MYC2. This is in line with previous studies, which established that AIB is dependent on and antagonistic to MYC2, thereby repressing JA signalling[50, 51]. Confirmation by both genetic data from the literature and our DAP-seq and ChIP-seq experiments indicates that our gene regulatory network modelling approach is a useful tool to identify new regulatory interactions within JA signalling and to better understand known regulatory interactions.

【参考译文15】基因调控网络中预测到的100个最重要的组分就包含许多已知的JA信号转导组分(例如,MYC2、ERF1、JAZ1、JAZ2、JAZ5、JAZ10和ATAF2等就位列4366个组分中使用标准化基序分数评估排序的前100位)(补充表17)。预测MYC2可调控26个组分的子网络,其中23个组分在ChIP测序分析中表明被MYC2直接结合(占88.5%;扩展数据图10a;补充表1和17)。我们通过比较先前收集的另外12个JA转录因子(TFs)的ChIP测序和DAP测序数据与其在基因调控网络中的靶基因,进一步证实了该网络(图2e, f;扩展数据图10b;补充表18)。基因调控网络鉴定出所有这些转录因子都是JA响应的组分,但MYC3除外(补充表17)。很可能MYC3没有被看作网络的一部分,因为它在JA处理后差异表达不显著,在(磷)蛋白质组分析中也未检测到(补充表4、13和14)。与MYC2靶基因相比,靶基因更广泛地被证实不强,程度从0%到33.3%都有。这反映了基因调控网络预测的互作可能无法鉴定所有中间成分。最后,我们检查了已知的遗传互作。MYC2子网络包括在JA刺激0.5 h内激活JAZ10,JAZ10与MYC2相互抑制(扩展数据图10a, b)。这与JAZ10在建立负反馈以衰减JA信号转导中的已知作用一致[49]。MYC2还被预测激活ABA-INDUCIBLE BHLH-TYPE TRANSCRIPTION FACTOR(AIB;也称为JAM1、bHLH017和AT2G46510)(扩展数据图10a, b),因此建立一个负反馈回路,其中AIB负调控MYC2。这与先前的研究一致,即AIB依赖于MYC2并与MYC2拮抗,从而抑制JA信号转导[50, 51]。文献中的遗传数据以及我们的ChIP测序和DAP测序实验都证实,我们的基因调控网络建模方法是鉴定JA信号转导中新的调控互作和更好地理解已知的调控互作的有用工具。

【原文16】Crosstalk between hormone response pathways permits fine-tuning of plant growth and development in response to diverse environmental signals[1]. We examined the potential points at which MYC2 may interface directly with other hormone signalling pathways, since MYC2 is the master regulator of JA responses and one of the first TFs activated by JA. The MYC2 subnetwork identified a potential route for JA signalling to cross-regulate auxin hormone signalling. MYC2 activated ARF18, and ARF18 reciprocally activated MYC2 (Extended Data Fig. 10a; Supplementary Table 17). It also indicated that MYC2 may promote ethylene signalling by activating MAP kinase kinase 9 (MKK9) (Extended Data Fig. 10a). Previous genetic studies have determined that MKK9 induces ethylene production, but had not examined a possible link with JA signalling[52]. Positive crosstalk exists between JA and auxin signalling; however, the mechanism is not clearly determined[53]. RGL3, a regulator of gibberellic acid (GA) signalling previously associated with JA-GA crosstalk[54], was also present within the MYC2 subnetwork (Extended Data Fig. 10a) and predicted to inhibit MYC2 but not to be reciprocally regulated by MYC2. These three interactions are potential points at which crosstalk can rapidly occur during a JA response with auxin, gibberellin and ethylene.

【参考译文16】激素响应通路之间的串扰允许植物生长和发育响应于不同的环境信号而作微调[1]。我们研究了MYC2作为与其他激素信号通路可能的直接连接点，因为MYC2是JA响应的主调控因子，也是JA激活的第一类转录因子(TFs)之一。MYC2子网络鉴定出JA信号转导交叉调控生长素激素信号的潜在途径。MYC2激活ARF18，ARF18又反过来激活MYC2(扩展数据图10a；补充表17)。还表明MYC2可能通过激活MAP激酶激酶9(MAP kinase kinase 9, MKK9)促进乙烯信号转导(扩展数据图10a)。先前的遗传学研究已经确定MKK9可诱导乙烯产生，但还没有研究与JA信号转导的可能联系[52]。JA和生长素信号转导之间存在正串扰，但其机制尚不清楚[53]。原先将与JA-GA串扰联系起来的赤霉素(GA)信号转导调控因子RGL3，也存在于MYC2子网络(扩展数据图10a)中，并预测能抑制MYC2，但不受MYC2的交互调控。这3种互作是JA响应与生长素、赤霉素和乙烯之间迅速发生串扰的潜在连接点。

【原文17】We next examined the broader gene regulatory network to identify additional predicted points of crosstalk between JA and other signalling pathways. The model predicted that STZ is a key early hub through which JA signalling is prioritized over several other hormone and stress response pathways (Fig. 5a; Supplementary Table 17). Genetic studies have shown that STZ is a transcriptional repressor[55], and, consistent with this, our model predicted that it inhibited the majority of genes it regulates (25 out of 34 genes). *WRKY40*, *WRKY70*, *DDF* and *ERF6* were all predicted to be inhibited by STZ within 0.25 h of a JA stimulus and *GRX480* within 1 h. Direct binding of STZ to ERF6 was detected in ChIP-seq assays (Supplementary Table 11). WRKY40 and WRKY70 are both early brassinosteroid response components that repress defence responses[56]. DDF1 promotes resistance to drought, cold, heat and salinity stress by reducing endogenous gibberellin abundance[57]. ERF6 similarly promotes drought resistance by reducing gibberellin abundance[58]. GRX480 regulates the negative crosstalk between salicylic acid and both JA and ethylene signalling through direct interactions with TGA TFs[59, 60]. The model also predicted that ERF6, WRKY70 and DDF1 exert negative feedback on STZ by activating JAZ8 within 0.25 h of the JA stimulus (Fig. 5a; Supplementary Table 17). JAZ8 is a repressor of JA signalling and is predicted to repress STZ[61]. In summary, the gene regulatory network predicts that STZ is an important hub for JA signalling to be prioritized over other hormone and stress response pathways (Fig. 5a).

【参考译文 17】 接下来，我们研究了更广泛的基因调控网络，以鉴定 JA 和其他信号通路之间串扰的另外预测连接点。该模型预测 STZ 是一个关键的早期枢纽，通过它 JA 信号转导优先于其他几种激素和胁迫反应通路（图 5a；补充表 17）。遗传研究表明 STZ 是一个转录抑制因子[55]，与此一致，我们的模型预测它抑制了它调控的绝大多数基因（34 个基因中的 25 个）。*WRKY40*、*WRKY70*、*DDF* 和 *ERF6* 在 JA 刺激 0.25 h 内，及 *GRX480* 在 JA 刺激 1 h 内均被 STZ 抑制，在 ChIP 测序分析中检测到 STZ 与 ERF6 的直接结合（补充表 11）。WRKY40 和 WRKY70 都是抑制防御反应的早期油菜素类固醇（brassinosteroid）响应组分[56]。DDF1 通过降低内源赤霉素丰度，提高对干旱、寒冷、高温和盐碱胁迫的抗性[57]。ERF6 同样通过减少赤霉素丰度来提高抗旱性[58]。GRX480 通过与 TGA 转录因子直接互作来调控水杨酸（salicylic acid）与 JA 和乙烯信号两者之间的负串扰[59, 60]。该模型还预测 ERF6、WRKY70 和 DDF1 通过在 JA 刺激的 0.25 h 内激活 JAZ8 对 STZ 实施负反馈（图 5a；补充表 17）。JAZ8 是 JA 信号转导的一个阻遏蛋白，被预测可以抑制 STZ[61]。总之，基因调控网络预测 STZ 是使 JA 信号转导优先于其他激素和胁迫响应通路的重要枢纽（图 5a）。

【原文 18】Large-scale data-mediated identification of new JA regulators

We next utilized our regulatory network and large-scale datasets to identify novel regulators of the JA pathway using the JA root-growth inhibition assay as our experimental readout. First, we focused on ABA overly sensitive 3 (ABO3), which is directly targeted by MYC2 and MYC3 (Supplementary Table 1) and whose subnetwork is composed of 26 predicted regulated genes, the majority of which are positively regulated (22 out of 26 genes; Fig. 5b). ABO3 encodes the *Arabidopsis* WRKY TF gene *WRKY63*, which is involved in stress gene expression and drought tolerance[62]. To investigate the importance of the ABO3 subnetwork in JA signalling, we tested *abo3* T-DNA mutant seedlings (SALK_075986C[63]) in a JA-induced root-growth inhibition assay. We found that *abo3* mutants show a weak JA hyposensitive root-growth inhibition phenotype (Fig. 5c-e), which indicates that ABO3 is positive regulator of JA signalling and that our network approach is able to identify new pathway components.

【参考译文 18】利用大规模数据鉴定新的 JA 调控因子

接下来,利用我们的调控网络和大规模数据集,以 JA 根生长抑制试验结果作为实验读出数据,鉴定 JA 通路新调控因子。首先,我们关注的是 ABA overly sensitive 3 (ABO3),它是 MYC2 和 MYC3 的直接靶蛋白(补充表 1),其子网络由 26 个预测的受调控的基因组成,其中大多数是正调控的基因(26 个基因中的 22 个;图 5b)。*ABO3* 编码拟南芥 WRKY 转录因子基因 WRKY63,该基因参与植物胁迫基因表达和抗旱性[62]。为了探讨 ABO3 子网络在 JA 信号转导中的重要性,我们在 JA 诱导的根系生长抑制试验中检测了 *ABO3* T-DNA 突变苗(SALK_075986C[63])。我们发现 *abo3* 突变体表现出弱的 JA 低敏感根系生长抑制表型(图 5c-e),这表明 ABO3 是 JA 信号转导的正调控因子,我们的网络方法能够鉴定新的通路成分。

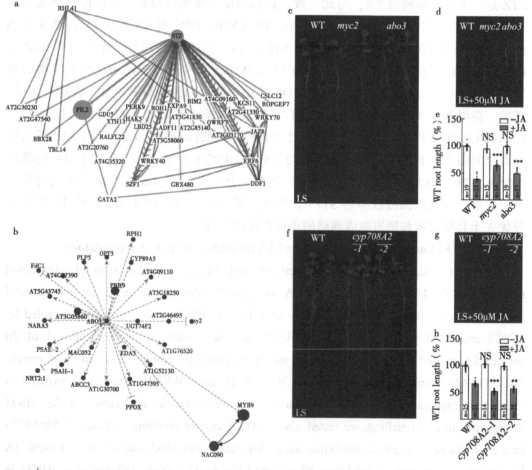

Fig. 5 | JA-response genome regulatory model positions: known and new components. a, b, Subnetworks of STZ(**a**) and ABO3(**b**). Edges are directed. Red edges exist at early time points(0.25-2 h), blue only at late time points(4-24 h). Thicker edges with chevrons indicate that MYC2 directly bound that gene in ChIP-seq experiments. **c, d,** JA-induced root-growth inhibition assays identified ABO3 as a positive

JA regulator. Seedlings were grown on LS media without(**c**)or with(**d**)50 μM JA. WT and *myc2* seedlings served as controls. **e**, Quantification (±s. e. m.) of JA-induced root-growth nhibition in WT, *myc2* and *abo3* seedlings. Sample size number (*n*) is shown within the respective bars. Data were derived from three independent experiments. Asterisks represent significant differ-ences between WT(with(+)or without(-)JA treatment)and *abo3* mutants(with or without JA treatment); two-way analysis of variance with Bonferroni post-test, *** $P<0.001$, NS, not significant. **f**, **g**, Root-growth inhibition assays identified two *cyp708A2* T-DNA alleles as JA hypersensitive. Seedlings were grown on LS media without(**f**)or with(**g**)50 μM JA, and WT seedlings served as controls. **h**, Quantification(±s. e. m.) of JA-induced root-growth inhibition in WT and *cyp708A2* seedlings. Sample size number is shown within the respective bars. Date were derived from three independent experiments. Asterisks represent significant differences between WT(with or without JA treatment) and *cyp708A2* (with or without JA treatment) seedlings. Significant differences were determined using two-way analysis of variance with Bonferroni post-hoc test; ** $P<0.01$, *** $P<0.001$。

图 5. JA 应答基因组调控模型位置：已知的组分和新组分。a，b，STZ(a)和 ABO3(b)的子网络。边线是有方向的。红色边线出现在早期时间点(0.25~2 h)，蓝色边线只出现在晚期时间点(4~24 h)。带 V 形标志的较粗边线表示在 ChIP 测序实验中 MYC2 直接结合该基因。c，d，JA 诱导的根系生长抑制试验表明 ABO3 是 JA 的正调控因子。幼苗在无 50 μM JA(c)或有 50 μM JA(d)的 LS 培养基上生长。WT 和 myc2 幼苗作为对照。e，对 WT、myc2 和 abo3 幼苗 JA 诱导的根系生长抑制进行定量分析(平均数±标准差)。样本大小数目(n)显示在相应的条内。数据来自 3 次独立的实验。星号表示 WT(用 JA 处理(+)或不用 JA 处理(-)和 abo3 突变体(用 JA 处理或不用 JA 处理)之间的显著差异；双因素方差分析，并用邦弗朗尼事后检验(Bonferroni post-test)，*** $P<0.001$，NS, 不显著。f，g，根生长抑制试验鉴定两个 cyp708A2 T-DNA 等位基因为 JA 超敏突变体。在不添加 50 μM JA(f)或添加(g)50 μM JA 的 LS 培养基上生长，野生型(WT)实生苗作为对照。h，JA 对 WT 和 cyp708A2 幼苗根系生长抑制作用的定量分析(平均数±标准差)。样本大小数目显示在相应的条中。数据来自 3 次独立的实验。星号代表 WT(用 JA 处理或不用 JA 处理)和 cyp708A2 突变体(用 JA 处理或不用 JA 处理)之间的显著差异。双因素方差分析，并用邦弗朗尼事后检验(Bonferroni post-test)；** $P<0.01$, ** $P<0.001$。

【原文 19】Next, we expanded our phenotyping analysis to T-DNA lines of genes that display the strongest binding of MYC2 and MYC3 in their promoters(Supplementary Tables 1 and 18). The rationale behind this approach is that master TFs target the majority of key signalling components in their regulated respective pathways and that these are often the most strongly bound targets[2,3,27]. Of the 99 genes tested(194 T-DNA lines in total; Supplementary Table 19), we discovered six genes that, when mutated, display mild JA root-growth phenotypes(Extended Data Fig. 10c; Supplementary Table 19). Mild phenotypes and their low frequency were not surprising, since gene redundancy is very common in the *Arabidopsis* genome, and even the mutation of the master TF MYC2 only causes a mild JA hyposensitive root-growth phenotype[15](Fig. 5c-e). Among these genes was the cytochrome P450 enzyme *CYP708A2* gene, from which both tested T-DNA mutant alleles exhibited a JA hypersensitive root phenotype (Fig. 5f-h). Interestingly, our network analysis also discovered CYP708A2 as a regulatory hub (Extended Data Figs. 9a and 10d). CYP708A2 is involved in triterpene synthesis, which is stimulated by JA[64]; future studies are, however, needed to further decipher the role of CYP708A2 in JA signalling. Another interesting uncharacterized gene that we discovered to cause a JA phenotype is a Sec14p-like phosphatidylinositol transfer family protein (*AT5G47730*; Extended Data Fig. 10c; Supplementary Table 19). Phosphatidylinositol transfer proteins are crucial for maintaining phosphatidylinositol homeostasis in plants[65], and inositol polyphosphates are implicated in COI1-mediated JA perception[66]. Taken together, these data show that our multi-omics approach goes beyond network description, ultimately enabling the identification of novel JA pathway regulators.

【参考译文19】接下来，我们将表型分析推广到哪些MYC2和MYC3与其启动子结合最强的T-DNA基因系（补充表1和18）。这种方法的基本原理是，主转录因子靶向结合其各自调控的通路中的绝大多数关键信号转导组分，而这些信号转导组分通常是结合最紧密的靶基因[2,3,27]。在测试的99个基因中（共194个T-DNA系；补充表19），我们发现了6个基因突变时，显示出较弱的JA根系生长表型（扩展数据图10c；补充表19）。轻弱的及低频率的根系生长表型并不奇怪，因为在拟南芥基因组中基因（功能）冗余十分常见，甚至主转录因子MYC2的突变也只会导致较弱的JA低敏感根生长表型[15]（图5c-e）。这些基因中有细胞色素P450酶*CYP708A2*基因，两种检测的T-DNA突变体等位基因均表现出JA超敏感根生长表型（图5f-h）。有意思的是，我们的网络分析还发现*CYP708A2*是一个调控枢纽（扩展数据图9a和10d）。CYP708A2参与JA64刺激的三萜合成；然而，需要进一步研究CYP708A2在JA信号转导中的作用。我们发现的另一个产生JA表型的有趣的未鉴定基因是一种Sec14p类磷脂酰肌醇转移家族蛋白（*AT5G47730*；扩展数据图10c；补充表19）。磷脂酰肌醇转移蛋白对维持植物中磷脂酰肌醇的稳态至关重要[65]，而肌醇多磷酸与COI1介导的JA感知有关[66]。综上所述，这些数据表明我们的多组学方法不只是能进行网络描述，最终能够鉴定新的JA通路调控因子。

说明：本论文中出现的"JA response"，一般译为"JA响应"，如果跟"gene"（基因）或"genome"（基因组）搭配时，翻译为"JA应答"。在"MYC2 controls JA-induced epigenomic reprogramming"为标题的小节中，有几个词或术语略加解释。

In line with the predominantly activating function of MYC2 (Extended Data Fig. 3c), the JA-induced genes had a stronger promoter enrichment of MYC2 than the JA-repressed genes (Fig. 3a). 这个句子中的"in line with"意思是"（与……）一致，（与……）相符（in agreement or alignment or accordance with...）"。

Strikingly, *myc2* mutants only displayed a compromised increase in H3K4me3 levels after JA treatment, which suggests that the JA-induced H3K4me3 depends on functional

MYC2(Fig. 3b-d; Extended Data Fig. 8a). 这个句子中的"compromised"是个多义词，这里的意思是"微弱的(weakened)"。

表观遗传学中经常用到一个词"gene body"，这里将其译为"基因本体"，指不包含基因上游调控区域(如启动子)和下游区域，只包含基因外显子(exon)和内含子(intron)在内的转录区域(transcriptional region)。或者说，从转录起始位点到转录终止位点之间的这一段可转录成 mRNA 的基因序列，称为基因本体(图 17-4)。

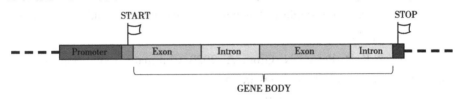

图 17-4　基因本体(gene body)示意图

图片来源：https://socratic.org/questions/what-is-a-gene-body#:~:text=The%20term%20%27gene%20body(%27%20is%20used%20in%20different, stop%20siteso%20the%20enzymes%20know%20what%20to%20do)

基因本体(gene body)图片还可参见下面文献中的图 3：Lou S, Lee H, Qin H, et al. Whole-genome bisulfite sequencing of multiple individuals reveals complementary roles of promoter and gene body methylation in transcriptional regulation. Genome Biol, 2014, 15：408.

这一节中出现的几个类似的词语 chromatin structure、chromatin architecture、chromatin landscape 和 chromatin states，这些词语还不是严格的专业术语，但在很多论文中使用，目前尚未有人对其区别进行论述。但根据这些词语使用的情况，似可这样理解：染色质结构(chromatin structure)和染色质架构(chromatin architecture)大致相同，指染色质在基本单位核小体(nucleosome)的基础上不同水平和维度的折叠与包装，后者尤指较高水平或高维度上的染色质结构或总体的染色质结构。Landscape 意思较多，有"地貌，景观，格局"等义，这里将其译为"格局"，其搭配能力也很强，目前在很多组学文章都可见到这个词的搭配形式。染色质格局(chromatin landscape)可以指染色质修饰格局(chromatin modification landscape)，也可以指染色质可接近性格局(chromatin accessibility landscape)，系染色质表观遗传修饰或染色质是否可接近的情况。染色质状态(chromatin states)一般指染色质是否处于开放(open)或否可接近(accessible)状态。从这个意义上讲，表观遗传学(epigenetics)可定义为有丝分裂遗传的染色质状态(mitotically inherited chromatin states)，而染色质状态传达细胞分裂之间的基因表达和阻抑信息(chromatin states convey gene expression and repression information between cell divisions)(Stewart-Morgan et al.，2020)。染色质可接近性在基因表达调控和核仁结构与组织等细胞核过程中发挥中心作用(Chromosomal accessibility plays a central role in several nuclear processes, including the regulation of gene expression and the structure and organization of the nucleus)(Gabitto et al.，2020)。

为了更好地理解这几个术语，读者可查阅以下相关的论文：

Black J C, Whetstine J R, 2011. Chromatin landscape: Methylation beyond transcription[J]. Epigenetics, 6(1): 13-19.

Chiarella A M, Lu D, Hathaway N A, 2020. Epigenetic control of a local chromatin landscape[J]. Int J Mol Sci, 21(3): 943.

Gabitto M I, Rasmussen A, Wapinski O, et al., 2020. Characterizing chromatin landscape from aggregate and single-cell genomic assays using flexible duration modeling[J]. Nat Commun, 11: 747.

Stewart-Morgan K R, Petryk N, Groth A, 2020. Chromatin replication and epigenetic cell memory[J]. Nature Cell Biology, 22: 361-371.

很多情况下，理解一个术语（尤其是尚未进入一般的教材和词典的术语），往往需要大量地查阅和阅读才能掌握其含义。也就是说，阅读的问题需要更多的阅读来解决。

接下来我们看一下结果部分的结构。这篇文章的结果由6个小节组成，小标题如下：

1. MYC2 and MYC3 target a large proportion of JA-responsive genes（MYC2和MYC3靶向结合大部分JA应答基因）

2. MYC2 and MYC3 activate the JA response through a large TF network（MYC2和MYC3通过一个大型转录因子网络激活JA响应）

3. MYC2 controls JA-induced epigenomic reprogramming（MYC2控制JA诱导的表观基因组重编程）

4. JA extensively remodels the (phospho) proteome[JA大量重塑（磷酸）蛋白质组]

5. Multi-omics modelling of the JA-response regulatory programme（JA响应调控程序的多组学建模）

6. Large-scale data-mediated identification of new JA regulators（利用大规模数据鉴定新的JA调控因子）

这6个小节的排列顺序基本按照分析的调控层级（profiled regulatory layers）顺序进行的，也就是首先分析转录因子结合（TF binding），这是第一小节的内容，然后分析转录组（transcriptome），这是第二小节的内容，接下来分析组蛋白修饰（Histone modifications），也就是第三小节关于表观基因组重编程（epigenomic reprogramming）的内容，再之后是分析全局磷酸蛋白组学（global phosphoproteme）和全局蛋白组学（global proteme），也就是第四小节的内容。第五小节为利用上述分析结果，整合多组学手段来建模（multi-omics modelling），第六节为模型的应用，也就是利用上述多组学得到的调控模型来鉴定新的JA调控因子（identification of new JA regulators）。

每一个小标题之下陈述一组相关的实验结果。按顺序陈述的内容包括做此项实验的直接目的和原因(也时需要简略地叙述背景信息)、主要实验方法(有时需要提供所用某种材料或方法的实验理据)、数据和结果(详尽的数据用图表呈现,用文字概括主要结果)、由这些数据和结果得出的结论。目前,在一些顶级期刊长文中,甚至原本属于讨论中的内容(例如,对某项具体结果的简要解释)也放在结果中,因此,论文结果部分也会征引文献来说明背景信息和解释印证结果。为了让读者理解结果部分写作的结构,我们以下面两个典型段落进行简要说明:

MYC2 and MYC3 activate the JA response through a large TF network

To study the MYC2 and MYC3-governed transcriptional regulatory network in more detail, we investigated the relationship between MYC2-bound and MYC3-bound TF-encoding genes and their transcriptional responsiveness to JA treatment【简述实验目的】. We conducted a JA time-course experiment(time points of 0, 0.25, 0.5, 1, 2, 4, 8, 12 and 24 h post JA treatment)【陈述所用的主要方法】and identified a total of 7,377 differentially expressed genes at one or more time points within 24 h of JA treatment(Supplementary Table 4). Differentially expressed genes were categorized into clusters with similar expression trends over time to facilitate the visualization of complex expression dynamics and enriched functional annotations (Extended Data Fig. 5a; Supplementary Table 7). The largest upregulated cluster was the "JA cluster", which was enriched for GO terms associated with JA responses (Fig. 2a). In contrast, the "Cell wall cluster" was the largest cluster of downregulated genes and enriched for GO terms associated with cell wall organization, development and differentiation (Fig. 2b)【简述主要实验结果】. These two main clusters illustrate the defence-growth trade-off when defence pathways are activated[31]【结论与解释】.

MYC2 controls JA-induced epigenomic reprogramming

Reprogramming of the epigenome is an integral part of development and environmental stimulus-induced gene expression[41]. For example, activation of the transcriptional JA response requires the formation of MYC2-MED25-mediated chromatin looping[42]【背景介绍】. To investigate the extent of JA-induced changes in chromatin architecture and the regulatory importance of MYC2 in this response, we conducted ChIP-seq assays to profile the genome-wide occupancy of the histone modification H3K4me3 (trimethylation of lysine 4 on histone H3) and the histone variant H2A.Z in untreated and in JA-treated (4 h) WT and *myc2* seedlings【简述实验目的与所用实验方法】. H3K4me3 marks active and poised genes whereas the histone variant H2A.Z confers gene responsiveness to environmental stimuli[43,44]. mRNA expression was monitored in parallel using RNA-seq【解释实验方法或陈述方法原理】. JA treatment led to a reprogrammed chromatin landscape, with several thousand differentially enriched H3K4me3 and H2A.Z domains (Extended Data Fig. 8a-c; Supplementary Table 12). We identified 826 differentially expressed genes (675 induced, 151 repressed; WT control versus JA treated) in that experiment. In line with the predominantly activating function of MYC2 (Extended Data Fig. 3c), the JA-induced genes had a stronger promoter enrichment of MYC2 than the JA-repressed genes (Fig. 3a). H3K4me3 levels were increased in JA-induced genes, whereas JA-repressed genes did not exhibit any dynamic change in H3K4me3 levels (Fig. 3b, d). Strikingly, *myc2* mutants only displayed a compromised increase in H3K4me3 levels after JA treatment, which suggests that the JA-induced H3K4me3 depends on functional MYC2 (Fig. 3b-d; Extended Data Fig. 8a). The impact of the *myc2* mutation on JA-induced H3K4me3 changes was also observed in JA-induced genes that are not directly targeted by MYC2 (Extended Data Fig. 8e, f), which is potentially caused by the decreased expression of MYC2-targeted TFs. The scenario of a direct MYC2 regulation network is illustrated by two JA-induced genes, *JAZ2* and *GRX480*, which are directly targeted by MYC2. Their expression depends on MYC2, and their JA-induced increase in gene-body-localized H3K4me3 partially depended on MYC2 (Fig. 3d; Extended Data Fig. 8d). However, whether the MYC2-dependent changes in H3K4me3 levels precede transcription or rather reflect increased transcriptional activity cannot be addressed by these experiments. In contrast, JA-induced changes in H2A.Z occupancy were only slightly affected in *myc2* mutants (Extended Data Fig. 8a, g, h), which suggests that JA-induced H2A.Z dynamics are either independent of MYC2 or precede MYC2 binding. Alternatively, other MYCs such as MYC3, MYC4 and MYC5 are functionally redundant in regulating H2A.Z dynamics【简述主要实验结果并做出解释,对结果的解释用下划线标出】。

图表是论文结果的重要组成部分。例文除第6小节外,每一小节都有一个包含多张结果相关的图片组成的图版。目前顶级期刊论文的长论文所包含的工作量相当大,因此很少用单张图片来说明结果,往往是利用多张图片的图版来说明一种情况或得出一个结论。由于图比表更为直观和容易理解,所以,用图更多,而表则多放在附件中。通常图和表的内容不能重复,但目前由于详细的数据可作为附件上传,因此,反映同一批数据的简单明了的图片可放在正文,而详细的数据可同时作为附件上传。由于图的标题和注解应该尽可能详细,具有自明性,因此,文字部分无须重复叙述图表,只需根据图表注释进行概括和解释即可,但要按顺序征引图表。

注意每一小节中节的标题与相应的图版标题需要对应,但最好不要重复。通常节的标题更具概括性,也就是概括这节内容的主要结果或结论语句,而图版的标题则相对具体一些。试比较例文前5个小节的节标题和图版标题:

【节标题】MYC2 and MYC3 target a large proportion of JA-responsive genes.

【图版标题】Fig. 1 | Design of our study and key datasets utilized.

【节标题】MYC2 and MYC3 activate the JA response through a large TF network.

【图版标题】Fig. 2 | MYC2 and MYC3 target a large proportion of JA-responsive genes that encode TFs.

【节标题】MYC2 controls JA-induced epigenomic reprogramming.

【图版标题】Fig. 3 | The JA-responsive epigenome.

【节标题】JA extensively remodels the (phospho) proteome.

【图版标题】Fig. 4 | Loss of functional MYC2 affects the global proteome and phosphoproteome.

【节标题】Multi-omics modelling of the JA-response regulatory programme.

【图版标题】Fig. 5 | JA-response genome regulatory model positions: known and new components.

另外要注意的是，图表除纯粹的照片外，用 Excel 等软件制作的折线图和条形图等都要包含反映误差和统计检验结果的内容。因为在实验设计之初就要考虑统计学处理，因此结果有必要反映出来。单纯的结果数据无法得出相对科学的结论，需要进行统计检验才能从数据中提炼出有科学意义的结论，也就是说，利用数量有限的样本处理得出有限的结果，是统计学分析给有限的结果赋予科学判断上的意义，并允许得出相对确定性的结论。论文图表所用的数据一般用"平均值±标准差"，在折线图和条形图中要用误差条（error bar）来反映标准差，数据分析要说明所采用的统计检验方法及具体的 P 值与统计检验结果。相应地，在正文中，描述统计学上的显著差异只能用"significant"，没有进行统计检验的结果不能用这个词来描述。此外，统计学上利用相关系数给出不同指标之间关联的强度，使我们能从给定样本中推断出适用于更广样本群体的结论。

最后，我们来了解一下结果部分常用的一些表达方法。

一般在小节或段落开头介绍实验的目的，并陈述（用了什么方法）做了什么实验，可以学习的语句有：

【例文 1】To decipher the JA-governed regulatory network with its high degree of dynamic interconnectivity with other signalling pathways, we applied a multi-omics network approach that comprised five newly generated high-quality large-scale datasets.

【例文 2】To better understand how the master TFs MYC2 and MYC3 control the JA-induced transcriptional cascade, we determined their genome-wide binding sites using chromatin immunoprecipitation (ChIP) with sequencing (ChIP-seq).

【例文 3】To study the MYC2 and MYC3-governed transcriptional regulatory network in more detail, we investigated the relationship between MYC2-bound and MYC3-bound TF-encoding genes and their transcriptional responsiveness to JA treatment.

【例文 4】To investigate this crosstalk function of MYC2 and MYC3 in more detail, we utilized our ChIP-seq data to determine the number of plant hormone TFs that are bound by

MYC2 and MYC3.

【例文5】To investigate the extent of JA-induced changes in chromatin architecture and the regulatory importance of MYC2 in this response, we conducted ChIP-seq assays to profile the genome-wide occupancy of the histone modification H3K4me3 (trimethylation of lysine 4 on histone H3) and the histone variant H2A.Z in untreated and in JA-treated (4 h) WT and myc2 seedlings.

【例文6】To investigate the importance of the ABO3 subnetwork in JA signalling, we tested abo3 T-DNA mutant seedlings (SALK_075986C) in a JA-induced root-growth inhibition assay.

【例文7】We examined isoform-switch events across our JA transcriptome time-series, for which the most abundant of two isoforms from a single gene changes, to determine the extent of JA-responsive alternative splicing.

【例文8】We next examined the broader gene regulatory network to identify additional predicted points of crosstalk between JA and other signalling pathways.

【例文9】We then wanted to characterize the broader JA-response genome regulatory programme so that we could increase our understanding of the roles of known JA TFs within this and to identify new potential regulatory interactions. To do so, we generated a gene regulatory network model encompassing the (phospho) proteomic and time-series transcriptomics data.

利用什么方法，做出什么结果，可以学习的语句有：

【例文1】Using RNA sequencing (RNA-seq), we determined that 2,522 genes were differently expressed (false discovery rate (FDR) <0.05) after 2 h of JA treatment.

【例文2】We next utilized our regulatory network and large-scale datasets to identify novel regulators of the JA pathway using the JA root-growth inhibition assay as our experimental readout.

【例文3】We identified putative partner TFs by determining DNA motifs enriched in MYC2 binding sites that did not contain a G-box motif.

【例文4】We examined the effect of removing MYC2 activity on JA-responsive transcriptional regulation by generating transcriptomes from a myc2 null mutant (jin1-8) in an early JA response time-series experiment (0, 0.5, 1 and 4 h).

解释方法原理可用的语句有：

【例文1】The rationale behind dissecting jasmonate signalling in etiolated seedlings is that although MYC2 is highly expressed in etiolated seedlings and regulates important processes such as photomorphogenesis and apical hook formation, a comprehensive characterization of this special developmental stage is still missing.

【例文 2】 The rationale behind this approach is that master TFs target the majority of key signalling components in their regulated respective pathways and that these are often the most strongly bound targets.

【例文 3】 Molecular investigations of these TFs would be required to determine whether they bind cooperatively with MYC2 to DNA.

陈述实验结果与发现，可以用第一人称（we）开头的主动语态，也可以用 our analysis 等开头的主动语态，还可以用物质名词或抽象名词做主语的被动语态或主动语态。

【例文 1】 We conducted a JA time-course experiment (time points of 0, 0.25, 0.5, 1, 2, 4, 8, 12 and 24 h post JA treatment) and identified a total of 7,377 differentially expressed genes at one or more time points within 24 h of JA treatment.

【例文 2】 We identified 6,736 MYC2 and 3,982 MYC3 high-confidence binding sites ($P \leq 1 \times 10^{-25}$ and conserved in at least two independent biological replicates), equating to 6,178 MYC2 and 4,092 MYC3 target genes (within 500 nucleotides of a binding site centre or nearest neighbouring gene).

【例文 3】 We identified 826 differentially expressed genes (675 induced, 151 repressed; WT control versus JA treated) in that experiment.

【例文 4】 We determined that the loss of MYC2 caused substantial changes to the JA-responsive proteome and phosphoproteome; 1,432 proteins and 939 phosphopeptides (corresponding to 567 genes) were significantly differentially abundant in WT seedlings relative to myc2 seedlings after 2 h of JA treatment.

【例文 5】 We found that approximately one-third of OPDA-specific response genes (45 genes) are targeted by MYC2.

【例文 6】 We found that 37%-59% of annotated hormone pathway genes are bound by MYC2 and MYC3 and that their expression changes in response to 24 h of JA treatment.

【例文 7】 We found that *abo3* mutants show a weak JA hyposensitive root-growth inhibition phenotype, which indicates that ABO3 is positive regulator of JA signalling and that our network approach is able to identify new pathway components.

【例文 8】 In addition, we discovered 122 annotated hormone TFs, with representatives from all hormone pathways, that are bound by MYC2 and MYC3, and 118 of these were differentially expressed.

【例文 9】 Of the 99 genes tested (194 T-DNA lines in total), we discovered six genes that, when mutated, display mild JA root-growth phenotypes.

【例文 10】 We observed that phosphorylation of proteins involved in RNA recognition and nucleotide binding was disrupted in JA-treated myc2 mutants compared with WT seedlings.

【例文 11】Our analysis also determined that 522 out of 1,717 known or predicted TFs were differentially expressed within 24 h of JA treatment.

【例文 12】Our MYC2 and MYC3 ChIP-seq analyses determined that approximately two-thirds of the genes encoding for known JA pathway components(112 out of 168 genes for MYC2, and 96 out of 168 genes for MYC3)were bound by MYC2 and MYC3.

【例文 13】Interestingly, our network analysis also discovered CYP708A2 as a regulatory hub.

【例文 14】Our ChIP-seq approach revealed that beyond the autoregulation of MYC2 and MYC3, these TFs also regulate JA biosynthesis either directly by targeting the JA biosynthesis genes LOX2, LOX3, LOX4, LOX6 and AOS or indirectly through binding to the AP2-ERF TF gene ORA47.

【例文 15】Genetic studies have shown that STZ is a transcriptional repressor, and, consistent with this, our model predicted that it inhibited the majority of genes it regulates(25 out of 34 genes).

【例文 16】The MYC2 subnetwork identified a potential route for JA signalling to cross-regulate auxin hormone signalling.

【例文 17】The gene regulatory network identified all of these TFs as components of the JA response, except MYC3.

【例文 18】The scenario of a direct MYC2 regulation network is illustrated by two JA-induced genes, JAZ2 and GRX480, which are directly targeted by MYC2.

【例文 19】Differentially abundant phosphopeptides were detected that corresponded to 15 differentially expressed transcripts.

【例文 20】No significant protein domain or GO term enrichment was detected among the small number of MYC3-only targets.

【例文 21】Differentially expressed genes were categorized into clusters with similar expression trends over time to facilitate the visualization of complex expression dynamics and enriched functional annotations.

【例文 22】MYC2 was predicted to regulate a subnetwork of 26 components, 23 of which were validated as directly bound by MYC2 in ChIP-seq assays.

【例文 23】Both transcripts and proteins encoded by 28 genes were differentially expressed in JA-treated WT seedlings relative to air controls.

【例文 24】Their target genes were enriched for JA-related gene ontology(GO) terms and for terms related to other hormones.

【例文 25】Target genes shared between MYC2 and MYC3 were significantly enriched

($P<0.05$) for more JA-related GO terms than for target genes unique to either TF.

【例文 26】 Proteins encoded by shared MYC2 and MYC3 target genes were enriched for DNA binding and transcriptional regulatory domains; in contrast, proteins encoded by MYC2-only target genes were enriched for kinase domains.

【例文 27】 A further 33 differentially expressed proteins in JA-treated WT seedlings had no corresponding differentially expressed transcript, but were encoded by genes that are targeted by MYC2 and MYC3.

【例文 28】 The *myc2* mutation also affected the expression of secondary, indirect MYC2 target genes (that is, genes targeted by MYC2-regulated TFs, but not by MYC2 itself).

【例文 29】 *ABO3* encodes the *Arabidopsis* WRKY TF gene WRKY63, which is involved in stress gene expression and drought tolerance.

描述结果（现象）与解释（结论）时，除了可利用两个单独的句子、主语和宾语从句表达外，还经常利用主句描述结果（现象），利用非限制性定语从句给出解释（结论）。

【例文 1】 Two of the genes exhibiting isoform switches had prior JA annotations (*RVE8* (also known as *AT3G09600*) and *SEN1* (also known as *AT4G35770*), and others were annotated to a variety of processes (including auxin, ABA, light signalling, disease response, among many others), but there was no significant enrichment of any GO terms or pathways. This indicates that MYC2 influences alternative splicing that diversifies the transcriptome in response to a JA stimulus.

【例文 2】 The wider validation of targets was less strong than for MYC2, ranging from 0% to 33.3%. This could reflect the possibility that interactions predicted by the gene regulatory network may not identify all intermediate components.

【例文 3】 Confirmation by both genetic data from the literature and our DAP-seq and ChIP-seq experiments indicates that our gene regulatory network modelling approach is a useful tool to identify new regulatory interactions within JA signalling and to better understand known regulatory interactions.

【例文 4】 Our MYC2 and MYC3 ChIP-seq dataset derived from a 2-h-long JA treatment revealed that up to 63% (0.5 h JA treatment) of differentially expressed genes at any given time point were potentially directly bound by MYC2 and/or MYC3, which highlights the important role of MYCs in transcriptionally regulating JA responses.

【例文 5】 The fact that only a single JA-regulated protein and no phosphoproteins were annotated as JA pathway components may indicate that existing annotations are overly dependent on transcriptome data and that consideration of (phospho) proteome data deepens our understanding of JA responses.

【例文 6】We found that *abo3* mutants show a weak JA hyposensitive root-growth inhibition phenotype, which indicates that ABO3 is positive regulator of JA signalling and that our network approach is able to identify new pathway components.

【例文 7】The (phospho) proteomics and transcript data shared 217 nodes within the network, a relatively small proportion, which indicates that these datasets complement one another when attempting to characterize the JA-response genome regulatory programme.

【例文 8】The majority of JA-responsive genes that are directly targeted by MYC2 and MYC3 were transcriptionally upregulated after JA application, which indicates that MYC2 and MYC3 predominantly act as transcriptional activators.

【例文 9】Overall, a majority of the MYC2 target genes differentially expressed between *myc2* and WT plants were more highly expressed in WT, which indicates that loss of MYC2 function reduces the JA responsiveness of these genes.

【例文 10】Half of these (268), representing 36 out of 58 TF families, were also direct MYC2 or MYC3 targets, which indicates that MYC2 and MYC3 cooperatively control a massive TF network.

【例文 11】The spliceosome was the only pathway significantly enriched among these differentially phosphorylated proteins ($P < 0.05$, 18 genes matched), which suggests that MYC2 may influence JA-responsive alternative splicing.

【例文 12】Strikingly, *myc2* mutants only displayed a compromised increase in H3K4me3 levels after JA treatment, which suggests that the JA-induced H3K4me3 depends on functional MYC2.

【例文 13】In contrast, JA-induced changes in H2A.Z occupancy were only slightly affected in *myc2* mutants, which suggests that JA-induced H2A.Z dynamics are either independent of MYC2 or precede MYC2 binding.

【例文 14】MYC2 was also predicted to activate ABA-INDUCIBLE BHLH-TYPE TRANSCRIPTION FACTOR (AIB; also known as JAM1, bHLH017 and AT2G46510), which establishes a negative feedback loop in which AIB negatively regulates MYC2.

【例文 15】The impact of the *myc2* mutation on JA-induced H3K4me3 changes were also observed in JA-induced genes that are not directly targeted by MYC2, which is potentially caused by the decreased expression of MYC2-targeted TFs.

描述某种结果与前人的结果或结论一致时，可用 be consistent/concordant/line with 或者 be in agreement with 来表示，但句型可以多样化，同样可利用两个单独的句子、主语或宾语从句表、介词结构、非限制性定语从句等。

【例文 1】One-third (843 genes) of JA-modulated genes were directly bound by MYC2 or MYC3. This is consistent with the important role of MYC2 and MYC3 in JA-responsive gene expression.

【例文 2】 Notably, ERF1 and ORA59 also shared significant enrichment of a separate set of GO terms with one another, but these were not enriched among MYC2 and MYC3 targets. This is consistent with the joint role of ERF1 and ORA59 in controlling a pathogen defence arm of JA signalling.

【例文 3】 These extensive changes in phosphopeptide abundance are consistent with the observation that 118 genes encoding protein kinases were differentially expressed between WT and *myc2* seedlings in our transcriptome experiments.

【例文 4】 Genetic studies have shown that STZ is a transcriptional repressor, and, consistent with this, our model predicted that it inhibited the majority of genes it regulates (25 out of 34 genes).

【例文 5】 Consistent with this, their target genes shared several significantly enriched GO terms (adjusted $P<0.05$), which suggests that there are related functions in jasmonate signalling.

【例文 6】 JA-responsive gene expression occurred in *myc2* plants, which is consistent with the partially redundant function of MYC2, MYC3 and MYC4.

【例文 7】 The G-box (CA[C/T]GT[G/T]) motif was the most common DNA sequence motif found at MYC2 or MYC3 binding sites, which is concordant with the observation that they shared a large proportion of their binding sites.

【例文 8】 The three most numerous families (ERFs, bHLHs and MYBs) in the *Arabidopsis* genome had the most JA-responsive members targeting MYC2 or MYC3, which is concordant with their previously annotated roles in JA responses.

【例文 9】 MYC2 was also predicted to activate ABA-INDUCIBLE BHLH-TYPE TRANSCRIPTION FACTOR (AIB; also known as JAM1, bHLH017 and AT2G46510), which establishes a negative feedback loop in which AIB negatively regulates MYC2. This is in line with previous studies, which established that AIB is dependent on and antagonistic to MYC2, thereby repressing JA signalling.

【例文 10】 In line with the predominantly activating function of MYC2, the JA-induced genes had a stronger promoter enrichment of MYC2 than the JA-repressed genes.

【例文 11】 Transcript and protein abundance was weakly positively correlated (Pearson's correlation value of 0.40341) in JA-treated WT seedlings, which is in agreement with previous studies.

【例文 12】 Transcript and protein abundance was weakly positively correlated (Pearson's correlation value of 0.40341) in JA-treated WT seedlings, which is in agreement with previous studies.

另外需要注意学习的是，为了小节与小节之间、段落与段落之间、句子与句子之间语义连贯、衔接自然，要使用适当的过渡词来表示顺序、转折、对比、选择、增补、举例、例外、强调、总结。

【例文1】First, we focused on ABA overly sensitive 3 (ABO3), which is directly targeted by MYC2 and MYC3 and whose subnetwork is composed of 26 predicted regulated genes, the majority of which are positively regulated (22 out of 26 genes). …Next, we expanded our phenotyping analysis to T-DNA lines of genes that display the strongest binding of MYC2 and MYC3 in their promoters. (表示顺序)

【例文2】We next set out to better understand the target genes of the network of TFs downstream of MYC2 and MYC3. (表示顺序)

【例文3】We next explored how JA remodels the proteome and phosphoproteome of etiolated seedlings. (表示顺序)

【例文4】We next examined the broader gene regulatory network to identify additional predicted points of crosstalk between JA and other signalling pathways. (表示顺序)

【例文5】We next utilized our regulatory network and large-scale datasets to identify novel regulators of the JA pathway using the JA root-growth inhibition assay as our experimental readout. (表示顺序)

【例文6】We then wanted to characterize the broader JA-response genome regulatory programme so that we could increase our understanding of the roles of known JA TFs within this and to identify new potential regulatory interactions. (表示顺序)

【例文7】We further validated the network by comparing the ChIP-seq and DAP-seq data previously collected for the remaining 12 JA TFs to their targets in the gene regulatory network. (表示顺序)

【例文8】Last, we examined known genetic interactions. The MYC2 subnetwork included activation of JAZ10 within 0.5 h of a JA stimulus, with JAZ10 reciprocally repressing MYC2. This is consistent with the known role of JAZ10 in establishing negative feedback to attenuate JA signalling. (表示顺序)

【例文9】Last, we examined known genetic interactions. The MYC2 subnetwork included activation of JAZ10 within 0.5 h of a JA stimulus, with JAZ10 reciprocally repressing MYC2. (表示顺序)

【例文10】*myc3* and *myc4* single mutants behave like wild-type (WT) plants with regards to JA-induced root growth inhibition. However, in combination with the *myc2* mutant, *myc2 myc3* double mutants exhibit an increased JA hyposensitivity, almost as pronounced as in *myc2 myc3 myc4* triple mutants. (表示转折)

【例文 11】The majority of MYC2 and MYC3 binding sites contained the G-box motif (4,240 out of 6,736 for MYC2, and 3,072 out of 3,982 for MYC3). However, the absence of the motif from a substantial number of MYC2 and MYC3 binding sites suggests that the TFs may bind indirectly to some sites through a partner protein(or proteins). (表示转折)

【例文 12】JA-responsive gene expression occurred in *myc2* plants, which is consistent with the partially redundant function of MYC2, MYC3 and MYC4. However, JA-responsive genes were upregulated more highly in WT than *myc2* plants. (表示转折)

【例文 13】It is central to the JA-mediated regulation of transcription, with an alternative isoform of the repressor JAZ10 creating a negative feedback loop that desensitizes cells to a JA stimulus. However, the extent of alternative splicing in JA signalling beyond the JAZ repressors is poorly characterized. (表示转折)

【例文 14】Positive crosstalk exists between JA and auxin signalling; however, the mechanism is not clearly determined. (表示转折)

【例文 15】CYP708A2 is involved in triterpene synthesis, which is stimulated by JA; future studies are, however, needed to further decipher the role of CYP708A2 in JA signalling. (表示转折)

【例文 16】Two of the genes exhibiting isoform switches had prior JA annotations (*RVE8*(also known as *AT3G09600*) and *SEN1*(also known as *AT4G35770*)), and others were annotated to a variety of processes (including auxin, ABA, light signalling, disease response, among many others), but there was no significant enrichment of any GO terms or pathways. (表示转折)

【例文 17】The largest upregulated cluster was the "JA cluster", which was enriched for GO terms associated with JA responses. In contrast, the "Cell wall cluster" was the largest cluster of downregulated genes and enriched for GO terms associated with cell wall organization, development and differentiation. (表示对比)

【例文 18】Interestingly, the majority of all known JA genes that were differentially expressed following JA treatment were bound by MYC2 or MYC3, whereas fewer non-differentially expressed known JA genes were directly targeted. (表示对比)

【例文 19】Their expression depends on MYC2, and their JA-induced increase in gene-body-localized H3K4me3 partially depended on MYC2. However, whether the MYC2-dependent changes in H3K4me3 levels precede transcription or rather reflect increased transcriptional activity cannot be addressed by these experiments. In contrast, JA-induced changes in H2A. Z occupancy were only slightly affected in *myc2* mutants, which suggests that JA-induced H2A. Z dynamics are either independent of MYC2 or precede MYC2 binding. Alternatively, other MYCs such as MYC3, MYC4 and MYC5 are functionally redundant in regulating H2A. Z dynamics. (依次表示转折、对比和选择)

【例文 20】 We also included the following TFs with known roles in JA signalling: ERF1 (also known as AT3G23240, ERF1B and AtERF092); ORA59 (also known as AT1G06160); ANAC055 (also known as NAC3); WRKY51 (also known as AT5G64810); and STZ (also known as ZAT10). (表示增补)

【例文 21】 The spliceosome was the only pathway significantly enriched among these differentially phosphorylated proteins ($P < 0.05$, 18 genes matched), which suggests that MYC2 may influence JA-responsive alternative splicing. Furthermore, 18 genes with splicing-related annotations were differentially expressed between *myc2* and WT seedlings in our transcriptome experiments. (表示增补)

【例文 22】 We found that 37%-59% of annotated hormone pathway genes are bound by MYC2 and MYC3 and that their expression changes in response to 24 h of JA treatment. In addition, we discovered 122 annotated hormone TFs, with representatives from all hormone pathways, that are bound by MYC2 and MYC3, and 118 of these were differentially expressed. (表示增补)

【例文 23】 Our ChIP-seq approach revealed that beyond the autoregulation of MYC2 and MYC3, these TFs also regulate JA biosynthesis either directly by targeting the JA biosynthesis genes *LOX2*, *LOX3*, *LOX4*, *LOX6* and *AOS* or indirectly through binding to the AP2-ERF TF gene *ORA47*. In addition, MYCs simultaneously target various negative regulators, enabling MYCs to efficiently dampen the JA response pattern. (表示增补)

【例文 24】 Reprogramming of the epigenome is an integral part of development and environmental stimulus-induced gene expression. For example, activation of the transcriptional JA response requires the formation of MYC2-MED25-mediated chromatin looping. (表示举例)

【例文 25】 These TFs formed a highly connected network, with all TFs except DREB2B targeting at least two TFs in the network and these two in turn targeted by two TFs. (表示例外)

【例文 26】 It is probable that MYC3 was not considered part of the network because it was only modestly differentially expressed following JA treatment and was not detected in the (phospho)proteome analyses. (表示因果)

【例文 27】 Mild phenotypes and their low frequency were not surprising, since gene redundancy is very common in the *Arabidopsis* genome, and even the mutation of the master TF MYC2 only causes a mild JA hyposensitive root-growth phenotype. (表示因果)

【例文 28】 We examined the potential points at which MYC2 may interface directly with other hormone signalling pathways, since MYC2 is the master regulator of JA responses and one of the first TFs activated by JA. (表示因果)

【例文 29】 Transcript abundance is also frequently weakly correlated with protein abundance. Consequently, proteomic and phosphoproteomic analyses yield additional insight into gene regulatory networks. (表示因果)

【例文 30】 Notably, ERF1 and ORA59 also shared significant enrichment of a separate set of GO terms with one another, but these were not enriched among MYC2 and MYC3 targets. (表示强调)

【例文 31】 Interestingly, *STZ* belongs to a group of genes that is inducible by the JA precursor 12-oxo-phytodienoic acid(OPDA)and not by JA. (表示强调)

【例文 32】 Interestingly, our network analysis also discovered CYP708A2 as a regulatory hub. (表示强调)

【例文 33】 Strikingly, *myc2* mutants only displayed a compromised increase in H3K4me3 levels after JA treatment, which suggests that the JA-induced H3K4me3 depends on functional MYC2. (表示强调)

【例文 34】 Strikingly, all JAZ members and NINJA are directly bound by MYC2 and MYC3, which probably leads to a dampening of the JA response and thereby preventing excessive activation of JA signalling. (表示强调)

【例文 35】 Collectively, these data indicate that MYC2 and MYC3 have the potential to regulate 23.2% of genes in the *Arabidopsis* genome (27, 655 coding genes). However, binding events are not necessarily regulatory. (表示总结)

【例文 36】 Overall, a majority of the MYC2 target genes differentially expressed between *myc2* and WT plants were more highly expressed in WT, which indicates that loss of MYC2 function reduces the JA responsiveness of these genes. (表示总结)

【例文 37】 In summary, the gene regulatory network predicts that STZ is an important hub for JA signalling to be prioritized over other hormone and stress response pathways. (表示总结)

【例文 38】 Taken together, our analyses determine that MYC2 and MYC3 shape the dynamic JA response through the activation of a large TF network that includes various potentially coupled feedforward and feedback loops and allows extensive cross-communication with other signalling pathways. (表示总结)

【例文 39】 Taken together, these data demonstrate that MYC2 regulates gene expression through a large network of downstream TFs during responses to a JA stimulus. (表示总结)

【例文 40】 Taken together, these data show that our multi-omics approach goes beyond network description, ultimately enabling the identification of novel JA pathway regulators. (表示总结)

另外，如果是不依赖于时间的原理和结论，或者描述现在的行为与动作，用一般现在时；如果是主体（人或物）过去的动作和行为，过一般过去时态。读者可对上述例句进行体会，不再举例说明。

（五）讨论

【原文1】

Discussion

An important unanswered question in plant biology is how multiple signalling pathways interact to coordinate the control of growth and development. In this study, we comprehensively characterized cellular responses to the plant hormone JA and generated a network-level understanding of the MYC2 and MYC3-regulated JA signalling pathway. We used this approach to identify several new points at which JA signalling may have cross-regulation with other hormone and stress response pathways to prioritize itself. The results increase our knowledge of how JA functions in the etiolated seedling, a less well-characterized model of JA responses. Moreover, the general principles described here provide a framework for analyses of cross-regulation between hormone and stress signalling pathways. We provide our data in a web-based genome and in network browsers to encourage deeper exploration (http: //signal. salk. edu/interactome/JA. php and http: // neomorph. salk. edu/MYC2).

【参考译文1】

讨论

植物生物学中一个重要的未解问题是，多种信号转导途径如何互作来协调对生长和发育的控制。在本研究中，我们全面鉴定了植物激素 JA 的细胞响应，并对 MYC2 和 MYC3 调控的 JA 信号转导通路产生了一种网络水平的理解。我们使用此方法鉴定出几个新的 JA 信号转导与其他激素和胁迫响应通路的交叉调控点，植物以此来优先进行 JA 信号转导。这一结果增进了我们对 JA 如何在黄化幼苗中发挥功能的了解，因为黄化幼苗的 JA 响应模型此前未得到充分鉴定。此外，本文描述的一般原理为分析激素和胁迫信号转导通路之间的交叉调控提供了框架。我们的基因组数据已上传到网络，可用网络浏览器来获取（ http: //signal. salk. edu/interactiome/JA. php 和 http: // neormph. salk. edu/MYC2），以便进行更深入的探索。

【原文2】A major insight provided by our study is that multiple points of crosstalk probably exist between JA signalling and other pathways. This was evident from the interactions within the genome regulatory network model and supported by our observation that many (37%-59%) genes from other hormone signalling pathways are bound by MYC2 and MYC3 and are regulated by JA. The WRKY family TF ABO3 was identified as a candidate JA response regulator, and genetic analyses determined a mutant of the gene was

JA hyposensitive. ABO3 is also a regulator of ABA responses[62], which suggests that ABO3 functions in cross-communication between the JA and ABA pathway. The repressive zinc-finger family TF STZ, working with JAZ8, emerged as a potentially important point of contact with salt and drought stress, as well as the salicylic acid, brassinosteroid and gibberellin hormone signalling pathways. Combined, these results illustrate the importance of transcriptional cross-regulation during a JA response in modulating the correct cellular output for the stimuli a plant perceives.

【参考译文2】我们的研究产生的一个主要见解是，JA信号转导和其他通路之间可能存在多个串扰点。这一结论从基因组调控网络模型内的互作来看是十分明显的；其他激素信号转导通路的许多基因（37%~59%）可以被MYC2和MYC3结合，并且受JA调控——这样的观察结果也支持该结论。WRKY家族转录因子ABO3被鉴定为JA响应的候选调控因子，遗传分析表明该基因的一个突变体是JA低敏感型的。ABO3也是ABA响应的调控因子62，这表明ABO3在JA和ABA通路的交叉通讯中发挥作用。阻遏性的锌指家族转录因子STZ与JAZ8一起，不仅可能是水杨酸、油菜素类固醇和赤霉素激素信号转导通路的重要交叉接触点，还可能是盐胁迫和干旱胁迫通路的重要交叉接触点。总之，这些结果说明，对于所感知的刺激，转录交叉调控在JA响应调控正确细胞输出中具有重要意义。

【原文3】Our multi-omics analysis determined that the master TF MYC2 and its relative MYC3 directly target thousands of JA-responsive genes, including hundreds of JA-responsive TFs, thereby enabling a robust cascade of transcriptional reprogramming. Secondary TFs downstream of MYC2 and MYC3 directly targeted overlapping but distinct cohorts of genes, indicating that they have distinct roles within the JA response. This illustrates the complexity of hormone-response genome regulatory programmes; we assayed only a fraction of the JA-responsive TFs and found that any individual JA-responsive gene may be bound by multiple TFs. How the final quantitative output of any individual gene is determined by combinatorial binding of TFs remains a major challenge to address. Achieving this will require analyses at cell-type resolution, resolving differences in TF activity between tissues that would be obscured by our bulk-tissue analyses. We further demonstrated the importance of MYC2 and MYC3 target genes in JA responses by analysing JA root-growth phenotypes in mutants of 99 genes strongly targeted by MYC2 or MYC3. Mutations in six genes caused clear disruptions in JA responses, both hypersensitivity and hyposensitivity. It is probable that genetic redundancy accounts for a proportion of the mutants not causing phenotype changes. The structure of hormone-response genome regulatory programmes will probably differ between cells and tissues and, while our findings can be translated between etiolated seedlings and seedlings grown in light, exploration of other developmental stage-specific regulatory programmes is needed to generalize these findings.

【参考译文 3】我们的多组学分析确定，主转录因子 MYC2 及其同源的 MYC3 直接靶向数千个 JA 响应基因，包括数百个 JA 响应转录因子，从而实现转录重编程的强大级联。MYC2 和 MYC3 下游的次级转录因子直接靶向重叠但不同的基因群，表明它们在 JA 响应中具有不同的作用。这说明了激素应答基因调控程序的复杂性；我们只分析了 JA 应答转录因子的一小部分，发现任何单个 JA 应答基因都可能被多个转录因子结合。如何通过转录因子组合形式结合来测定单个基因的最终定量输出仍是一个有待解决的重大挑战。要做到这一点，需要在细胞类型分辨率上进行分析，解决组织之间存在的转录因子活性差异问题，而这些转录因子活性差异会被我们的大块组织分析所掩盖。通过对 99 个 MYC2 或 MYC3 靶向结合较强的基因的突变体进行 JA 根系生长表型分析，进一步证明了 MYC2 和 MYC3 靶基因在 JA 响应中的重要性。6 个基因突变明显破坏了 JA 响应（包括超敏反应和低敏反应）。没有引起表型变化的突变体占一定的比例，这可用遗传冗余来解释。激素应答基因组调控程序的结构可能在细胞之间和组织之间有所不同。虽然我们的发现可以变换应用于黄化幼苗和光照下生长的幼苗，但需要探索其他特定发育阶段的调控程序来加以归纳推广。

【原文 4】Our study also highlighted that many different regulatory mechanisms are utilized by JA to exert its effects on the cell. Expression of a large number of protein kinases was regulated by MYC2. Consistent with this, substantial MYC2-dependent changes in phosphopeptide abundance occurred in JA-treated seedlings. It is also probable that JA modulates alternative splicing through MYC2. Genes encoding splicing factors were differentially expressed between *myc2* and WT plants, and the spliceosome pathway was enriched among *myc2*-dependent JA-regulated phosphopeptides. Accordingly, isoform-switch events occurred following JA treatment. Collectively, these findings indicate that investigation of post-transcriptional and post-translational layers of regulation are required to better understand the complexity of JA signalling. The targets of JA-regulated protein kinases are a notable prospect.

【参考译文 4】我们的研究还突出表明 JA 利用许多不同的调控机制对细胞发挥作用。大量蛋白激酶的表达受 MYC2 调控。与此一致的是，经 JA 处理的幼苗中磷酸肽丰度发生 MYC2 依赖性变化。JA 也可通过 MYC2 来调控选择性剪接。编码剪接因子的基因在 *myc2* 和 WT 植株间差异表达，剪接体途径在 *myc2* 依赖性 JA 调控的磷酸肽中富集。因此，JA 处理后发生了同源蛋白异构体转换（isoform-switch）事件。总之，这些发现表明，为了更好地理解 JA 信号转导的复杂性，需要对转录后和翻译后调控层进行研究。对于受 JA 调控的蛋白激酶的靶蛋白研究前景值得关注。

【原文 5】Another layer of regulatory complexity within the JA signalling pathway, and within signalling pathways in general, is the presence of multiple feedforward and feedback loops that are simultaneously activated. The interactions between these subnetworks through their kinetics and the strength of their regulatory impact on the broader networkare not well understood. For example, we discovered that MYC2 and MYC3 stimulate JA biosynthesis and target the entire JAZ repressor family from which the majority of members are also transcriptionally activated. Uncoupling these subnetworks would be an effective way to determine how they interact to drive very robust activation of the JA pathway. The combination of our multi-omics framework approach coupled with powerful genetic approaches, such as the generation of the *jaz* decuple mutant[29], should significantly contribute to a better understanding of JA response pathways.

【参考译文 5】 JA 信号转导通路和一般信号转导通路内另外一层调控复杂性在于，存在多个同时激活的前馈和反馈回路。这些子网络之间通如何过它们的动态变化互作，以及子网络对范围更广的网络的调控影响的强度，都还不清楚。例如，我们发现 MYC2 和 MYC3 刺激 JA 生物合成，并靶向结合全部 JAZ 阻遏蛋白家族，大多数家族成员也被转录激活。分析这些子网络将是确定它们如何互作以驱动 JA 通路稳定激活的有效方法。

说明：本文的讨论部分并没有出现新的难理解的术语。注意在下面 "Secondary TFs downstream of MYC2 and MYC3 directly targeted overlapping but distinct cohorts of genes, indicating that they have distinct roles within the JA response" 这一句中的 cohort，原义是 "古罗马的步兵队"（an ancient Roman military unit），后引申为 "（有共同特点或举止类同的）一群人，一批人"（a group of people banded together or treated as a group），目前最常用的意思是 "组"（group）或 "群"（company）。

不同期刊文章的风格和写作要求存在很大的变异。《自然》和《自然植物》的长论文与《植物细胞》的长论文风格就有很大的差别。前者的讨论简略（有一部分内容移到结果中），而后者的讨论会有相当的篇幅，并且分若干标题和小节来进行。就这篇文章而论，相当一部分属于讨论的内容被移到结果部分。也就是说，从结构方面而论，前面的结果部分已经通过征引文献对具体的结果进行解释，置于现有的文献背景下对其有效性或确定性进行评价，例如引述前人的文献，来支持论文得出的结果或结论，因此，讨论部分主要是针对重要结果或结论的意义（也包括不足和局限性）进行讨论，也就是重点讨论论文结果如何增进了人们对相关知识领域的认识。

在讨论部分的第一段，对论文的中心贡献或核心结果进行概括。简析其结构如下：

An important unanswered question in plant biology is how multiple signalling pathways interact to coordinate the control of growth and development. ［陈述目前植物生物学领域最重要的一个问题，设定为理解论文中心贡献或核心结果的背景］In this study, we comprehensively characterized cellular responses to the plant hormone JA and generated anetwork-level understanding of the MYC2 and MYC3-regulated JA signalling pathway. We used this approach to identify several new points at which JA signalling may have cross-regulation with other hormone and stress response pathways to prioritize itself.【概括论文的中心贡献或核心结果】The results increase our knowledge of how JA functions in the etiolated seedling, a less well-characterized model of JA responses. Moreover, the general principles described here provide a framework for analyses of cross-regulation between hormone and stress signalling pathways.【论述本论文结果的意义和价值】We provide our data in a web-based genome and in network browsers to encourage deeper exploration (http://signal.salk.edu/interactome/JA.php and http://neomorph.salk.edu/MYC2).【给出论文数据的使用方式】

接下来的几个段落对论文的重要结果进行讨论，根据结果的重要性来顺序分段讨论。第二段讨论 JA 信号转导和其他通路之间可能存在多个串扰点，第三段讨论主转录因子 MYC2 及其同源的 MYC3 直接靶向数千个 JA 响应基因，包括数百个 JA 响应转录因子，从而实现转录重编程的强大级联，第四段讨论我们的研究还强调了 JA 利用许多不同的调控机制对细胞发挥作用，最后一段讨论 JA 信号转导通路和一般信号转导通路内另外一层调控复杂性在于，存在多个同时激活的前馈和反馈回路。这些段落的通常将讨论的要点放在段首作为主题句，接下来主要利用论文本身的结果对其进行证实或解释，然后得出一定的结论，并指出本研究存在的局限性与下一步努力的方向或前景。

最后，我们看一下讨论部分可以学习的词汇和句子。

在某些语境中，例如，解释一个理论或一个想法，可以使用 demonstrate 和 illustrate 这两个动词。它们意义接近，在一些上下文中可以互换使用，但却存在细微差别：demonstrate 强调通过推理或证据来证明或论证结论的正误；illustrate 指利用实物、图片或实例进行说明。

【例文1】We further demonstrated the importance of MYC2 and MYC3 target genes in JA responses by analysing JA root-growth phenotypes in mutants of 99 genes strongly targeted by MYC2 or MYC3.

【例文2】Combined, these results illustrate the importance of transcriptional cross-regulation during a JA response in modulating the correct cellular output for the stimuli a plant perceives.

【例文3】This illustrates the complexity of hormone-response genome regulatory programmes.

表示结论得到某项证据支持时可参考以下例文：

【例文】This was evident from the interactions within the genome regulatory network model and supported by our observation that many (37%-59%) genes from other hormone signalling pathways are bound by MYC2 and MYC3 and are regulated by JA.

表示仍有什么问题没有解决或某件事尚不了解时可参考以下例文：

【例文1】How the final quantitative output of any individual gene is determined by combinatorial binding of TFs remains a major challenge to address.

【例文2】The interactions between these subnetworks through their kinetics and the strength of their regulatory impact on the broader network are not well understood.

表示需用什么方法来解决某个问题时可参考以下例文：

【例文1】Achieving this will require analyses at cell-type resolution, resolving differences in TF activity between tissues that would be obscured by our bulk-tissue analyses.

【例文2】Exploration of other developmental stage-specific regulatory programmes is needed to generalize these findings.

【例文3】Investigation of post-transcriptional and post-translational layers of regulation are required to better understand the complexity of JA signalling.

【例文4】Uncoupling these subnetworks would be an effective way to determine how they interact to drive very robust activation of the JA pathway.

【例文5】The combination of our multi-omics framework approach coupled with powerful genetic approaches, such as the generation of the *jaz* decuple mutant, should significantly contribute to a better understanding of JA response pathways.

(六) 方法

【原文】

Methods

Plant material and growth conditions. The *myc2* mutant *jin1-8*(SALK_061267)[15] was obtained from the Arabidopsis Biological Resource Center. Col-0 *MYC2*::*MYC2-YPet* and Col-0 *MYC3*::*MYC3-YPet*, generated by recombineering, have been previously described[67]. For the generation of all large-scale datasets, 3-day-old etiolated seedlings were used [Col-0 (WT), *myc2*, *MYC2*::*MYC2-YPet* and *MYC3*::*MYC3-YPet*]. Seedlings were grown in the dark in closed lightproof containers. Gaseous methyl jasmonate treatments for the respective times were performed in these containers, as previously described[17], with 1 μl of methyl jasmonate (95% purity; Sigma-Aldrich) per 1 litre of container volume dropped onto Whatman paper. For the JA-induced root-growth inhibition assay, surface-sterilized WT, *myc2* and T-DNA mutant seeds (Supplementary Table 19) were grown on agar plates containing Linsmaier and Skoog (LS) medium supplemented with or without 20 μM methyl jasmonate (392707, Millipore Sigma) for 9 days. Plates were scanned afterwards and root lengths were measured using ImageJ.

ChIP-seq. Three-day-old etiolated Col-0*MYC2*::*MYC2-YPet*, Col-0 *MYC3*::*MYC3-YPet*, Col-0 and *myc2* seedlings were used for ChIP-seq experiments. ChIP assays were performed as previously described[68]. ChIP-seq assays were conducted with antibodies against H2A.Z (39647, Active Motif), H3K4me3 (04-745, Millipore Sigma) and green fluorescent protein (GFP; 11814460001, Millipore Sigma or goat anti-GFP supplied by D. Dreschel, Max Planck Institute of Molecular Cell Biology and Genetics). As a negative control, mouse or goat IgG (015-000-003 or 005-000-003, Jackson ImmunoResearch) was used. The respective antibodies or IgG were coupled for 4-6 h to Protein G Dynabeads (50 μl, 10004D, Thermo Fisher Scientific) and subsequently incubated overnight with equal amounts of sonicated chromatin. Beads were washed twice with high-salt buffer (50 mM Tris-HCl pH 7.4, 150 mM NaCl, 2 mM EDTA, 0.5% Triton X-100), low-salt buffer (50 mM Tris-HCl pH 7.4, 500 mM NaCl, 2 mM EDTA, 0.5% Triton X-100) and wash buffer (50 mM Tris-HCl pH 7.4, 50 mM NaCl, 2 mM EDTA) before samples were decrosslinked, digested with proteinase K and DNA precipitated. Sequencing libraries were generated following the manufacturer's instructions (Illumina). Libraries were sequenced on a Illumina HiSeq 2500 and HiSeq 4000 Sequencing system, and sequencing reads were aligned to the TAIR10 genome assembly using Bowtie2 (ref.[69]).

DAP-seq. DAP-seq assays were carried out as previously described[70, 71] using recombinantly expressed ERF1, ORA59, ATAF1 (also known as AT1G01720), DREB2B, ZAT18, RVE2, WRKY51, HY5 and TCP23.

RNA-seq. Three-day-old etiolated seedlings were used for expression analyses. Total RNA was extracted using a RNeasy Plant Mini kit (74903, Qiagen). Complementary DNA library preparation and subsequent single-read sequencing were carried as previously described[3].

RNA-seq analyses. Sequencing reads were quality trimmed using TrimGalore 0.4.5 (https://github.com/FelixKrueger/TrimGalore) then aligned to the TAIR10 genome assembly using TopHat 2.1.1 (ref.[72]). Reads within gene models were counted using HTSeq[73]. Differentially expressed genes in time-series RNA-seq were identified using EdgeR 3.6.2 with a likelihood ratio test (using the functions glmFit and glmLRT), and batch correction using Benjamini-Hochberg correction was used for multiple tests[74]. Differentially expressed genes in the Col-0 versus *myc2* mutant RNA-seq were determined using EdgeR 3.18.1 and quasi-likelihood *F*-tests (using the function glmQLFit)[75]. Temporal co-regulation of transcripts was determined using Short Time-Series Expression Miner (STEM)[76]. A minimum correlation coefficient of 0.7 was applied, and up to 50 permutations were permitted to identify correct cluster/gene matches. Significant clusters were those having a Bonferroni-corrected $P<0.05$.

Full STEM model parameters are given in Supplementary Table 7. Known *A. thaliana* TFs were identified by reference to PlantTFDB 4.0 (ref. [77]).

ChIP-seq and DAP-seq analyses. ChIP-seq and DAP-seq sequence reads were mapped to the TAIR10 reference genome using Bowtie2 v. 2-2.0.5 with default parameters[78]. For TF and histone ChIP-seq, we first assessed the quality of the ChIP data by using PhantomPeak QualTools v. 2.0 to calculate normalized strand correlation, relative strand correlation and shift size[79]. Enriched binding sites were then identified using MACS2 v. 2.1 (options-p 99e-2-nomodel-shiftsize-down-sample-call-summits) against sequence reads from whole IgG control samples[80]. Subsequent analyses used summits only. Summit lists were filtered with a cut-off of $P \leq 1 \times 10^{-25}$, and remaining summits expanded from single nucleotides to 150 nt. Only summits with at least 10% nucleotide overlap between at least two biological replicates were retained. These overlapping summits were merged between replicates using BEDtools v. 2.17.0 to give the final set of high-confidence binding sites, which were then annotated using ChIPpeakAnno v. 2.2.0 to any gene within 500 nt of the centre of the summit or, alternatively, the nearest neighbour if there was no gene within 500 nt[81,82]. Venn diagrams were drawn using Venny and Intervene (http://bioinfogp.cnb.csic.es/tools/venny/)[83]. Top-ranked MYC2 and MYC3 binding sites were identified by applying irreproducible discovery rate to the summits from the two biological replicates that had the greatest number of summits above the MACS2 cut-off of $P \leq 1 \times 10^{-25}$. TF binding motifs were determined using the MEME-ChIP webserver with default parameters on the sequences of the high-stringency MYC2 summits[84]. To identify potential partner TFs that may enable indirect MYC2 binding, we removed all MYC2 high-stringency summits that contained the MYC2 motif (CACGTG, CATGTG or CACGTT). This was done by scanning them with FIMO set to default parameters (http://meme-suite.org/tools/fimo) against the position weight matrix for the MYC2 motif we previously identified by MEME-ChIP. We then conducted MEME-ChIP analyses on the remaining high-stringency summits as described above. The Genome wide Event finding and Motif discovery (GEM) tool[85] was used to identify the target summits in DAP-seq data. Significant enrichments of histone modifications and histone variants were identified with the software SICER[86] using the TAIR10 genome assembly. The Intersect tool from BEDtools[81] was used to identify the genes in the histone ChIP-seq datasets most proximal to the binding sites. The fraction of reads in peak score was calculated for DAP-seq and histone ChIP-seq data using BEDtools and SAMtools[86,87]. For both ChIP-seq and DAP-seq, GO enrichment was assessed using clusterProfiler with default parameters[88]. Protein domain enrichment was assessed using Thalemine (https://apps.araport.org/thalemine/) with default parameters[89].

Mass spectrometry analysis. Untreated and JA-treated Col-0 and *myc2* seedling tissue samples were ground and lysed in YeastBuster(71186, Millipore Sigma). Proteins(100 μg per sample) were precipitated using methanol-chloroform. Dried pellets were dissolved in 8 M urea, 100 mM triethylammonium bicarbonate (TEAB), reduced with 5 mM Tris(2-carboxyethyl) phosphine hydrochloride (TCEP) and alkylated with 50 mM chloroacetamide. Proteins were then trypsin digested overnight at 37 °C. The digested peptides were labelled using a TMT10plex Isobaric Label Reagent set(90309, Thermo Fisher Scientific, lot no. TE264412) and combined. One hundred micrograms (the pre-enriched sample) was fractionated using a basic reverse-phase kit (84868, Thermo Fisher Scientific). Phosphopeptides were enriched from the remaining sample (900 μg) using a High-Select Fe-NTA Phospho-peptide Enrichment kit (A32992, Thermo Fisher Scientific). The TMT labelled samples were analysed on a Fusion Lumos mass spectrometer (Thermo Fisher Scientific). Samples were injected directly onto a 25 cm, 100-μm inner diameter column packed with BEH 1.7-μm C18 resin(186002350, Waters) and subsequently separated at a flow rate of 300 nl min^{-1} on a nLC 1200 (LC140, Thermo Fisher Scientific). Buffer A and B were 0.1% formic acid in water and 90% acetonitrile, respectively. A gradient of 1%-20% B over 180 min, an increase to 40% B over 30 min, an increase to 100% B over another 20 min and held at 90% B for a final 10 min of washing was used for a total run time of 240 min. The column was re-equilibrated with 20 μl of buffer A before the injection of sample. Peptides were eluted directly from the tip of the column and nano sprayed directly into the mass spectrometer by application of 2.8 kV voltage at the back of the column. The Lumos was operated in the data-dependent mode. Full MS1 scans were collected in the Orbitrap at 120,000 resolution. The cycle time was set to 3 s, and within this 3 s, the most abundant ions per scan were selected for tandem mass spectrometry with collision-induced dissociation in the ion trap. MS3 analysis with multinotch isolation(SPS3) was utilized for detection of TMT reporter ions at 60,000 resolution. Monoisotopic precursor selection was enabled and dynamic exclusion was used with an exclusion duration of 10 s.

The raw data were analysed using MaxQuant (v. 1.6.3.3)[90]. Spectra were searched using the Andromeda search engine[91] against the TAIR10 proteome file entitled "TAIR10_pep_20101214" that was downloaded from the TAIR website (https://www.arabidopsis.org/download/indexauto.jsp?dir=%2Fdownload_files%2FProteins%2FTAIR10_protein_lists) and was complemented with reverse decoy sequences and common contaminants by MaxQuant. Carbamidomethyl cysteine was set as a fixed modification, while methionine oxidation and protein amino-terminal acetylation were set as variable modifications. For the phoshoproteome, "Phosho STY" was also set as a variable modification. The sample type was set to "Reporter

Ion MS3" with "10plex TMT selected for both lysine and N-termini". Digestion parameters were set to "specific" and "Trypsin/P;LysC". Up to two missed cleavages were allowed. A FDR, calculated in MaxQuant using a target-decoy strategy[92], value of less than 0.01 at both the peptide spectral match and protein identification level was required. The 'second peptide' option to identify co-fragmented peptides was not used. Differentially expressed proteins and phospho-sites were identified using PoissonSeq[93] with a q-value cut-off of 0.1. Sample loading normalization was performed before differential expression analysis.

Transcript quantification and identification of isoform switches. Quantification of transcripts was performed using Salmon v.0.8.1 in conjunction with the AtRTD2-QUASI transcript reference[94, 95]. The quasi mapping-based index was built using an auxiliary k-mer hash over k-mers of length 31 ($k = 31$). For quantification, all parameters of Salmon were kept at default; however, the option to correct for the fragment-level GC biases ("-gcBias") was turned on. The TSIS R package[96], which is designed for detecting alternatively spliced isoform-switch events in time-series transcriptome data, was used to perform the isoform-switch analysis. Only transcripts whose average TPM across all time points was >1 were included in the TSIS analysis. The mean expression approach was used to search interaction points. Significant switch events were identified using the following filtering parameters: (1) probability cut-off value of >0.5; (2) differences cut-off value of >1; (3) P cut-off value of <0.05; (4) minimum time in interval of >1.

Gene regulatory network inference. All gene regulatory network inferences were constructed using the Regression Tree Pipeline for Spatial, Temporal, and Replicate data (RTP-STAR)[97, 98]. Before gene regulatory network inference, genes were clustered on the basis of transcriptome, proteome or phosphoproteome data using Dynamic Time Warping and the dtwclust package in R[99]. These clusters were then used in the RTP-STAR pipeline. For the transcriptome networks, one network was inferred for genes differentially expressed at each time point (eight networks in total), and then the networks were combined in a union. For each network, the biological replicates for that individual time point and the 0 h (control) time point were used to infer the network. The sign (activation/repression) of each edge was inferred using all of the time points in the time course. For the proteome and phosphoproteome networks, one network was inferred for genes differentially expressed in any of the comparisons. The biological replicates for all of the (phospho)proteome samples were used to infer the network. The sign of each edge was not inferred, as the (phospho)proteome data only consisted of one time point. After the transcriptome, proteome and phosphoproteome networks were combined in a union, a Network Motif Score (NMS)[100] was calculated to determine the importance of each gene. Feedback loop, feedforward loop, bi-fan and diamond motifs were used in this score as they have been previously shown to contain genes important for biological processes[101,102,103]. All motifs that were significantly enriched in the combined network were compared to a randomly generated network of the same size. The number of times each gene appeared in each motif was counted, the counts were normalized to a scale of 0 to 1, and the counts were summed to calculate the NMS. The higher the NMS, the more functionally important the gene. All code for RTP-STAR is available at https://github.com/nmclark2/RTP-STAR. The parameters used for all networks in this paper are provided in Supplementary Table 20.

Reporting Summary. Further information on research design is available in theNature Research Reporting Summary linked to this article.

Data availability. All described lines can be requested from the corresponding authors. Sequence data can be downloaded from the Gene Expression Omnibus repository (GSE133408). Proteomics data are deposited at the ProteomeXchange under the accession ID PXD013592. Visualized data can be found at http://neomorph.salk.edu/MYC2 and http://signal.salk.edu/interactome/JA.php. Source data for Figs. 1-5 and Extended Data Figs. 1-10 are provided with the paper.

说明：方法部分没有什么生词与新出现的术语，但其中提到的ChIP-seq、DAP-seq、RNA-seq 和 Mass spectrometry analysis 等具体的方法原理和一般实验步骤如果不了解，需要阅读相关的教科书和综述论文。

从结构上说，方法部分分若干小节进行论述，除 Plant material and growth conditions 一般放在方法部分的前面，Reporting summary 和 Data availability 放在方法部分的末尾外，主要的方法按照论文中出现的先后顺序（也是实验的先后顺序）进行排列：ChIP-seq, DAP-seq, RNA-seq, RNA-seq analyses, ChIP-seq and DAP-seq analyses, Mass spectrometry analysis, Transcript quantification and identification of isoform switches, Gene regulatory network inference.

每个小节内也按实验步骤的顺序进行描述。因此，必要之处需要使用表示顺序的过渡词来明确表示。另外，描述实验方法和步骤时，要注意介绍实验目的，以便于读者理解。例如，

For TF and histone ChIP-seq, we first assessed the quality of the ChIP data by using PhantomPeakQualTools v.2.0 to calculate normalized strand correlation, relative strand correlation and shift size[79]. Enriched binding sites were then identified using MACS2 v.2.1 (options-p 99e-2-nomodel-shiftsize-down-sample-call-summits) against sequence reads from whole IgG control samples[80]. Subsequent analyses used summits only.

方法部分应该包含足够的细节信息，以便于其他研究者能重复论文的实验结果或参考使用论文描述的方法。如果重要的细节信息遗漏，致使别人无法重复论文的实验

结果，不仅会影响科学研究向前推进，而且会让人怀疑作者的学术诚信。因此，在方法写作中，不仅步骤描述要正确，描述所用的统计学方法（包括判断显著性的阈值等）。诸如时间、温度、质量、体积、浓度等细节条件信息也要详细提供。此外，重要试剂的纯度、供应商，以及关键设备的型号和厂家（包括地址）都要尽可能给出。

如果实验方法是本课题组或前人曾经使用过的（要给出参考文献），或者是生产商的操作手册，那么可用下述方法加以表示。

【例文1】Col-0 *MYC2*::*MYC2-YPet* and Col-0 *MYC3*::*MYC3-YPet*, generated by recombineering, have been previously described[67].

【例文2】Gaseous methyl jasmonate treatments for the respective times were performed in these containers, as previously described[17], with 1 μl of methyl jasmonate (95% purity; Sigma-Aldrich) per 1 litre of container volume dropped onto Whatman paper.

【例文3】Three-day-old etiolated Col-0 *MYC2*::*MYC2-YPet*, Col-0 *MYC3*::*MYC3-YPet*, Col-0 and *myc2* seedlings were used for ChIP-seq experiments. ChIP assays were performed as previously described[68].

【例文4】DAP-seq assays were carried out as previously described[70,71] using recombinantly expressed ERF1, ORA59, ATAF1 (also known as AT1G01720), DREB2B, ZAT18, RVE2, WRKY51, HY5 and TCP23.

【例文5】Complementary DNA library preparation and subsequent single-read sequencing were carried as previously described[3].

【例文6】Sequencing libraries were generated following the manufacturer's instructions (Illumina).

最后，需要注意的是，论文中使用前人的方法要给出参考文献，如果使用分析和应用程序要给出版本信息，生物信息存储网络、在线分析和应用程序还需要提供网址。例如，

【例文1】Libraries were sequenced on a Illumina HiSeq 2500 and HiSeq 4000 Sequencing system, and sequencing reads were aligned to the TAIR10 genome assembly using Bowtie2 (ref.[69]).

【例文2】The fraction of reads in peak score was calculated for DAP-seq and histone ChIP-seq data using BED tools and SAM tools[86,87].

【例文3】For both ChIP-seq and DAP-seq, GO enrichment was assessed using clusterProfiler with default parameters[88].

【例文4】Spectra were searched using the Andromeda search engine[91] against the TAIR10 proteome file entitled "TAIR10_pep_20101214" that was downloaded from the TAIR website (https://www.arabidopsis.org/download/indexauto.jsp?dir=%2Fdownload_files%2FProteins%2FTAIR10_protein_lists) and was complemented with reverse decoy sequences and common contaminants by MaxQuant.

【例文5】All code for RTP-STAR is available at https://github.com/nmclark2/RTP-STAR.

【例文6】Sequencing reads were quality trimmed using TrimGalore 0.4.5 (https://github.com/FelixKrueger/TrimGalore) then aligned to the TAIR10 genome assembly using TopHat 2.1.1(ref.[72]).

【例文7】Venn diagrams were drawn using Venny and Intervene (http://bioinfogp.cnb.csic.es/tools/venny/)[83].

【例文8】Protein domain enrichment was assessed using Thalemine (https://apps.araport.org/thalemine/) with default parameters[89].

由于论文作者一般被为实验者，且方法描述宜突出实验动作、材料和条件，因此，此部分多用被动句。此外，由于实验是过去进行的，动作是过去发生的，所以，方法描述应该使用过去时态，但描述现在的状态或不受时间限制的原理或情况，用现在时（一般现在时或现在完成时）。

（七）参考文献

References

1. Vanstraelen, M. & Benkova, E. Hormonal interactions in the regulation of plant development. *Annu. Rev. Cell Dev. Biol.* 28, 463-487(2012).

2. Chang, K. N. et al. Temporal transcriptional response to ethylene gas drives growth hormone cross-regulation in *Arabidopsis. eLife* 2, e00675(2013).

注：由上面2条参考文献可知，本文采用顺序编码法（citation-order system 或 citation-sequence system），就是在正文中按照顺序来征引参考文献。篇末参考文献按正文中出现或引用顺序先后来排列。只有两个作者采用"&"连接，3个作者以上用"首作者 et al."的方法表示。期刊名用缩写，出版年用括号括住，置于最后。

第十八章　SCI 论文阅读法之泛读法

一、概述

文献浩如烟海，光靠精读是不够的。大量文献阅读还必须学会泛读。泛读也称为快读，是指为获取文章内容而进行的快速阅读。在初级阶段，应以精读为主，等到精读了三五十篇有了一定的基础之后，就可以短时间内对大量文献进行泛读了。泛读法的前提是，读者已经基本掌握本领域的专业术语，没有语言文字障碍，对相关专业知识和问题背景有一定的了解。泛读法不仅阅读速度快，也是一种目的性很强的阅读方式，这使我们在海量的文献面前能够快速抓取自己感兴趣的学术内容。此外，论文总是有这样那样的优点，有的论文设计很巧妙，角度很独特；有的论文方法很新颖，技术很先进；有的论文证据很充分，结论很坚实。泛读法也可以使我们快速学习不同论文的优点，获得最大的收益。泛读的题材不一定局限于自己的小领域。定时泛读 CNS 文章，可以了解本领域及相关领域的重大发现、研究进展及最新动态；对其他领域文章的泛读也有可能无意中获得对自己研究有用的信息、技术或启发。

SCI 论文快速阅读与普通英语快速阅读一样，都是有一定技巧的。例如，最常用的推测法（prediction），熟悉本领域的读者根据论文标题就可大致推断出研究内容和结果。如果根据标题仍不能了解论文的大致情况，那么读摘要就足以明白作者在这篇论文中表述的主要结果和结论。因为摘要实质上就是一篇微型或迷你论文（mini-paper），而结构式摘要通常分为背景、目的、方法、结果和结论几个要素，只是更加简洁和概括，不包含细节和讨论罢了。关键词和主题句法（key word and topic sentences）是指在阅读时关注摘要后面的关键词以及正文中能反映文章主要内容的关键词，同时，重点关注结果部分（有时也包括讨论部分）每一节前面小标题（小标题都是每节内容的概括和论点）或段落的主题句和结论句，以求很快了解论文的主要内容。略读法（skimming）或跳读法（reading and skipping）是指根据论文的整体结构（例如论文正文分引言、方法、结果、讨论和结论）、每个部分的结构（例如，引言的"倒三角形"或"倒金字塔"结构、结果的分节论述结构等），以及段落中反映的写作思路（例如，过渡词 however, moreover, in addition, collectively 和序列词 firstly, secondly, thirdly, finally 的使用等），有意识地忽略一些不重要的细节，选择关键性的结构部分和重要内容来阅读，或者选择最感兴趣的部分（如图表或方法）来阅读。扫读法（scanning）就是一目十行地快速扫过句子阅读。SCI 论文（也包括自然科学领域的专著）一般句式简单，没有复杂的长句和难句，这种扫读是很容易实现的。扫读法有时也称寻读法，因为该法可从很长的篇幅或海量的资料中迅速查找与定位某一具体的数据或结论。在实际泛读过程中，集中注意力，根据论文结构和自己关心的内容，灵活使用这几种方法，可以取得很好的效果。

多数情况下，人们对论文的阅读方式是这样的：看到标题后，确定论文是否与自己的研究问题相关，或者自己是否有兴趣了解。如果答案是肯定的，那么，接下来阅读摘要。摘要读完，文章大致内容也就了解了。如果觉得有必要继续阅读，通常也不会从引言部分从头读起，而是跳到结果的图表部分。一般认为，图表是一篇文章中最重要的部分，论文的结果实质是对图表的解释；图表能清楚、直观地反映论文结果。图表对于论文而言，相当于人的衣着，图表做得漂亮，就会有足够的吸引力使读者继续阅读，如果图表平平，读者就没有继续阅读的兴趣。事实上，由于图表具有自足性，也就是单看图表，不看正文，读者就足以直观地了解文章的主要结果。图表读完，有基础的读者就会得出论文的结论，当然也能对论文水平有大致的判断。这时候，再来对照论文最后的结论，看与论文的结论是否一致，再读讨论部分，看作者如何评价论文结果及如何论证或推导论文的结论。如前所述，批判性阅读的要义就是读者根据自己的判断来确定文章结论是否可靠，方法是否可行。那么，读者可根据自己对论文结果所提供的证据，来确定是否足以得出论文一致的新观点或新结论，以及根据材料和方法是否有瑕疵，来确定论文的结果是否可靠。如果从论文引言开始按部就班地阅读，很容易滑入作者的论证思路，因此，为了避免作者的逻辑对自己的判断造成干扰，批判性阅读就不一定从引言开始读起。

事实上，SCI 论文各部分具有清晰的结构和功能：引言是描述论文要解决的问题，也就是说明为什么要做这项研究，方法是描述作者采用了哪些方法和手段，结果是描述研究产生了什么样的发现，讨论则是论述结果有什么意义。那么，读者看哪部分不看哪部分，先看哪部分后看哪部分，既取决于读者的阅读目标和阅读兴趣，也取决于论文的性质及读者对论文相关工作的熟悉程度。如果想快速了解论文的结果，那就阅读图表；如果想了解论文传递的最重要的信息或学术贡献，就读结论；如果想了解技术细节，那就阅读材料和方法；如果想知道问题的来龙去脉，那就阅读引言；如果想了解作者对论文发现的解释和论证，就读讨论。一般而言，如果论文是读者熟悉的领域，那么很可能最感兴趣的是结果部分（了解论文的新发现，对自己的课题有所启发）、方法部分（了解论文采用的实验设计、实验材料和分析方法，以便参考学习）或者讨论部分（寻找研究结果的局限性或还有哪些问题没有解决，也许可作为选题参考）；如果论文不是读者熟悉的领域，那么除了结果与方法外，引言和讨论部分也很重要，因为引言提供了理解论文的专业背景，而讨论则对论文结果进行了解释和评价。在实际阅读中，读者可以在读完论文标题后，从自己感兴趣的任意部分开始，如从图表、结果的小标题或方法等处开始阅读。

二、第一条泛读路线

第一条泛读路线为论文标题→摘要→图表→结论。这条泛读路线是很多人泛读论文的路线，首先阅读标题，对于感兴趣的题目，就阅读摘要了解大概情况，其次阅读图表，最后跳到结论部分。中间如果不懂结果是怎么来的，就读方法部分。

以短论文或简报（Reports）形式发表在《科学》（2006 年 314 卷）上的文章"A NAC Gene Regulating Senescence Improves Grain Protein, Zinc, and Iron Content in Wheat"为例，来说明这种阅读路线。

案例全文

这篇文章的标题为陈述句，意思是"调控小麦衰老的 NAC 基因提高了籽粒蛋白质、锌、铁的含量"。吸引我们的是这个 NAC 基因提高了小麦的籽粒蛋白质、锌、铁的含量，接下来看摘要，了解一下提高到什么程度。

摘要如下：

【原文】Enhancing the nutritional value of food crops is a means of improving human nutrition and health. We report here the positional cloning of *Gpc-B1*, a wheat quantitative trait locus associated with increased grain protein, zinc, and iron content. The ancestral wild wheat allele encodes a NAC transcription factor (NAM-B1) that accelerates senescence and increases nutrient remobilization from leaves to developing grains, whereas modern wheat varieties carry a nonfunctional *NAM-B1* allele. Reduction in RNA levels of the multiple *NAM* homologs by RNA interference delayed senescence by more than 3 weeks and reduced wheat grain protein, zinc, and iron content by more than 30%.

说明：从摘要我们了解到：①这个数量性状基因 *Gpc-B1* 是利用图位克隆从古老的小麦中获得的，它编码 NAC 转录因子 NAM-B1。这个基因能加速小麦衰老，提高从叶片到发育中的籽粒的养分转运（remobilization）。②现代小麦品种则携带一种无功能的 *NAM-B1* 等位基因，利用 RNA 干扰使多个 *NAM* 同源基因 RNA 水平降低后，延缓衰老可达 3 周以上，并使小麦籽粒蛋白质、锌和铁含量降低 30%以上。

由上可知，这篇文章之所以能够发表在《科学》期刊上，一是因为它能提高最主要的粮食作物小麦的营养价值，这对改善人类营养和健康十分重要；二是利用图位克隆法从非模式植物小麦上克隆一个数量性状基因，在 2006 年是一件很新很难的事；三是不论方法还是结果都可能推广到其他粮食作物上，具有普遍意义。

由于是一篇短论文或简报，正文没有明确划分为引言、方法、结果、讨论等几个部分，如果我们还想进一步阅读，可直接看该文的两个图和一个表，这样更为直观易懂。该例文图 1 讲的是 *Gpc-B1* 的图位克隆，图 2 主要是利用 RNA 干扰技术的转基因和非转基因小麦植株内源 *TaNAM* 基因的相对转录水平、旗叶叶绿素含量、植株及穗形态对比。至于转基因和非转基因小麦植株籽粒蛋白质、锌和铁含量的对比，利用表来表示更为具体、精确，因此，作者在表 1 中给出了这些指标的精确数据。

想了解这篇文章的一般性结论，可以看最后一段。

The cloning of *Gpc-B1* provides a direct link between the regulation of senescence and nutrient remobilization and an entry point to characterize the genes regulating these two processes. This may contribute to their more efficient manipulation in crops and translate into food with enhanced nutritional value.

大意为：对 *Gpc-B1* 基因的克隆为衰老调控和营养转运提供了直接的联系，同时也为研究这两个过程的调控基因提供了切入点。这可能有助于在作物中更有效地遗传操作，转化为营养价值更高的粮食作物。

三、第二条泛读路线

第二条泛读路线是论文标题→结果部分的小标题→结果（包括图表）。对于熟悉专业背景的读者来说，可以采取这条泛读路线。首先阅读标题，就知道论文的核心论点，其次阅读结果部分的小标题，就大致了解其论证路线，最后再阅读结果（包括图表），详细考察其证据的可靠性。

案例全文

以下以《植物杂志》（2006 年 46 卷）标题为 "AtNAP, a NAC family transcription factor, has an important role in leaf senescence" 论文为例，说明泛读法的第二条路线。

从这篇论文的题目来看，意思是 "NAC 家族转录因子 AtNAP 在叶片衰老中发挥重要作用"，标题很简单朴素。粗略看一下，发现这篇论文的结果部分最值得我们学习，那我们就看一下文章是怎样论证其中心结论（也就是其标题）。该文结果共有下面 8 个小标题，每个小标题分别是下面小节中要论证的结论。

AtNAP is upregulated during leaf senescence in *Arabidopsis*

AtNAP is targeted to nuclei

The *AtNAP* expression is knocked out in one T-DNA line and knocked down in another line

Leaf senescence is significantly delayed in the atnap null mutant plants

AtNAP restores the atnap null mutant plants to wild type

Inducible overexpression of *AtNAP* causes precocious senescence

AtNAP homologs in rice and kidney bean are specifically expressed in senescing leaves

AtNAP homologs in rice and kidney bean are able to restore the Arabidopsis atnap null mutant to wild-type

在 "*AtNAP* is upregulated during leaf senescence in *Arabidopsis*" 小节中，作者利用

RNA 凝胶印迹分析（RNA gel blot analysis）或 RNA 凝胶杂交分析表明，*AtNAP* 基因在拟南芥莲座叶中的表达与叶片衰老进程密切相关，表明 *AtNAP* 在拟南芥叶片衰老过程中表达上调。重点证明了 *AtNAP* 与叶片衰老有关。但是有关不等于发挥重要作用，有关不等于有因果关系。

接下来作者在"AtNAP is targeted to nuclei"小节中，利用 35S 启动子驱动 GFP-AtNAP 的嵌合基因在洋葱表皮细胞中瞬时表达来进行亚细胞定位，证明 AtNAP 是定位于细胞核的转录因子。

在"The AtNAP expression is knocked out in one T-DNA line and knocked down in another line"小节中，利用 RNA 凝胶印迹分析表明 *AtNAP* 基因在一个 T-DNA 插入系中被敲除（knocked out）功能，在另一个插入系中被敲低（knocked down）功能。

在"Leaf senescence is significantly delayed in the atnap null mutant plants"小节中，作者不仅通过表型（叶片黄化）观测、单个莲座丛中的叶绿素水平测定，而且使用叶片衰老的分子标记基因（拟南芥衰老特异基因）*SAG12* 和 Rubisco 小亚单位基因（*RBCS*）表达分析监测，表明 *atnap* 的缺失突变植株中，叶片衰老明显延迟。

在"*AtNAP* restores the atnap null mutant plants to wild type"标题的小节中，利用功能互补实验（complementation test experiment），证明 *AtNAP* 能使 *AtNAP* 插入缺失突变植株恢复到野生型，证明了 *AtNAP* 基因的 T-DNA 缺失突变是导致延迟衰老表型的原因。这一步已经足以证明这种相关关系是一种因果关系。

接下来，作者在"Inducible overexpression of *AtNAP* causes precocious senescence"小节中，利用获得功能分析（gain-of-function analysis），即化学诱导基因表达系统（chemical inducible gene expression system），表明诱导的 *AtNAP* 过表达导致叶片早衰。上一步加上这一步，就从正反两方面（功能缺失和互补实验，以及功能获得实验）证明了 *AtNAP* 在叶片衰老中发挥重要促进作用。至此，这个结论就已立于不败之地，论证实现无懈可击。

再接下来，作者在"*AtNAP* homologs in rice and kidney bean are specifically expressed in senescing leaves"和"*AtNAP* homologs in rice and kidney bean are able to restore the Arabidopsis atnap null mutant to wild-type"小节中，表明不仅是在拟南芥中，在水稻和芸豆中，*AtNAP* 及其同源基因（homologs）也在叶片衰老中起着重要作用。

这篇文章虽然内容不算太多，但从几个方面说是一篇很好的论文。首先，它研究的是一个非常重要的科学问题。因为叶片衰老与作物的产量和抗逆关系很大，对于植物生产而言是一个重要问题。第一，有不少研究表明，NAC 家族转录因子基因在衰老的叶片中表达，但 NAC 家族转录因子基因在叶片衰老中有什么重要作用呢？这篇文章回答了这个问题。第二，它有创新的内容，它是第一个证明 NAC 家族转录因子基因在叶片衰老中发挥重要作用（促进作用）的论文。第三，它是一个完整的科学研究，所得结论具有普遍性，论文讲述了一个完整的故事。作者不仅证明 NAC 家族转录因子基因在拟南芥叶片衰老中发挥重要作用，更难能可贵的是，作者还证明这个结论在水稻和芸豆中也成立，这表明它可能具有普遍性。如果让一些学生来做，很可能不会想到来证明 AtNAP 同源基因在水稻和芸豆中叶片衰老中也发挥重要作用，因为做到拟南芥就已经算完整了。作者将结论外推到拟南芥以外的其他植物，使论文的核心结论得到加强。因为结论的普遍性越强，文章的意义就越大。作者选择拟南芥、水稻和芸豆这 3 种植物也是匠心独具，因为它们分别是双子叶植物、单子叶植物和豆科植物的模式植物，利用代表性植物来进行试验，可保证结论的普遍性。第四，作者提供了足够的证据来证明论文的结论，使结论十分可靠。作者不仅表明 AtNAP 基因的表达与叶片衰老具有某种相关性，还利用插入突变体的表型观测及互补试验恢复其野生型表型来证明 AtNAP 基因在拟南芥叶片衰老中发挥促进作用。作者又进一步用功能获得实验证实了这个结论。好的科研工作就是要利用多种方法从多个角度来证明其结果的可靠性，事实上，很多论文的薄弱之处就是证据不足。综上可知，一篇好的论文不仅要研究一个重要的科学问题，还要以创新、完整和可靠为标志，做不到这些，就不是一篇好的论文。

案例全文

以下再举一例，《分子植物》(2013 年 6 卷)标题为"NAC Transcription Factor ORE1 and Senescence-Induced *BIFUNCTIONAL NUCLEASE1*(BFN1)Constitute a Regulatory Cascade in Arabidopsis"。

这篇论文的标题可译为"拟南芥 NAC 转录因子 ORE1 和衰老诱导的 *BIFUNCTIONAL NUCLEASE1*(BFN1)构成一个调控级联(线路)"。同样，我们最感兴趣的是作者如何论证其中心结论(也就是其标题)。该文结果共有下面 7 个小标题，每个小标题分别是下面小节中要论证的结论。

BFN1 Expression Is Rapidly Induced by ORE1

Overlapping Patterns of Transcriptional Activities of *ORE1* and *BFN1* Promoters

Senescence-Specific Expression of *BFN1* Is ORE1-Dependent

ORE1 Binding Site

In Vitro Binding of ORE1 Transcription Factor to the *BFN1* Promoter

Transactivation of the *BFN1* Promoter in Mesophyll Cell Protoplasts

In Vivo Binding of ORE1 to the *BFN1* Promoter

Altered Level of BFN1 Protein in *ORE1* Transgenic Plants

作者首先采用过表达 *ORE1/ANAC092* 转基因植株的转录组数据，表明 ORE1 能快速诱导 BFN1 表达(*BFN1* Expression Is Rapidly Induced by ORE1)，BFN1 在细胞和转基因植株中的高表达，表明 ORE1 这个 NAC-TF 基因是 BFN1 的上游正调控因子。

其次，作者根据以前的资料表明，ORE1 和 BFN1 在自然衰老、黑暗和盐胁迫诱导衰老及 ABA 处理植株中共表达，利用 ORE1 和 BFN1 基因启动子驱动 GUS 基因表现组织特异性表达模式比较发现，NAC 转录因子基因 *ORE1* 与其推定的下游靶基因

BFN1 的表达模式有很大重叠（Overlapping Patterns of Transcriptional Activities of *ORE1* and *BFN1* Promoters）。

然后，作者用野生型与 *ORE1* 基因和 *miR164* 突变体衰老过程中 *BFN1* 基因表达水平，来表明 *BFN1* 的衰老特异性表达是 ORE1 依赖性的（Senescence-Specific Expression of *BFN1* Is ORE1-Dependent），同时用 *Prom-BFN1：GUS* 构件来转化 *anac092-1* 突变体来分析 *BFN1* 启动子活性来进一步证实这一点。

接下来作者结合 ORE1 的结合位点序列分析和结合位点诱变资料，了解了 ORE1 结合位点（ORE1 Binding Site）的核心基序。

在上述结果的基础上，作者利用研究核酸与蛋白质相互作用的凝胶电泳迁移阻滞实验（electrophoretic mobility shift assays, EMSAs）研究了 ORE1 转录因子与 *BFN1* 启动子直接的物理相互作用，并表明 ORE1 转录因子与 *BFN1* 启动子体外结合（In Vitro Binding of ORE1 Transcription Factor to the *BFN1* Promoter）这种互作是特异性的。

此外，作者利用 35S：*ORE1* 和 *PromBFN1-FLuc* 构件单独或共同转化拟南芥叶肉原生质体，即基于荧光素酶的反式激活分析（luciferase-based transactivation assays），*BFN1* 启动子在叶肉细胞原生质体的反式激活（Transactivation of the BFN1 Promoter in Mesophyll Cell Protoplasts）进一步表明 *BFN1* 基因是 ORE1 转录因子的直接的下游靶基因。

最后，作者对 *ORE1* 转录因子基因突变体和过表达植株的 BFN1 蛋白水平进行了分析，表明 *ORE1* 转录因子基因表达水平改变确实会引起 *BFN1* 基因的蛋白质表达水平变化（Altered Level of BFN1 Protein in *ORE1* Transgenic Plants）。至此，作者就充分证明了拟南芥 NAC 转录因子 ORE1 和衰老诱导的 *BIFUNCTIONAL NUCLEASE1*（BFN1）构成一个调控级联（线路）。

四、第三条泛读路线

第三条泛读路线为论文标题→摘要→材料与方法。对于一些重要的方法类论文，我们最感兴趣的是其材料与方法，因此，首先阅读标题和摘要，然后就阅读材料与方法部分。如在植物生长素研究中，观测生长素运输的经典文献如：

Friml J, Benkova E, Mayer U, et al., 2003. Automated whole-mount localization techniques for plant seedlings[J].Plant J. 34: 115-124.

Steinmann T, Geldner N, Grebe M, et al., 1999.Coordinated polar localization of auxin efflux carrier PIN1 by GNOM ARF GEF[J].Science, 286: 316-318.

观测植物生长素分布动态变化的经典文献如：

Sabatini S, Beis D, Wolkenfelt H, et al., 1999.An auxin-dependent distal organizer of pattern and polarity in the Arabidopsis root[J].Cell, 99: 463-472.

Ulmasov T, Murfett J, Hagen G, et al., 1997.Aux/IAA proteins repress expression of reporter genes containing natural and highly active synthetic auxin response elements [J]. Plant Cell, 9:1963-1971.

Brunoud G, Wells D M, Oliva M, et al., 2012. A novel sensor to map auxin response and distribution at high spatiotemporal resolution[J].Nature, 482: 103-106.

另外，对于某些结论较为"惊人"的论文，也需要仔细考察其材料与方法部分，看其方法是否合理。例如，arXiv 网站上有一篇标题为"Hemolithin：a Meteoritic Protein containing Iron and Lithium"的论文（arXiv: 2002.11688 或 arXiv: 2002.11688v1），作者声称在陨石中发现了一种蛋白质——血石蛋白（Hemolithin）。如果证实，这将是有史以来从地球以外发现的第一种蛋白质。那么其结论是否可靠呢？这就需要考察其方法是否合理、是否支持这样的结论。

五、为评审论文进行的泛读

该类泛读是对期刊文章进行同行评议（peer review）而进行的一种特殊形式的阅读方式，其特点是重在"挑刺"。Stiller-Reeve（2018）认为，同行评议需要读 3 遍论文，每次阅读都会有不同的侧重点。第一次阅读主要是根据对论文的科学理解而获得一种"印象"，例如，了解论文的研究目的、结果和新颖性如何，尤其要关注自己最在行的那一部分内容。如果没有致命缺陷（如方法有误、缺少关键证据或存在写作问题）而完全无法阅读，那么就进行第二次阅读。第二次阅读按顺序阅读论文的基本组成部分，对下面的问题作出判断：①摘要和引言是否清楚地表明这项研究的必要性及相关性；②方法是否对主要问题具有针对性和恰当性；③论文的结果或数据是否清楚、合理和完整；④结论是否合理地、正确地回答了作者在引言中所提出的主要问题。第三次阅读主要关注写作和结果呈现，重点关注各部分（也包括每个段落）的组织和结构是否混乱，句子和段落写作是否通畅和连贯，推理是否严密，用词和造句是否恰当，格式是否规范和统一，然后据此写作同行评议。

第十九章 SCI 论文阅读法之串读法

对于初学者而言，精读和泛读还不够，还需要学会对某一领域或某一类文章进行串读。所谓串读，就是检索或下载与某一类主题相关的论文，对其实验设计和写作方法进行归纳，找出规律性或模式性，以便在自己的论文设计或写作中加以模仿。

一、学习做论文工作的套路

有两种方式：第一种是总结；第二种是借鉴。总结是指对与主题相关的一类文章进行串读，总结其"套路"。从论文设计角度而言，每一类文章或多或少有一个"套路"存在。武术套路就是一连串的动作组合，练武的人一般在掌握某一门派的常规套路后，熟练到形成条件反射，才能在实战中加以变化或发挥。科研也是这样，初学者应该在大量阅读的基础上，归纳论文设计的套路，也就是某一类论文工作的常规分析步骤（其实也是这类文章的写作思路）。如果做某一类工作，而对此类工作的常规套路一无所知，不仅论文做不到一定深度或者做不完整，写起来也很困难，更谈不上发表在 SCI 期刊上了。相反，如果按一定的套路来做、来写，那么不能发表 SCI 论文的风险就会很低。借鉴是指植物领域向微生物、医学和动物学领域，非模式生物向模式生物，或者研究不充分的领域向研究较充分、较先进的领域学习。例如，植物领域广泛采用的 CRISPR（clustered regularly interspaced short palindromic repeats，规律成簇间隔短回文重复）基因编辑技术和单细胞测序技术就是从医学、动物学和微生物学领域借鉴学习的。就我所知，研究植物器官衰老通常以植物的叶片、果实和花瓣为对象，目前，植物叶片衰老研究较花瓣衰老研究更为先进，所以，研究花瓣衰老的科学工作者就经常借鉴植物叶片衰老的研究成果。由于生物都是由细胞构成（除病毒外），组成和代谢也都类似，都由遗传物质表达来控制，生物之间或多或少存在一定的同源性，那么，研究方法及研究思路的借鉴就不可避免。因此，研究人员还不能局限于一隅，只读自己领域的文献，而是应该广泛涉猎，及时关注本领域与相关领域的研究进展，正所谓"他山之石，可以攻玉"。

(一)基因克隆和表达分析的套路

首先是克隆相关基因全长序列，方法可以采用图位克隆法，也可以采用 cDNA 末端快速扩增技术(rapid amplification of cDNA ends, RACE)。

基因克隆后进行生物信息学分析，内容包括系统发育树构建、编码蛋白质的理化性质、蛋白质的二维结构、蛋白质的三维结构等。

接下来是基因表达模式分析，即利用实时荧光定量核酸扩增技术(real-time quantitative PCR, qPCR)，对基因在植物体不同组织部位进行表达模式分析，在整株或具体组织器官中不同发育阶段表达分析。如果该基因涉及生物或非生物胁迫，或者与激素反应有关，还需在不同条件处理下进行表达分析。

最重要的工作是鉴定基因功能。方法可以是利用相应的拟南芥或水稻突变体观测表型，同时利用互补测验观察是否能使其恢复野生型表型。此外，利用 CRISPR 基因编辑技术删除目的基因，观测其表型。采用反义基因表达技术，观测基因表达水平降低之后的表型。某些植物的表型分析还可利用近年来一种重要且更为简便的植物基因功能的反向遗传学手段，即病毒诱导的基因沉默(virus-induced gene silencing, VIGS)技术来直接(不经遗传转化)对目的基因进行沉默。利用 35S 强启动子连接目的基因进行组成型表达，观测其表型。为了避免 35S 强启动子导致的整株超表达的有害影响，可利用组织特异性启动子连接，或者利用化学诱导的超表达系统(chemical inducible overexpression)，如地塞米松(dexamethasone, DEX)诱导的超表达系统，观测植株在表达水平增强后的表现型。如果某个物种遗传转化困难，可利用异源转化到拟南芥或水稻中来确定基因的功能。此外，还可利用原核表达、酶活测定、酵母双杂(鉴定蛋白-蛋白的相互作用)或双分子荧光互补(bimolecular fluorescent complimentary, BiFC)技术(表征蛋白质互作及其发生的空间位置)等分析其表达产物蛋白质的结构、活性与功能。

此外，还可以做的工作包括基因启动子全长序列克隆与表达分析，即利用染色体步移试剂盒或巢式 PCR 克隆启动子全长序列，连接 GUS 基因，转化拟南芥，分析不同组织部位及不同发育时期表达强度，观察其表达是否具有时空特异性或发育与组织特异性。

对于转录因子基因或膜蛋白基因，还需要分析其是否在细胞核内或细胞膜上定位表达。那么可做的工作还有亚细胞定位分析，即利用基因启动子全长序列，连接 GUS 基因，转化洋葱表皮细胞或拟南芥原生质体，分析其亚细胞表达情况。

更进一步，还可对基因所在的调控途径(通路)或调控网络进行解析，鉴定目的基因受到上游哪些基因调控(如转录调控或表观遗传修饰等)。如果目的基因为转录因子基因，还可分析目的基因对下游哪些基因调控，其中哪些基因是直接作用的靶基因等。

(二)RNA 测序与转录组学研究套路

RNA 测序与转录组学研究的基本数据来自测序公司，但这些数据是否对研究目的有用，很大程度上取决于实验设计，也就是使用什么样的处理样本与什么样的对照样本，或者使用哪几组不同发育阶段或时间进程的样本进行比较分析，要确保由此获得的差异表达基因及代谢途径能说明问题。可借助结合形态结构分析、生理生化指标检测或指示基因表达等数据来划分不同发育阶段或时间进程；表型分析也可作为 RNA 测序与转录组学研究要解释的现象。此外，要注意设置 3 次测序重复，这样的结果才能进行统计学处理或具有统计学意义。

首先需要对转录组测序数据进行整体分析和介绍，例如，获得的原始 Reads 片段和过滤后 reads 片段的数量与质量（如片段长度大于 20 个碱基的百分比），组装和拼接成的 Contig 片段及 Unigene 片段的数量与质量（如不同 nt 长度的比率和分布），测序深度（reads 碱基数/序列长度）和覆盖度（reads 覆盖的碱基数/序列长度），Unigene 的 COG 功能分类、GO 功能分类和 KEGG 代谢途径分类等。

然后对不同样本之间的差异表达基因筛选，上调和下调基因分析，差异基因进行 GO 功能富集和 KEGG 通路分析，重点分析处理与对照或不同时间序列样本间的基因表达变化模式，特别是可能与具体生物学过程（如脂肪酸代谢途径、天然橡胶生物合成途径）或相关机理（如激素的生物合成与信号转导、转录因子、活性氧）相关的差异表达基因要进行详细分析与直观呈现，从而揭示相关生物学过程或调控的分子机理。对于 5 组以上的复杂数据（如 5 个不同发育阶段），还可用 WGCNA 进行基因共表达网络模块分析，分析不同基因模块之间的相互关系及其与表型的关联性，并获得每个模块的关键基因。

最后是进行验证。最简单的是利用实时定量 PCR（qRT-PCR）、Northern 印迹杂交（Northern blot）等验证候选基因的表达水平变化是否与 RNA 测序数据一致。更进一步还可利用前述基因克隆与表达分析方法，对候选目的基因的功能进行验证。

基本的套路如此，如果想获得更详细的数据和发表点数更高的论文，那么需要采取以下几种方法：①丰富 RNA 测序的样本数量（例如，由 3 或 5 个发育阶段细分到 10 或 20 个发育阶段）。样本数量越多，得出的信息就越丰富。②转录组学方法结合基因组学、蛋白组学、代谢组学、表观组学等所谓多组学手段，研究相关的生物学过程或调控的分子机理，并对候选基因进行功能验证。③对数据进行深度挖掘，例如，分析可变剪接和融合基因，或者与长链非编码 RNA（lncRNA）、环状 RNA（circRNA）、小 RNA、甲基化等进行联合分析。

(三) 基因家族分析的套路

首先，只有植物物种基因组完成测序，才能对基因家族进行分析。从相关的数据库检索和下载目的物种的基因组相关数据（如基因家族的所有成员蛋白序列文件）。

接着对蛋白序列进行过滤，分析蛋白结构和理化性质，如氨基酸数目、分子量、等电点、疏水性、结构域、二级和三级结构等。

再通过家族基因的多序列比对构建系统进化树，然后对进化树、基序及基因结构

(内含子和外显子、剪接内含子模式、特定结构域和序列长度、非翻译区等)进行分析;进行家族基因的染色体定位分析和共线性分析。

然后,使用已发表的转录组数据,绘制家族基因的表达量热图。

最后,根据研究目的,对材料进行处理,用qRT-PCR对家族基因在不同处理条件下的表达进行定量分析,鉴定可能参与某个生物过程或具有某种功能的家族基因。

二、推敲论文标题

论文标题是读者最先读到的部分,决定读者的第一印象。好的论文须设定一个吸引人的论文标题。注重论文写作应当经常留心好的论文标题,以便为我所用。

(一)分析和总结论文的标题结构

名词结构作为论文标题最为常见,有前置修饰语+名词、名词中心语+后置修饰语(介词、分词、不定式、从句)、前置修饰语+名词+后置修饰语结构、名词+and+名词、动名词短语等多种结构,但以(前置修饰语+)名词中心语+后置修饰语(介词、分词、不定式、从句)结构较为普遍。此外,以简单句作为标题也较为普遍,一般采用现在时。初学者需要特别注意学习标题句子中常用的动词。以《自然》等期刊论义的标题为例,结构如下:

1. 名词结构

①前置修饰语+名词:

One-dimensional van der Waals heterostructures

Highly active cationic cobalt(Ⅱ)hydroformylation catalysts

Fully hardware-implemented memristor convolutional neural network

②(前置修饰语+)名词中心词+后置修饰语(介词、分词、不定式、从句):

Structure of the transcription coactivator SAGA

The transcriptional landscape of polyploid wheat

Proton-assisted growth of ultra-flat graphene films

The biochemical basis of microRNA targeting efficacy

Signatures of self-organized criticality in an ultracold atomic gas

The emergence of transcriptional identity in somatosensory neurons

International evaluation of an AI system for breast cancer screening

Individual and population benefits of marine reserves for reef sharks

A genome-wide transcriptomic analysis of protein-coding genes in human blood cells

Synchrotron infrared spectroscopic evidence of the probable transition to metal hydrogen

Selective functionalization of methane, ethane, and higher alkanes by cerium photocatalysis

Late development of navigationally relevant motion processing in the occipital place area

The expansion and diversification of pentatricopeptide repeat RNA-editing factors in plants

Structure of the human metapneumovirus polymerase phosphoprotein complex

Prevention of tuberculosis in macaques after intravenous BCG immunization

Adaptive mutability of colorectal cancers in response to targeted therapies

Superstructure control of first-cycle voltage hysteresis in oxygen-redox cathodes

Last appearance of *Homo erectus* at Ngandong, Java, 117,000-108,000 years ago

A genome-wide transcriptomic analysis of protein-coding genes in human blood cells

Rapid non-uniform adaptation to conformation-specific KRAS(G12C) inhibition

Palaeoclimate evidence of vulnerable permafrost during times of low sea ice

Insulator-metal transition in dense fluid deuterium

Ultrahigh thermal conductivity in isotope-enriched cubic boron nitride

Long-term cyclic persistence in an experimental predator-prey system

Ancient West African foragers in the context of African population history

Coherent vortex dynamics in a strongly interacting superfluid on a silicon chip

Potassium channel dysfunction in human neuronal models of Angelman syndrome

Genomic and fitness consequences of genetic rescue in wild populations

3D printed polyamide membranes for desalination

A molecular mechanism for Wnt ligand-specific signaling

A distributional code for value in dopamine-based reinforcement learning

Constructive molecular configurations for surface-defect passivation of perovskite photovoltaics

Classification with a disordered dopant-atom network in silicon

Resonant microwave-mediated interactions between distant electron spins

A population of dust-enshrouded objects orbiting the Galactic black hole

Crystal symmetry determination in electron diffraction using machine learning

Circuit mechanisms underlying chromatic encoding in drosophila photoreceptors

Structural basis of DNA targeting by a transposon-encoded CRISPR-Cas system

Plant iron acquisition strategy exploited by an insect herbivore

Mechanism of adrenergic CaV1.2 stimulation revealed by proximity proteomics

A dominant autoinflammatory disease caused by non-cleavable variants of RIPK1

A repeating fast radio burst source localized to a nearby spiral galaxy

Origin of the bright photoluminescence of few-atom silver clusters confined in LTA zeolites

Frequent mutations that converge on the NFKBIZ pathway in ulcerative colitis

Mutations that prevent caspase cleavage of RIPK1 cause autoinflammatory disease

③名词+同位语：

SIR1, an upstream component in auxin signaling identified by chemical genetics

GARNet, the genomic arabidopsis resource network

④名词+and+名词：

Dualities and non-Abelian mechanics

Oceanic forcing of penultimate deglacial and last interglacial sea-level rise

The water lily genome and the early evolution of flowering plants

Mechanotransduction-Dependent Control of Stereocilia Dimensions and Row Identity in Inner Hair Cells

2. 动名词短语

Sleeping with hippocampal damage

Molecular tuning of CO_2-to-ethylene conversion

Decoding the development of the human hippocampus

Assessing progress towards sustainable development over space and time

Mapping child growth failure across low-and middle-income countries

Mapping disparities in education across low-and middle-income countries

Producing adipic acid without the nitrous oxide

Host monitoring of quorum sensing during *Pseudomonas aeruginosa* infection

Therapeutic targeting of preleukemia cells in a mouse model of NPM1 mutant acute myeloid leukemia

Delineating the rules for structural adaptation of membrane-associated proteins to evolutionary changes in membrane lipidome

Lense-Thirring frame dragging induced by a fast-rotating white dwarf in a binary pulsar system

3. 简单句标题

Fragile X mental retardation 1 gene <u>enhances</u> the translation of large autism-related proteins

Tertiary lymphoid structures <u>improve</u> immunotherapy and survival in melanoma

Cell death in cells overlying lateral root primordia <u>facilitates</u> organ growth in *Arabidopsis*

Engineered symbionts <u>activate</u> honey bee immunity and limit pathogens

DNA-induced liquid phase condensation of cGAS <u>activates</u> innate immune signaling

Modifications during early plant development <u>promote</u> the evolution of nature's most complex woods

Hyperactivation of sympathetic nerves <u>drives</u> depletion of melanocyte stem cells

Changing climate drives divergent and nonlinear shifts in flowering phenology across elevations

RGF1 controls root meristem size through ROS signalling

Microbial bile acid metabolites modulate gut RORγ$^+$ regulatory T cell homeostasis

A feedforward circuit regulates action selection of pre-mating courtship behavior in female *Drosophila*

Metabolic heterogeneity confers differences in melanoma metastatic potential

Aberrant tonic inhibition of dopaminergic neuronal activity causes motor symptoms in animal models of Parkinson's disease

An acute immune response underlies the benefit of cardiac stem cell therapy

Internal state dynamics shape brainwide activity and foraging behaviour

New predictors for immunotherapy responses sharpen our view of the tumour microenvironment

Salicylic acid targets protein phosphatase 2A to attenuate growth in plants

Clonally expanded CD8 T cells patrol the cerebrospinal fluid in Alzheimer's disease

HBO1 is required for the maintenance of leukaemia stem cells

The origin of land plants is rooted in two bursts of genomic novelty

Protein phosphatase 1 is a molecular constraint for learning and memory

Extraocular vision in a brittle star is mediated by chromatophore movement in response to ambient light

Comparison of independent evolutionary origins reveals both convergence and divergence in the metabolic mechanisms of symbiosis

The coix genome provides insights into panicoideae evolution and papery hull domestication

Do cytokinins and strigolactones crosstalk during drought adaptation?

4. 主标题：副标题

The BAP module: A multisignal integrator orchestrating growth

Evolution of guard-cell theories: The story of sugars

Yeast-bacterium interactions: The next frontier in nectar research

Acquiring control: The evolution of stomatal signalling pathways

Tuning the orchestra: miRNAs in plant immunity

Allelopathic plants: Models for studying plant-interkingdom interactions

Single-cell transcriptomics: A high-resolution avenue for plant functional genomics

Crop phenomics and high-throughput phenotyping: Past decades, current challenges, and future perspectives

Feeling the heat: Searching for plant thermosensors

Plant immunity: Thinking outside and inside the box

Collective clog control: Optimizing traffic flow in confined biological and robophysical excavation

The strawberry tales: Size matters

Light emission in betalains: From fluorescent flowers to biotechnological applications

Molecular recognition: How photosynthesis anchors the mobile antenna?

Polar transport of auxin: Carrier-mediated flux across the plasma membrane or neurotransmitter-like secretion?

在分析论文标题时,标题属于名词结构还是句子,就看它是否有动词,如果没有动词,一般来说就不是句子。对于一个名词结构,后面的修饰成分可以有很多变化。以下面一个题目为例"Identification of a novel melon transcription factor CmNAC60 as a potential regulator of leaf senescence",这是一个名词结构,结构通式为:Identification of...as...(将……鉴定为……)。翻译成中文为:"甜瓜新转录因子 CmNAC60 鉴定为叶片衰老潜在调控蛋白"或"作为叶片衰老潜在调控蛋白的甜瓜新转录因子 CmNAC60 的鉴定"。如果我们留意生物农业或生物医学期刊论文,以名词结构 Identification of...as... 作为论文标题相当普遍。例如,

Identification of PRDX6 as a regulator of ferroptosis

Identification of erythroferrone as an erythroid regulator of iron metabolism

Identification of RBPMS as a smooth muscle master splicing regulator via proximity of its gene with super-enhancers

Identification of XBP1-u as a novel regulator of the MDM2/p53 axis using an shRNA library

Identification of IL-27 as potent regulator of inflammatory osteolysis associated with vitamin E-blended ultra-high molecular weight polyethylene debris of orthopedic implants

Identification of microRNA-27a as a key regulator of cholesterol homeostasis

Identification of the novel role of CD24 as an oncogenesis regulator and therapeutic target for triple-negative breast cancer

……

当然,还可采用这样的结构:Identification of+名词+形容词结构或分词结构(来说明前面名词的功能)。

以名词结构 Identification of...responsible for... 作为论文标题:

Identification of genes responsible for sex-related differences in cancer aggressiveness

Identification of major active ingredients responsible for burn wound healing of *Centella asiatica* Herbs

Identification of transcription factors responsible for dysregulated networks in human osteoarthritis cartilage by global gene expression analysis

Identification of the mechanism responsible for the boron oxygen light induced degradation in silicon photovoltaic cells

……

以名词结构 Identification of...involved in... 作为论文标题：

Identification of miRNAs potentially involved in bronchiolitis obliterans syndrome: A computational study

Identification of protein interactions involved in cellular signaling

Identification of genes involved in the differentiation of R7y and R7p photoreceptor cells in *Drosophila*

Identification of microRNAs involved in pathogen-associated molecular pattern-triggered plant innate immunity

……

以名词结构 Identification of...associated with... 作为论文标题：

Identification of genes associated with chlorophyll accumulation in flower petals

Identification of a novel antibody associated with autoimmune pancreatitis

Identification of potential key genes associated with osteosarcoma based on integrated bioinformatics analyses

Identification of proteins associated with the *Pseudomonas aeruginosa* biofilm extracellular Matrix

Identification of genetic variants associated with skeletal muscle function deficit in childhood acute lymphoblastic leukemia survivors

Identification of modifiable factors associated with owner-reported equine laminitis in Britain using a web-based cohort study approach

Identification of genes that are associated with DNA repeats in prokaryotes

Systematic identification of regulatory variants associated with cancer risk

Efficient identification of mutated cancer antigens recognized by T cells associated with durable tumor regressions

Molecular identification of bacteria associated with bacterial vaginosis

Identification of H3K4me1-associated proteins at mammalian enhancers

Identification of early senescence-associated genes in rice flag leaves

Identification of mouse embryonic stem cell-associated proteins

Identification of a novel arthritis-associated osteoclast precursor macrophage regulated by FoxM1

Identification of multiple cancer-associated myositis-specific autoantibodies in idiopathic inflammatory myopathies: A large longitudinal cohort study

Identification of tumor-associated antigens with diagnostic ability of colorectal cancer by in-depth immunomic and seroproteomic analysis

Identification and analysis of ribosome-associated lncRNAs using ribosome profiling data
……

（二）研究性论文和综述性论文的标题分析

以下是近百年来《自然》期刊影响力最大的十篇论文（10 extraordinary *Nature* papers：https：//www.nature.com/collections/fajcgfjdgh）的标题：

Evidence for the existence of new unstable elementary particles

Continuous cultures of fused cells secreting antibody of predefined specificity

Australopithecus africanus the man-ape of South Africa

C_{60}: Buckminsterfullerene

Large losses of total ozone in Antarctica reveal seasonal ClO_x/NO_x interaction

Single-channel currents recorded from membrane of denervated frog muscle fibres

Ordered mesoporous molecular sieves synthesized by a liquid-crystal template mechanism

Sexually mature individuals of *Xenopus laevis* from the transplantation of single somatic Nuclei

Molecular structure of nucleic acids: A structure for deoxyribose nucleic acid

A Jupiter-mass companion to a solar-type star

由上可知，顶级期刊上研究性论文的标题一般简短、平实，并无过分夸张之词。论文的好坏主要还是由内容来决定，至于论文标题的长短，宜长则长，宜短则短，无一定之规，要视具体情况而定。上面《自然》期刊论文的标题以简短的名词性结构为主，更具有概括性。事实上，与之相对应的是，论文标题越长，内容可能越贫乏。

尽管研究性论文的标题一般比较简短、平实，但评论性论文或综述性论文的标题的修辞手段则丰富多样，更具文采，也更吸引人。有的标题引经据典，有的形象生动，有的推敲炼字。不少标题相当讲究，以下举例说明。

【例文1】Auxin binding protein: curiouser and curiouse

说明：其中 curiouser and curiouse 出自英国数学家、逻辑学家、童话作家刘易斯·卡罗尔（Lewis Carroll，1832—1898）的《爱丽丝漫游奇境记》（*Alice's Adventures in Wonderland & Through the Looking-Glass*），其意思是"越来越奇怪"（stranger and stranger）。

【例文2】Auxin transport: Why plants like to think BIG

说明：think big 指"目光远大，雄心勃勃"（To have grand or ambitious plans or ideas）。这里语义双关，表面意思是"往大处想"，实质上 BIG 是"一种体积巨大的拟南芥蛋白,是已经得到鉴定的另一种潜在的生长素转运调节因子"(An *Arabidopsis* protein of enormous size, another potential regulator of auxin transport has been characterized)。

【例文3】Auxin distribution and plant pattern formation: How many angels can dance on the point of PIN?

说明:这里语义双关,How many angels can stand(dance) on the head of a PIN? [多少个天使能站在一个大头针上(跳舞)?],原指中世纪的宗教争论。这里的PIN蛋白是植物信号分子生长素从细胞中流出的次级转运蛋白。它们在细胞内不对称分布,其极性决定细胞间生长素流动的方向。整个标题的意思是指PIN蛋白在生长素分布和植物格式形成方面还有多少功能。

【例文4】Auxin transport: ABC proteins join the club

说明:这里的 join the club 原来是个俗语,意指"表示和别人遇到了同样糟糕的情况或问题、彼此彼此、都一样"(An expression used when two people have something unpleasant in common 或 an expression indicating that the person spoken to is in the same, or a similar, unfortunate state as the speaker)。这里指植物ABC蛋白质发现也介导生长素的细胞内运输和长距离运输。

【例文5】Plant biomechanics: No Pain, no Gain for birch tree stems

说明:No Pain, no Gain 是一个俗语,意思是"没有付出就没有收获;没有痛苦,没有收获;不劳则无获"(Suffering is needed to make progress 或 it is necessary to suffer or work hard in order to succeed or make progress 或 Only by facing, dealing with, or subjecting oneself to difficulty or hardship will one truly improve or progress),这里指生物体大小和形状之间的异速生长关系(allometric relationships)。

【例文6】Auxin signals-turning genes on and turning cells around

说明:标题中 turn on(转动,旋转;打开开关)与 turn around(使调转方向,使转向,改变方向)结构对称且十分形象。turning genes on 指 auxin signals regulate gene activities in individual cells, 而 turning cells around 指 the polar transport of auxin could impact on patterning processes throughout the plant. 类似对称的标题还有:Auxin-cytokinin interactions in higher plants: old problems and new tools 和 The fall and rise of apical dominance.

【例文7】Plant tropisms: The ins and outs of auxin

说明:The ins and outs 有两个意思:一指"复杂详情,底细"(The intricate details of a situation or process; intricacies; particulars; peculiarities);二指"在具有某个位置和影响及不具有某个位置和影响的人或物"(Those with position and influence and those without)。此处的意思可能二者兼有。

【例文8】Auxin and embryo axis formation: the ends in sight?

说明:英语有 no end in sight(to something)的说法,意思是"没有可预见的结局或结论"(No foreseeable end or conclusion to something. The phrase indicates that one expects the thing to continue indefinitely.）。此处反其意而用之。

【例文 9】Genetic dissection of auxin action: More questions than answers?

说明：此处采用了英语中的一种常用说法"问题比答案多"（more questions than answers），说明生长素作用的遗传分析表明还存在很多不理解的问题。

【例文 10】Auxin Action: Slogging out of the Swamp

说明：Slogging out of the swamp 的意思是"艰难地走出沼泽"，此处用来形象地说明对生长素运出载体（efflux carrier）的定位，以及生长素对转录因子降解的影响等方面的最新证据已经揭示生长素影响植物生长发育的许多方面的可能机制。

【例文 11】AGC kinases tell the auxin tale

说明：英语中 tell the tale 的意思是"描述或揭示一种情况的真相"（If something tells the tale about a particular situation, it shows the truth about it; To depict or reveal the truth about a situation.）。

【例文 12】Unveiling the molecular arms race between two conflicting genomes in cytoplasmic male sterility

说明：英语中 arms race 意思是"军备竞赛"，尤其是指冷战时期美国和苏联之间为取得优势而进行的武器研制方面的竞争。此处形象地指细胞核基因组与线粒体基因组之间的遗传冲突，因此产生细胞质雄性不育（cytoplasmic male sterility）。使用 arms race 的论文标题还有 The arms race between bacteria and their phage foes.

其他比较形象的标题还有：

A pump for the auxin fountain: AUX1 and root gravitropism

Development: Painting flowers with MYBs

Auxin begins to give up its secrets

Axillary bud outgrowth: Sending a message

The high road and the low road: Trafficking choices in plants

Arabidopsis endogenous small RNAs: Highways and byways

注重选词炼字的标题有：

Funneling auxin action: Specificity in signal transduction（Funnel：汇集，使流经狭窄空间）

Eph receptors: Two ways to sharpen boundaries（Sharpen：变得清晰）

Plant development: Auxin in loops（In loops：环形运动）

Receptors for auxin: Will it all end in TIRs?（End in：以……告终，终结于……，以……为结局）

三、用集句法来学习表达

写作 SCI 论文总是从模仿起步的，不仅是措辞和造句，即便谋篇布局也是如此。

既可以在平时阅读文献时日积月累常用的表达法,也可以有意识地从已下载的文献或利用网络搜索来辑录某一类表达法。

集句原指古人摘取并集合前人的诗句拼成一首诗或词的方法。这里指从一批论文中摘取和辑录一类表述方法的语句,或描述一类现象、机制或功能的语句。集句法是很好的串读方法,对于迅速了解和掌握表达方法并用于论文写作极为有效。初学者可以多做此类练习,在论文写作中会获益良多。

(一)表达方法集句

以下是从有关植物不育性(sterility)相关的4篇文献:

A separation defect of tapetum cells and microspore mother cells results in male sterility in *Brassica napus*: The role of abscisic acid in early anther development

ABNORMAL POLLEN VACUOLATION1 (APV1) is required for male fertility by contributing to anther cuticle and pollen exine formation in maize

Control of abscisic acid catabolism and abscisic acid homeostasis is important for reproductive stage stress tolerance in cereals

Tapetum and middle layer control male fertility in *Actinidia deliciosa*

以上文献辑录了若干种常用的表达方法。

1. 表述因果关系

英语中有十分丰富的表达因果关系的方式,常使用连词(because, since, so, therefore, thus, hence, then, consequently, accordingly)、介词短语或形容词短语(because of, for this reason, due to, owing to, thanks to, as a result of, responsible for)、动词或动词短语(cause, lead to, result in, trigger, account for, explain, make, determine)、名词和名词短语(the reason for, the result of, contributor to)。

【例文1】The 7-7365A line with the genotype *Bnms3ms3ms4ms4RfRf* is male-sterile, while the 7-7365B line with the genotype *BnMs3ms3ms4ms4RfRf* is male-fertile, and 7-7365C with homozygous recessive genotypes at the three loci shows male fertility <u>because</u> the loss function of *Bnrf* gene causes the inhibition of the genetic trait of the double mutant Bnms3 Bnms4.

【例文2】<u>Since</u> the anthers in 7-7365A successfully complete tapetum differentiation, B15 and B37 could not be upstream of EMS1 and therefore work in a different pathway from EMS1.

【例文3】B15 and B37 were downregulated in the spl mutant but not affected in the *ems1* and *ms1* mutants, <u>so</u> they are upstream of *EMS1* or work in a different pathway.

【例文4】<u>Therefore</u>, the *BnRf* gene should negatively regulate the expression of these seven genes (Table 2) because their expression levels in 7-7365A were much lower than in 7-

7365C.

【例文 5】The genic male sterility (GMS) system is widely used in hybrid seed production <u>because of</u> its stability and no negative cytoplasmic effect compared with cytoplasmic male sterility (CMS).

【例文 6】The mutant male sterility 8 (*ms8*) shows meiotic dyad abortion <u>due to</u> the deposition of extra callose between them.

【例文 7】Sterility in the OsNCED3-TaABA8#OH1 transgenic lines may have been <u>due to</u> the absence of pollen dehiscence.

【例文 8】The fact that expression of the endogenous OsG6B gene is lower in the transgenic lines suggests that the endogenous gene may be partially suppressed <u>as a result of</u> sequence homology with the promoter of the transgene (translational fusion).

【例文 9】As the deletion involves two neighboring genes, we used clustered regularly interspaced short palindromic repeats (CRISPR/Cas9) to independently knock out the genes in the HiII inbred line background to identify the gene <u>responsible for</u> the male-sterile phenotype.

【例文 10】Both cold and drought stresses <u>cause</u> abscisic acid (ABA) accumulation.

【例文 11】These results indicate that the mutant phenotype <u>is caused by</u> a single recessive nuclear locus.

【例文 12】ABA treatment of the spike mimics the effect of drought, <u>causing</u> high levels of sterility.

【例文 13】In the male-sterile line 7-7365A, tapetum cell and microspore mother cell separation were affected, and this <u>led to</u> failure of microspore release.

【例文 14】Defects in any layer can <u>result in</u> a failure to produce such microspores.

【例文 15】Both cold and drought stresses were shown to <u>trigger</u> a premature cell death response in the tapetum.

【例文 16】Therefore, cold-induced accumulation of ABA, resulting in the repression of cell wall invertase expression in the tapetum, may <u>account for</u> pollen abortion.

【例文 17】This may <u>explain</u> the higher vulnerability of pollen development to abiotic stresses.

【例文 18】Furthermore, temperature treatment <u>made</u> some sterile 7-7365A flowers become fertile.

【例文 19】The delicate balance between ABA synthesis and catabolism <u>determines</u> ABA levels in plant tissues.

【例文 20】The fact that ABA down-regulates cell wall invertase expression suggests that repression of cell wall invertase expression in the vascular parenchyma cells may be <u>the main</u>

reason for the abortion of pollen development.

【例文 21】ABA levels in plants are the result of a balance between biosynthesis and catabolism.

【例文 22】Male sterility is an important contributor to heterosis in *Brassica napus* L.

2. 表述功能和用途

表达功能和用途最常用的方式有 be widely used for, plays an important role in, is vital/ critical/ important for 等。

【例文 1】Arabidopsis microarrays have been widely used for analysis of gene expression in Brassica species

【例文 2】We found that ABA plays an important role in the male sterility of 7-7365A and that the sterility can suppressed by heat shock.

【例文 3】Therefore, each layer has a unique role and coordinating functions for proper anther development.

【例文 4】The proper functioning of genes expressed in the tapetum is vital for the development of pollen exine and anther cuticle.

【例文 5】In self-fertilizing cereals, such as rice (*Oryza sativa*), wheat (*Triticum aestivum*), barley (*Hordeum vulgare*), and grain sorghum (*Sorghum bicolor*), successful pollen development is critical for grain production, and abiotic stresses interfering with the earliest stages of pollen formation lead to massive losses in grain number.

【例文 6】ABA homeostasis, therefore, is important for controlling abiotic stress tolerance and pollen fertility in wheat and rice.

【例文 7】The endothecium can be involved in secreting materials that are essential for pollen grain development.

【例文 8】Altogether, we suggest that APV1 functions in the fatty acid hydroxylation pathway which is involved in forming sporopollenin precursors and cutin monomers that are essential for the development of pollen exine and anther cuticle in maize.

【例文 9】Male fertility requires functional microspores that are formed during normal anther developmental processes

【例文 10】In addition, the ABCG16 and ABCG27/WBC27 transporters are required for normal pollen wall formation in Arabidopsis

【例文 11】They help to protect the internal functional layers against various stresses.

【例文 12】The world's most important staple crops depend on successful reproductive development for grain production.

3. 表述存在知识空白

表示某些方面了解不多，可用 ...be/remain (virtually/largely) unknown/elusive/unclear/

unsolved, ...be/remain less/scarcely/poorly/not well understood, 也可用 little/scant/limited information/data is available on..., less/little is known about..., very few attempts have been made to explore..., very few studies/investigations have been done about..., very few investigations have been conducted/made concerning/regarding/on..., our understanding of...remains surprisingly limited, we know little about... 或 there are few reports on... 等。

【例文1】In fact, this complexity of anther ontology is poorly understood in maize.

【例文2】However, the function of ABA in early anther development remains unknown.

【例文3】However, their functions in the mutant remain to be explored.

【例文4】It remains to be established whether cold tolerance in rice can be further improved to the level observed in cold-tolerant rice lines by using other tapetum-specific promoters.

【例文5】Less is known about the role of the middle layer.

【例文6】However, very limited information exists about the kiwifruit tapetum (Messina, 1993) and there is no information about the possible roles of other anther wall tissues.

【例文7】Additional biochemical experiments will be required to complete the assignment of the function to APV1.

4. 表述研究目的

表示研究目的除了可用名词(objective, goal, aim, attempt, effort 等)或动词(aim to 等)表达外，更多是使用动词不定式，如 to study/investigate/ understand/verify/determine/test... 或 "for + 名词或动名词" 形式表示，如 for studying/investigating/understanding/verifying/determining/testing...。

【例文1】Our research aimed to elucidate the REGMS malesterile mechanism at the molecular level.

【例文2】The aim of this study was to determine whether the anther wall controls male fertility in kiwifruit, providing calcium and carbohydrates to the microspores.

【例文3】The purpose of the present study was to determine the type of control of male sterility in this plant.

【例文4】In order to understand the network controlled by the *BnRf* and *BnMS3* genes in REGMS lines, we constructed an SSH library to identify genes expressed differentially in 7-7365A and 7-7365C.

【例文5】To determine whether the failure of PMCs to separate from tapetum cells was caused by a lack of cell wall-degrading enzymes, we assayed the activity of polygalacturonase (PG), which is a primary pectin degradation enzyme.

【例文6】To explain the role of heat shock treatment in male sterility restoration, we used the seven genes identified by SSH as markers to investigate the influence of heat shock on their expression.

【例文 7】To examine the morphological defects in the apv1 mutant anthers, transverse sections were analyzed to compare the cytology of wild-type and mutant anthers.

【例文 8】To compare these results in wheat with rice, we carried out a time-course experiment for cold stress in rice.

【例文 9】To assess the tissue and cell specificity of ABA biosynthesis, we analyzed the expression pattern of *OsNCED3*-GUS and *OsNCED3*-ECFP constructs in transgenic rice.

【例文 10】For SSH construction, we collected flower buds<1, 1-2 and 2-3 mm long.

【例文 11】For detailed information, we investigated anther surface and pollen surface using scanning electron microscopy(SEM).

5. 表述进行某项实验

表述进行某项实验既可以用主动语态，也可用被动语态。常用的实义动词有 perform, conduct, carry out, study, investigate, explore, identify, characterize, examine, test, measure, quantify, assess, evaluate, estimate 等。

【例文 1】We studied the effect of drought stress at the YM stage on ABA accumulation in wheat ears.

【例文 2】We measured the chloroform-extractable cuticular wax constituents of both wild-type and apv1 by gas chromatography-mass spectrometry(GC-MS).

【例文 3】We tested the effect of reducing anther ABA levels on cold tolerance in rice by manipulating expression levels of the ABA catabolic gene ABA 8#-hydroxylase using the wheat TaABA8#OH1 gene.

【例文 4】To investigate transcripts that were specifically expressed in the apv1 at the uninucleate stage, we performed RNA sequencing and determined the transcriptome profile of wild-type and *apv1*(two biological replicates each).

【例文 5】To confirm this possibility, we examined the DEGs in the RNA-seq data and found that some genes in this pathway were down-regulated in the mutant with log2-fold change ranging from-1 to-11.

【例文 6】In this article, we investigate the role of ABA in controlling abiotic stress tolerance in cereals.

【例文 7】The events occurring in the anther wall and microspores of male-fertile and male-sterile anthers were investigated by analyses of light microscopy, epifluorescence, terminal deoxynucleotidyl transferase-mediated dUTP nick-end labelling(TUNEL assay)and transmission electron microscopy coupled with electron spectroscopy.

【例文 8】To understand the function of APV1 during anther development, the expression of APV1 was analyzed in different tissues and at different stages of anther development.

【例文 9】Assays were conducted at 45℃ in 0.05 M sodium acetate (pH 5.0) at a substrate concentration of 0.1% (wt/vol) polygalacturonate with 2 ml fresh sample or 2 ml sample spoiled for 5 min to inactivate PG(control) and 2 ml substrate for 30 min.

【例文 10】Array dot-blot analysis was performed to confirm differential expression of the clones.

【例文 11】To determine the tissue specificity of APV1 at a cellular level during anther development, *in situ* hybridization was performed at different stages of wild-type using sense and anti-sense probes.

【例文 12】RT-PCR was carried out using the QIAGEN one step RT-PCR kit, (Cat. no. 210210) according to the manufacturer's instructions, in combination with the real-time primers and additional primers to pectin methylesterase(5-GACGGATACCAAGACACC-3 5-CACCTACTAAGA ACCTACCC-3) from a published paper(Kang et al., 2008).

【例文 13】Observations were carried out with the same epifluorescence microscope as mentioned above, equipped with a 50WHBOmercury lamp, using BP 395-440, FT 460 and LP 470 filter sets.

【例文 14】ABA levels were measured for control and drought-stressed spikes of the drought-sensitive varieties Sundor and Cranbrook and the drought-tolerant varieties Halberd and SYN604(Ji et al., 2010)

6. 表达实验结果

表达实验结果可用主动语态，也可用被动语态；可用人称，也可用物称。常用的实义动词有 found, discover, identify, detect, observe, show, indicate, demonstrate, reveal, illustrate, display, exhibit 等。另外，结果具有统计学意义上的显著性，要用 significance, significant, statistically significant, significantly 等来表述。

【例文 1】After sequencing, we found that the apv1 mutation has an 848-bp deletion which spanned the following two neighboring genes: GRMZM5G830329 and GRMZM2G439268.

【例文 2】We identified nine genes that were strongly downregulated in 7-7365A compared to 7-7365C and 7-7365B(Fig. 4).

【例文 3】In this research, we noticed that the separation of tapetum cells and PMCs was delayed at the early meiotic stage and that this resulted in male sterility.

【例文 4】We show that ABA controls anther sink strength and abortion of pollen development under drought conditions in wheat.

【例文 5】The fertile lines 7-7365B and 7-7365C show normal vegetative growth in the field; the sterile line 7-7365A also shows normal vegetative growth.

【例文6】The transgenic lines showed that anther sink strength (OsINV4) was maintained under cold conditions and that this correlated with improved cold stress tolerance.

【例文7】The results showed that PG activity in 7-7365A was significantly lower than that in 7-7365C or 7-7365B at the <1 mm anther length stage, but there was no difference in PG activity by the 1-2 mm anther length stage(Fig. 3b).

【例文8】ABA measurements in the spike of the TaABA8#OH1 deletion lines show that ABA content was significantly increased compared with variety Sunstate(Fig. 4A).

【例文9】It has been shown that low sugar levels inmale-sterile anthersmay be related to reduced amylolytic activity, i. e. the breakdown of starch in the stamen, as in a malesterile mutant of tomato(Bhadula and Sawhney, 1989).

【例文10】Gene expression studies using semiquantitative reverse transcription (RT)-PCR indicate that the biosynthetic genes TaZEP1, TaNCED1, and TaNCED2 are significantly induced(2-to 2.5-fold)by drought stress in wheat anthers of the drought-sensitive varieties Sundor and Cranbrook(Fig. 2).

【例文11】It also indicated that MYC2 may promote ethylene signalling by activating MAP kinase kinase 9(MKK9).

【例文12】In contrast with previous results (Messina, 1993; Biasi et al., 2001), the present results demonstrate that male fertility is controlled exclusively by the sporophyte in kiwifruit.

【例文13】However, some studies have also demonstrated that calcium ion distribution and content are related to male sterility(Tian et al., 1998; Kong and Jia, 2004; Chen et al., 2008), carbohydrate metabolism(Brauer et al., 1990)and signalling leading to PCD(Ning et al., 1999;Wang et al., 2001).

【例文14】Histological analysis revealed a separation failure between microspore mother cells during the meiotic stage leading to complete male sterility in 7-7365A.

【例文15】This clearly illustrates that the OsG6B-TaABA8#OH1 construct works: spike ABA accumulation is reduced under cold conditions, and these lower ABA levels result in the maintenance of OSINV4 expression.

【例文16】The rice cyp703a3 mutant displays complete male sterility, whereas its Arabidopsis orthologous cyp703a2 mutant produces partially sterile pollen grains that display an abnormal exine with no obvious sporopollenin deposition.

【例文17】The aborted microspores of male-sterile kiwifruit flowers exhibit reduced glucose, galactose and galacturonic acid levels in the cytoplasm and in the cell wall in comparison with the functional pollen of male-fertile flowers(Biasi et al., 2001).

【例文18】A significant difference was observed at the vacuolated stage of microspore development.

【例文19】At the pre-meiotic stage, no hybridization signal was detected using the antisense probe(Figure 5b).

【例文20】There was no significant difference in the spike ABA levels for the four wheat lines under unstressed control conditions(Fig. 1A).

【例文21】After 5 d of drought stress, ABA levels were significantly increased in spikes of both drought-sensitive varieties, Sundor and Cranbrook.

7. 表示推测

表示推测既可用实义动词(believe, infer, predict, seem, appear 等),也可用形容词(potential, possible 等)表示,更常用的是情态动词(will, may, could, should, might)和副词(likely, perhaps probably, possible 等)来表示。

【例文1】This gene is believed to play an important role in cell wall degradation before the tetrad stage in B. oleracea(Kang et al. 2008).

【例文2】We infer that the expression of certain important genes encoding cell wall degradation enzymes is reduced at the stage of anther length<1 mm in 7-7365A.

【例文3】These observations support the prediction that APA1 is localized to the ER in tapetal cells and consistent with its presumed function of fatty acids hydroxylation catalysis in the ER during the synthesis of sporopollenin precursors.

【例文4】The model predicted that STZ is a key early hub through which JA signalling is prioritized over several other hormone and stress response pathways.

【例文5】This deletion is predicted to lead to loss of function of the D genome allele of the TaABA8#OH1 gene due to the loss of the region that spans across intron 3 and exon 4 of the gene.

【例文6】It seems that the exine-thickening process did not occur following tetrad release in apv1 mutant anthers(Figure 2p).

【例文7】Tolerant lines appear to react quicker to changes in endogenous ABA levels than sensitive varieties.

【例文8】Moreover, it is possible that calcium continued to accumulate in the exine of male-sterile microspores even after their death, due to continued secretion activity by the not-yet degenerated middle layer.

【例文9】These three interactions are potential points at which crosstalk can rapidly occur during a JA response with auxin, gibberellin and ethylene.

【例文10】Our comprehensive transcriptome analysis will provide potential explanation for the reduction of hydroxylated fatty acids, fatty acid alcohols, x-hydroxylated fatty acids, and x-di/tri hydroxylated fatty acids for each reaction.

【例文 11】ABA may be involved in the desiccation response that is required for pollen dehiscence.

【例文 12】It might facilitate the transmission of intercellular signals for normal anther development to have certain cell wall components digested.

【例文 13】The induction of the TaABA8#OH1 transgene in the cold-stressed transgenic lines is likely due to the fact that endogenous ABA levels in the transgenic lines are reduced.

【例文 14】Down-regulation of a transporter, such as ABCG11/WBC11, likely causes reduced transport of the cutin/wax constituents to the anther surface. Similarly, down-regulation of ABCG31, ABCG16, and ABCG26/WBC27 transporters may lead to less sporopollenin transport to the pollen wall, which would explain the observations for our transverse sections and SEM analysis showing impaired anther cuticle and pollen exine formation in the apv1 mutant.

8. 表述证据

"证据"英语表达为 evidence，表示"证据支持、证实"用 support, confirmed, validated 等，表示"某一结果与另一结果一致"用 agree (well) with, consistent with, consistently, in accordance with, in line with, compatible with, match with 等，表示"结果或现象与某种原因有关"用 associated with, a correlation with, a clear relation 等，表示"结果类似"用 similar to 等。

【例文 1】There is evidence of interactions between ABA and sugar signaling (Arenas-Huertero et al., 2000; Laby et al., 2000; Rook et al., 2001; Arroyo et al., 2003).

【例文 2】Analysis of wheat TaABA8#OH1 deletion lines provides genetic evidence that higher ABA levels in these lines cause increased sensitivity to drought stress.

【例文 3】Some evidence suggests that ABA catabolism plays an important role in controlling tissue ABA levels and ABA homeostasis (Chono et al., 2006; Millar et al., 2006; Okamoto et al., 2006; Umezawa et al., 2006; Yang and Zeevaart, 2006; Ren et al., 2007; Zhu et al., 2009).

【例文 4】In vitro culture results support the sporophytic control of male fertility in kiwifruit and open the way to applications to overcome dioecism and optimize kiwifruit production.

【例文 5】This point is supported by the fact that A3, A9 and MS1 are specifically expressed in tapetum, and are greatly downregulated in 7-7365A.

【例文 6】This result confirmed that the deletion of GRMZM5G830329 causes male sterility in apv1.

【例文 7】The deletions were confirmed using Southern-blot hybridization (Supplemental Fig. S1).

【例文8】These APV1 expression patterns are consistent with data from the maize eFP browser(http://bar.utoronto.ca/efp_maize/cgi-bin/efpWeb.cgi) and are similar to the rice CYP703A3 expression patterns.

【例文9】The present results show variations in calcium levels in anther wall tissues during microspore development, suggesting that calcium ions were transported from the middle layer to the tapetum and secreted by the tapetum into the locule, finally accumulating in the exine and the internal membranes (plasma membrane and tonoplast) of the microspores. Consistent with these results, calcium is provided by tapetum and middle layer in gymnosperms and other dicotyledons(Kong and Jia, 2004; Chen et al., 2008; Qiu et al., 2009).

【例文10】The existence of the middle layer and the secretory function of the tapetum in kiwifruit is in accordance with the characteristics of other members of the family(Watson and Dallwitz, 1992).

【例文11】Induction of sterility is associated with the absence of starch accumulation in mature pollen and the accumulation of nonreducing sugars in anthers

【例文12】This observation is similar to what we previously observed for cold-tolerant rice lines(Oliver et al., 2007).

9. 表述论文结论

表述"得出结论"用动词 conclude, propose, suggest, indicate, demonstrate, reveal, found, show, identify, report, discover, detect, validate 等，也可用表示总结性的短语如 in conclusion, in summary, in a word, in brief, in short, in total, as a result, on the whole, taken together, to sum up, to conclude, to summarize, collectively, briefly, eventually, ultimately, overall, altogether, together, consequently, therefore, thereby, thus, hence 等引导出结论。

【例文1】We concluded that the infertility of the *OsNCED3*-TaABA8#OH1 transgenic lines may have been due to pollen indehiscence at anthesis.

【例文2】Together with qRT-PCR results, we concluded that APV1 is preferentially expressed in uninucleate anthers and is strongly transcribed in the tapetum when the microspores are becoming vacuolated.

【例文3】Therefore, we propose that APV1 is involved in the hydroxylation of lauric acid in maize.

【例文4】This means that separation of the different cells, including that between sporophytic and gametophytic cells, plays an important role in normal anther development.

【例文5】Coupling this information with the present results from in vitro culture, we suggest that fine regulation of the supply of calcium and carbohydrate by the anther wall to the microspores must be functioning in planta and causes male fertility in kiwifruit.

【例文 6】These result suggests that heat shock followed by low temperature can partially restore male fertility in 7-7365A and also that the KIN1 gene may respond to low temperature and ABA.

【例文 7】ABA in these deletion lines accumulates to high levels, and there is no effect on expression of the TaNCED biosynthetic genes, suggesting that there is no feedback regulation system restricting ABA biosynthesis in response to environmental stimuli like drought stress.

【例文 8】These results indicate that endogenous ABA levels, expression of the ABA 8#-hydroxylase gene, and drought stress tolerance are correlated in wheat.

【例文 9】Our data indicate that ABA and ABA 8#-hydroxylase play an important role in controlling anther ABA homeostasis and reproductive stage abiotic stress tolerance in cereals.

【例文 10】Comparison of ABA biosynthesis in cold-sensitive and cold-tolerant lines indicated that cold-tolerant rice accumulated less ABA in response to cold treatment.

【例文 11】The amino acids in the heme-binding domain are identical among maize, sorghum, rice, and Arabidopsis(Figure S4b), indicating the functional conservation of APV1 between monocots and dicots, and even among flowering plants.

【例文 12】Polygalacturonase(PG), an important cell wall degradation enzyme, showed lower activity in 7-77365A than in 7-7365B and 7-7365C, indicating that downregulation of pectin degradation enzyme genes was a direct cause of the cell separation defect(Fig. 6).

【例文 13】In conclusion, the middle layer and tapetum control male fertility in *Actinidia deliciosa*, and a delay in the PCD of these tissues results in male-sterile plants.

(二) 内容描述集句

很多情况下，初学者在写作 SCI 论文时，不仅不知道如何用英语来表达某个意思，甚至不知道表达什么意思。在这种情况下，利用集句的方式来学习选题内容相关的句子，有助于初学者找到恰当和地道的表达方式。当然，这不能是简单的拷贝，而是借用别人的表达方式来表述我们自己想要却不会表达的意思。

例如，我们克隆了一个器官衰老和成熟相关基因，并利用反义基因技术转化某种植物，拟对其意义进行表述。在不清楚如何表述时，就可利用集句法，从一组相关的文章中辑录相关的句子。

【例文 1】These results demonstrate the potential of antisense techniques for assigning functions to gene sequences. The generation of plants in which ethylene production is inhibited offers the opportunity of evaluating the role of the gas in regulating several developmental processes such as leaf senescence, abscission, ripening and response to pathogens, and raise the possibility of being able to manipulate these genetically to improve the quality, storage life and nutritional value of many plants and plant products.

【例文 2】These results raise the possibility of manipulating ripening of many fruits and also of controlling processes such as abscission and senescence of leaves and flowers.

【例文 3】This result demonstrates that ethylene is the trigger and not the by-product of ripening and raises the prospect that the life-span of plant tissues can be extended, thereby preventing spoilage.

【例文 4】The ability to obtain specific expression of foreign genes in ripening tomatoes opens up the possibility of genetic manipulation of this important crop.

【例文 5】These results extend our understanding of the hormone interactions that regulate flower senescence and provide a means of increasing flower longevity

【例文 6】The altered characteristics of fruit transformed with specific antisense genes, such as retarded ripening and resistance to splitting, may prove to be of value to fruit growers, processors and ultimately the consumer.

【例文 7】The generation of transgenic carnation plants in which the ability to synthesize ethylene has been reduced or eliminated by use of the antisense technique reflects similar findings in tomato and reinforces the concept of improving properties, such as postharvest qualities, by genetic engineering rather than by long-term classical breeding or the application of chemicals.

【例文 8】A combination of marker-assisted breeding, underpinned by advances in next generation sequencing technologies and in concert with GM approaches, provides the opportunities for a step-change in breeding new varieties that combine health-promoting traits, excellent quality and long postharvest shelf life in a competitively priced product.

【例文 9】Not only will these transgenic plants be a boon to post-harvest physiology and crop improvement but, it will also help us in discovering the mechanism of regulation of ethylene sensitivity.

【例文 10】Antisense RNA technology has allowed the production of a novel tomato mutant line with useful changes in fruit quality. This methodology has allowed a specific change in one enzyme while leaving other ripening related changes and the general plant morphology and performance substantially unaltered.

【例文 11】This opens up the possibility of being able to regulate the rate of ripening of tomatoes and other climacteric fruits, to reduce over-ripening and spoilage, without resorting to refrigeration, controlled atmosphere storage, or other treatments. It also raises the prospect of developing leafy vegetables and flowers with increased longevity, since in many plants these processes are also influenced by ethylene(Abeles, 1973).

【例文 12】This study provides new dimension in light of other reports in the literature (and some mentioned above) showing that suppression of ethylene has measurable impact on the metabolome and aroma of a commodity. Thus, altering ethylene biosynthesis or signaling in plants, be that by a chemical treatment or using genetic means (mutants or transgenes), to prolong shelf life of fruits limits the metabolic potential (nutrition) of such fruit, which needs to be ascertained and then rectified/salvaged by additional treatments including applying exogenous ethylene or creating a double transgenic event as shown here.

【例文 13】Our method of producing transgenic torenia plants with extended flower longevity will be useful for breeding flower longevity in torenia. We expect that this experimental system will be also valuable for analysis of ethylene biosynthesis and flower longevity, because torenia is easier to transform than other ethylene-sensitive ornamental plants such as carnation.

【例文 14】In this study, we identified a key regulator of PCD in petal senescence, which will facilitate further elucidation of the regulatory network of petal senescence.

【例文 15】Therefore, understanding what controls these processes in non-climacteric ripening may prove pertinent to gaining full understanding of climacteric fruit ripening and vice versa.

【例文 16】Deciphering the function of ERF genes in both ethylene-dependent and ethylene-independent processes during ripening and identifying the target genes of individual ERFs will be instrumental to better clarify their specific contribution to fruit ripening. Moreover, deciphering the ethylene receptor subfunctionalization and assigning specific roles to ERF members will open new avenues toward engineering fruit development and ripening via targeted approaches, especially when aiming to enhance some desirable traits and metabolic pathways and to reduce unwanted ones.

【例文 17】We showed that InPSR26 is a putative membrane protein that is involved in the progression of PCD during petal senescence. Our results highlight a link between autophagy and PCD in petal senescence, although the biochemical function of InPSR26 remains largely unknown. Analyses on the function of this protein will provide new insights on PCD and autophagy in petal senescence.

【例文 18】These studies, in combination with proteomic (Bai et al., 2010) and metabolomic investigations, will help us to further our understanding of the biological relevance of nutrient remobilization during petal senescence, and allow us to determine how petal senescence is regulated by ethylene, during development and under stress.

【例文 19】The increase in these polypeptides during flower senescence is of particular interest because they may be linked to flower longevity. Understanding the nature of these proteins can provide new insights into the pathways that execute senescence and the post-transcriptional regulation of senescence in this flower system.

【例文 20】We also highlight the possible contribution of epigenetic changes including the role of plant microRNAs, which is opening new avenues and great possibilities in the fields of fruit-ripening research and postharvest biology.

(三) 搜索法集句

除了通过串读文献来归纳和学习各种不同的表述方法外,我们还可利用浏览器(如 Google、Google Scholar、Bing 和 Yahoo)的搜索功能来选择合适的词语搭配和包含特定词语的句子。尤其是 Google Scholar 的高级搜索功能,还可帮助初学者搜索包含特定词语的某一期刊的句子,如输入:"目标词语" source:Nature,可找到《自然》期刊文章中包含"目标词语"的所有句子。利用当代美国英语语料库,也可搜索到大量包含特定词语的句子。另外,目前还出现了一些网站与 App 来帮助寻找多样的或地道的表述方法,例如,

Ludwig(https://ludwig.guru/)
Linggle(http://www.linggle.com)
Academic Phrasebank(http://www.phrasebank.manchester.ac.uk/)
NetSpeak(http://www.netspeak.org)
Hemingway Editor(http://www.hemingwayapp.com/)
Power thesaurus(https://www.powerthesaurus.org/)
Thesaurus(https://www.thesaurus.com/)
Wordhippo(https://www.wordhippo.com/)

下面的例子是在 ludwig.guru 网站查找到的关于 "previous research studies have failed to" 的例文。

【例文 1】Previous studies and reviews have failed to show consistent clinical benefits of extending the infusion time.

【例文 2】Previous synergy studies have failed to take account of the species of Bcc isolates.

【例文 3】Most previous research studies have failed to acknowledge this societal change.

【例文 4】Previous studies have failed to demonstrate haemodynamic effects on the VA in simulated pre-thrust positions.

【例文 5】Previous studies have failed to identify any clear seasonal distribution of GBS cases in Europe and North America.

【例文 6】Previous studies have failed to find a significant difference in intraocular pressure(IOP)between one-and two-site phacotrabeculectomy.

【例文 7】 Previous studies have failed to show a survival benefit following implementation of ACLS in the out-of-hospital setting.

总之，语言学习的方式本质在于模仿。在没有掌握一定数量的语言素材之前，还谈不上创造性使用语言来表达。但是，学习借鉴不等于直接拷贝，其目的主要是学习和借用别人的句式、常用词语、短语来表达我们自己的意思。

四、对论文进行归纳和总结，进而写作综述论文

为了提高论文阅读效果，可以对阅读过的论文进行归纳和总结。例如，利用图和表对每一篇文章的来源、主题、所用方法和主要发现进行归纳梳理，这不仅有利于记忆阅读所得，也有利于需要时查找，就同学者过去所做的阅读卡片那样。

新手在阅读大量文献后，可以写成一篇综述论文（未必要发表）。综述论文的写作不仅是检验阅读成效和成果的方法，也是真正了解某个问题或领域的途径。

综述写作需要建立在广泛阅读的基础上，对某个问题或领域的相关论文进行归纳、分析和总结，并在此基础上作出判断和评述。一篇好的综述论文首先需要征引大量文献，但又不能是文献的简单罗列和堆砌，作者应该在阅读论文之后形成自己的观点和论述角度，并据此对文献加以整理和论述。其次，不能只述不评，从而将综述变成论文摘抄，要用自己的话来总结论文，对论文的研究结果进行比较分析，指出研究工作的贡献和局限，并给出全面、准确、客观的判断和评述。另外，要识别本领域哪些问题解决了，哪些问题还没有解决，未来的出路和希望何在，也就是说，既要描述研究的历史和现状，又不忽视发展趋势和前景。综述论文最后的展望部分要论述领域存在的问题或尚未解决的难题，并提出将来的研究方向和解决之道。

参 考 文 献

阿卜杜斯·萨拉姆国际理论物理中心，2006. 成为科学家的100个理由[M]. 赵乐静，译. 上海：上海科学技术出版社.

阿瑟·科恩伯格，2006. 酶的情人——一位生物化学家的奥德赛[M]. 崔学军，倪红梅，王伟，等译. 上海：上海科学技术出版社.

伯纳德·伍德，2016. 人类进化简史[M]. 冯兴无，译. 北京：外语教学与研究出版社.

弗吉尼亚·伍尔夫，2016. 伍尔夫读书笔记[M]. 黄梅，刘炳善，译. 南京：译林出版社.

拉尔夫·罗斯诺、米米·罗斯诺，2020. 心理学论文写作——基于APA格式的指导手册[M]. 9版. 刘文，译. 重庆：重庆大学出版社.

梁甜甜，刘佳，刘艳红，2018. 科技英语翻译[M]. 北京：中国纺织出版社.

刘进平，2021. 学术英语写作技巧[M]. 北京：中国林业出版社.

刘进平，2018. 英语阅读理解科技英语翻译和SCI论文写作技巧[M]. 北京：中国林业出版社.

阮亚妹，果笑非，2015. 科技英语写作策略与技巧[M]. 北京：国防工业出版社.

斯坦利·费什，2020. 如何遣词造句[M]. 杨逸，译. 北京：译林出版社.

王金发，陈中健，杨琳，2000. TIG遗传命名指南[M]. 北京：科学出版社.

王智弘，2015. 中外名家教你学英语[M]. 北京：金盾出版社.

吴志根，2019. 国际高水平SCI论文写作和发表指南[M]. 杭州：浙江大学出版社.

杨仁宇，2012. 科技英语写作[M]. 王多，译. 上海：复旦大学出版社.

《英语世界》杂志社，2018. 如何学好英语——专家、教授谈英语学习方法[M]. 北京：商务印书馆.

张干周，2018. 科技英语应用文本翻译：理论探讨、问题分析、翻译方法及教学[M]. 北京：北京交通大学出版社.

张建，陈赟，2017. SCI/EI学术论文写作与发表攻略[M]. 北京：机械工业出版社.

FALASCA G, D'ANGELI S, BIASI R, et al., 2013. Tapetum and middle layer control male fertility in *Actinidia deliciosa*[J]. Annals of Botany, 112(6): 1045-1055.

GUO Y, GAN S, 2006. AtNAP, a NAC family transcription factor, has an important role in leaf senescence[J]. Plant Journal, 46(4): 601-612.

GWILYM L, 2016. Academic clickbait: Articles with positively-framed titles, interesting phrasing, and no wordplay get more attention online[J]. The Winnower, 7: e146723. 36330.

JI X, DONG B, SHIRAN B, et al., 2011. Control of abscisic acid catabolism and abscisic acid homeostasis is important for reproductive stage stress tolerance in cereals[J]. Plant Physiol, 156(2): 647-662.

KNISELY K, 2009. A student handbook for writing in biology[M]. 3rd ed. Massachusetts: Sinauer Associates, Inc.

MARTÍNEZ A, MAMMOLA S, 2021. Specialized terminology reduces the number of citations of scientific papers[J]. Proceedings of the Royal Society B(Biological Sciences), 288 (1948): 20202581.

MATALLANA-RAMIREZ L P, RAUF M, FARAGE-BARHOM S, et al., 2013. NAC transcription factor ORE1 and senescence-induced BIFUNCTIONAL NUCLEASE1 (BFN1) constitute a regulatory cascade in Arabidopsis[J]. Molecular Plant, 6(5): 1438-1452.

MATHEW S R, 2018. How to write a thorough peer review [J]. Nature, doi: 10.1038/d41586-018-06991-0.

SCHIMEL J, 2021. Writing science: How to write papers that get cited and proposals that get funded[M]. Oxford: Oxford University Press.

SOMARATNE Y, TIAN Y, ZHANG H, et al., 2017. Abnormal pollen vacuolation1 (APV1) is required for male fertility by contributing to anther cuticle and pollen exine formation in maize[J]. Plant Journal, 90 (1): 96-110.

UAUY C, DISTELFELD A, FAHIMA T, et al., 2006. A NAC gene regulating senescence improves grain protein, zinc, and iron content in wheat[J]. Science, 314(5803): 1298-1301.

WANG S, LI Y, 2019. How to write effectively for international journals[J]. Nature, doi: 10.1038/d41586-019-00359-8.

ZANDER M, LEWSEY M G, CLARK N M, et al., 2020. Integrated multi-omics framework of the plant response to jasmonic acid[J]. Nature Plants, 6(3): 290-302.

ZHU Y, DUN X, ZHOU Z, et al., 2010. A separation defect of tapetum cells and microspore mother cells results in male sterility in *Brassica napus*: the role of abscisic acid in early anther development[J]. Plant Molecular Biology, 72: 111-123.